Requirements for success-
full performer:

1. Personality
2. Looks
3. Talent

Acting: Onstage and Off

Acting: Onstage and Off

Robert Barton

University of Oregon

Holt, Rinehart and Winston, Inc.
Fort Worth   Chicago   San Francisco   Philadelphia
Montreal   Toronto   London   Sydney   Tokyo

Cover photo by Joseph A. Acosta
Cover design by Fred Pusterla

Library of Congress Cataloging-in-Publication Data

Barton, Robert, 1946–
    Acting : onstage and off / Robert Barton.
      p. cm.
    Bibliography: p.
    Includes index.
    ISBN 0-03-009904-8
    1. Acting. 2. Method (Acting) I. Title.
  PN2061.B294   1988
  792'.028—dc19   88-23519
                                      CIP

ISBN 0-03-009904-8

Printed in the United States of America
9 0 1 2   016   9 8 7 6 5 4 3 2

Holt, Rinehart and Winston, Inc.
The Dryden Press
Saunders College Publishing

TO MY SON ANDREW, WHOSE SENSE OF
WONDER RENEWED MY OWN

Preface

Acting to Understand

Acting is one of the best ways to learn about being alive. Because actors get to *become* other people, they have stronger opportunities than most to understand more and co-exist better. We stop making instant judgments of others if we are given the chance to play those others. Only shallow caricaturists can portray other humans, however strange or villainous, without gaining some lasting empathy for their pain and some feeling for their perspective. A worthwhile performance class does more than pass on information: It humanizes. An acting class can help each participant become less narrow and provincial, more a citizen of the entire world. Actors can find out more about themselves, others, and how selves and others connect. Each can learn the art of compromise and collaboration. Throughout these heady, high-sounding lessons, there can be a lot of laughs.

This book is designed for the beginning acting student, for whom the life-enhancing aspects of actor training are a higher priority than technical skills. The basic assumptions are (1) offstage performance can be comfortably adapted for the theater, (2) onstage training can be applied towards leading a full life outside the theater, and (3) the two can feed each other in a way that can be both illuminating and amusing, which is a pretty good combination.

Acting: Onstage and Off is divided into seven chapters that address areas of greatest concern to those just starting to study acting. The book begins by exploring each student's past and present offstage life, finding confidence, experience, and texture to be used in class. Once the actor no longer feels inexperienced and inept, the text moves in chapter 2 into learning to warm up (body, voice, and mind, individually and collectively), then to understanding the actor's own equipment (chapter 3). The assumption is that attaining *self*-awareness is crucial before *others*-awareness can be accomplished, whether those others are living or fictional.

Warmed up and self-aware, the actor next pursues in chapter 4 the basic means for putting together a character, as designed by Stanislavski and extended by the behavioral sciences. Once these fundamental principles of performing as someone *else* are established, chapter 5 explores the need to balance honesty with precision and considers methods for blending the two. At this stage, the actor is ready to tackle the unique traditions and history of this particular art form. Chapter 6 establishes rehearsal/performance etiquette and unwritten standards of behavior and support in the theater. This chapter is designed to aid the new actor in quickly settling nagging procedural questions, getting the help he or she needs, and avoiding, as one of my students put it, "blowing it without knowing it." It is also geared towards picking up quick survival information when entering any new world. The book's final chapter is designed to help the student decide some options for more involvement and some ways of applying all that has been learned, even if this class is the student's last direct contact with the art form.

Each chapter involves a more complex level of understanding than the one before. An attempt has been made to anticipate the actor's next question, as if in completing one chapter, the reader would say, "Okay, this is fine, but what if . . . ?" More than anything else, this book aims to help each actor find some joy and wonder in himself or herself as a performer. An actor needs many skills eventually, but joy and wonder should come first.

Using This Text

Acting classes vary from meeting only three hours a week for one term to as many as six hours plus lab sessions for a full year. It is useless for a fundamentals text to try to serve everyone equally. There are three different ways to employ this text, however, that may assist adapting to varying time structures and changing class enrollments. It is possible to work through the book in sequence for a full year of activity. It is also possible to move by subject or skill (such as voice, which is dealt with through separate sections in each chapter) or by sampling every chapter, doing the work suggested in the earlier portions of each. This last alternative is suggested for short-term classes, so that students get to at least taste each of the areas that concerns them. Most acting students enroll with a desire to do scene study work, for the chance to work with scripts. I sympathize with those students who find themselves in a class that accomplishes nothing but warm-ups and improvisations before suddenly the term is over. These students did not get what they came for. They have not really acted.

The book has far more exercises and more questions within these exercises than most readers will wish to handle. An excess of choice is offered so that teacher *and* reader can pick, choose, reject and modify. These exercises can easily be cut back in scope and written assignments can be adapted into thought/discussion questions and improvisations, in those instances where a minimum of academic work is deemed appropriate.

An unusually focused group of actors might be able to move quickly over the background examination and warm-up activities of the first two chapters, but most students need training in relaxation and channeling of energy prior to the relatively sophisticated demands of chapter 3. The activities in chapter 1 are largely passive and undemanding. By chapter 3, each student is asked to accomplish acute and systematic analysis of not only himself or herself but also others in the class. An entire chapter on warm-ups helps increase confidence and provide the calm necessary for these greater challenges.

An extensive list of scene suggestions appears in chapter 5 and a sample scene called "The Rehearsal" appears in an appendix. This scene can be employed for applying all the concepts discussed. However, examples in this book are otherwise drawn entirely from the actor's own life rather than plays. The book's basic approach focuses on life experience rather than dramatic literature for instances and background material. Some instructors may wish to supplement with a scene anthology.

The text aims for a sound and traditional approach to principles of acting. Five elements that are, however, uncommon to most basic texts include:

1. The constant connection between life in the theater and life removed from it
2. The personal examination of one's self and one's classmates as initial pathways to characterization

3. The extended development of an actor's responsibility for in-rehearsal active contribution and out-of-rehearsal exploration
4. The treatment of auditions as a basic rather than advanced concern
5. An emphasis on the actor's need to become self-sufficient

This last area involves knowledge of script analysis and staging, sometimes restricted to directing courses, but in my opinion essential tools for the actor when a director is unavailable or unqualified to guide and structure.

The subject of auditions is considered by many to be an advanced or "pre-professional" program consideration, outside the appropriate scope of a beginning acting class. I strongly disagree. Auditioning is what you do to get into another class, to apply what you have just learned in a show, to get a job, a scholarship, to make any temporary, tentative condition in your life more permanent and definite. Far too often beginning classes whet the appetite of novice actors without giving them any help in getting more chances to pursue this art. I believe it is this very postponing of auditioning that makes it so terrifying to an actor.

Acknowledgments

Wandalee Henshaw for permission to use open scene materials; Kathleen George for open scene concepts; Jack Watson for expertly running the University of Oregon acting program in my absence; Sovfoto agency for permission to use Stanislavski photos. For their manuscript suggestions, James A. Panowski, Northern Michigan University; Norman J. Myers, Bowling Green State University; Theodore Herstand, The University of Oklahoma; Kate Beckman, St. John's University; Barbara O'Neill, The University of North Dakota; Tom O. Mitchell, University of Illinois; Jon Beryl, Indiana University; Robert L. Amsden, Bethany College; Marc Powers, The Ohio State University; Tod Fortner, Santa Barbara City College; Pauline E. Peotter, Portland State University. Finally, Carrol Barton for assistance in locating sources and for abiding support.

Contents

2   Relaxed Readiness   24

(getting calm enough, yet energized enough, to perform fully)

Exercises

3   Individual Inventory   59

(knowing enough about yourself and your equipment to use everything you have)

Body Awareness   60

4   Stanislavski's System   104

(understanding the only complete process by which actors build characters)

Myth and Reality   105

Ten System Steps   114

Open Scenes   128

Stanislavski Extended   139

Exercises

5   Truth/Technique   151

*(balancing honest, open spontaneity with
steady, polished consistency)*

Character Analysis   156

Body Maneuvers   166

Voice Maneuvers   178

Improvisation and Freedom   183

Basic Awareness Improvs   184

Script Awareness Improvs   194

Exercises

6 Performance Process   200

(recognizing standard procedure and appropriate behavior from first audition through closing night)

Acting Etiquette   201

Adaptations   211

Shaking Up the Scene   221

Exercises

7   Acting Anticipated   236

(setting goals for the future which allow both artistic growth and personal satisfaction)

Training Objectives   237

Acting: Onstage and Off

1

Acting
Acknowledged

(recognizing that you are already
an experienced actor and are
almost always acting)

Jessica Lange: *At the age of eight or nine, I'd create scenes for myself and I'd act out all the parts.*[1]

Meryl Streep: *My first successful characterization is what I devised for myself in high school. I played the blond homecoming queen for several years. I laid out my clothes for the week every Sunday so that I wouldn't repeat.*[2]

Peter O'Toole: *Acting is just a matter of farting about in disguises.*[3]

Everyone acts almost all the time. You are a highly experienced actor even if you have never taken a class or been in a show. You may not be a *skilled* actor, but you are experienced. Acting is what we each do within groups—to survive in an old group, to gain membership in a new group, or even to be left alone by a group we do not wish to join. We are learning to act all our lives. We are always trying to figure out how *they* (current group members) want us to behave, what qualities to punch up or play down, which feelings to show or hide, what behavior will be rewarded or punished. We try to give our audience what it wants and still stay as much *ourselves* as possible, to avoid feeling cheap and compromised. This is called acting. This is what we do to survive.

All the World's a Stage

The world is full of actors, but it is also full of acting critics. Consider these lines of dialog, spoken so often that you will be able, at a glance, to place them in familiar situations:

"That's no way to act."
"Stay in your room until you learn to act like a young lady."
"He's been acting so strange lately."
"You don't need to act as if you own the place."
"I can't go there. I just wouldn't know how to act."
"Stop acting as if the whole thing was my fault."
"Oh yeah, she acts innocent, but I know better."
"O.K., so how would you have acted if you'd been there?"
"Do you think maybe this is all some kind of act?"
"He acts like he hasn't got a care in the world."
"When are you going to start acting like yourself again?"
"Don't worry about it. Just act natural."

And of course this all-time favorite we may hear anytime between birth and death:

"Act your age."

As with countless subjects, no one has said it better than William Shakespeare:

> All the world's a stage,
> And all the men and women merely players:
> They have their exits and their entrances;
> And one man in his time plays many parts,
> His acts being seven ages. As first the infant,
> Mewling and puking in the nurse's arms.
> And then the whining schoolboy, with his satchel
> And shining morning face, creeping like snail
> Unwillingly to school. And then the lover,
> Sighing like furnace, with a woeful ballad
> Made to his mistress' eyebrow. Then the soldier,
> Full of strange oaths and bearded like the pard,
> Jealous in honour, sudden and quick in quarrel,
> Seeking the bubble reputation
> Even in the cannon's mouth. And then the justice,
> In fair round belly with good capon lined,
> With eyes severe and beard of formal cut,
> Full of wise saws and modern instances;

And so he plays his part. The sixth age shifts
Into the lean and slipper'd pantaloon,
With spectacles on nose and pouch on side,
His youthful hose, well saved, a world too wide
For his shrunk shank; and his big manly voice,
Turning again toward childish treble, pipes
And whistles in his sound. Last scene of all,
That ends this strange eventful history,
Is second childishness and mere oblivion,
Sans teeth, sans eyes, sans taste, sans everything.[4]

Jaques' famous words from *As You Like It* strike a deep, responsive chord every time someone hears them for the first time. We "players" recognize ourselves and others going through each phase.

Seven Ages

1 Mewling infant

At some point every infant learns to mewl (bawl, shout, cry, complain) in order to get picked up, loved, fed, and changed; later actually learning to create the *impression* of need, whether need truly exists or not. My own infant son sits blissfully with me while I am writing. But if my wife passes through the room, he focuses suddenly on her breasts and breaks into a fairly convincing imitation of all the starving children of three, maybe four South African countries. Since we both know he has eaten within the hour, she continues on her way, and he sighs and gurgles happily again, as if to say there was no harm trying.

Some people, of course, never recover from this very early lesson in acting, and are deceiving others forever. More often, one simply learns to *enhance* the feeling of need. One also learns very early when the audience is not paying enough attention, and how to get it. This phase, while used less with time, is never really left behind. Any of us, in desperation, may resort to mewling, anywhere along the life journey.

2 Whining schoolboy

We all give performances surrounding school. Is there anyone who has never pretended to be sick (or sicker than for real) in order not to go to school? And then later pretended to be well (or better than for real) in order to go to some function he really wanted to attend? Is there anyone who has not whined and pouted through some responsibility that has been forced on her ? Often we really do not mind doing it that much, but we would like to let everyone around know how much we are suffering, what a great sacrifice this is, how noble we are for plugging on, how much they owe us for being such a brick. This performance can expand into a whole series of victim or "poor me" routines for those who enjoy casting themselves as martyrs.

School is also where one learns that even in group avoidance, some acting is required. If you are a bookish, artistic wimp who does not want to join the jock bullies at recess, you still need to figure out how to act, so they will not make your jocklessness the focus of their bullydom.

3   Sighing lover

When smitten by somebody, many of our actions are guided by what we feel a lover *should* act like, by our observations of other, more experienced lovers. If you do not have a clue how to respond, it is the most natural thing in the world to turn to some movie or book for a role model. Being in love is a great excuse for behaving irrationally and extravagantly, knowing everyone will tolerate your acting silly.

Then there are the performances you give *for* the object of affection. You are trying to act in such a way that the adored one is never disappointed, always pleasantly surprised. ("Maybe if I write her an eyebrow poem. I'll bet nobody else has done that . . .") If you really have it bad, you will give an extended performance, trying for wittier, smoother, better read, stronger and wilder than you have ever been in your life—whatever your beloved seems to admire. After a while, if the relationship is worth it, the forced acting begins to fade, with much mutual relief, into the sunset.

4   Reputation-seeking soldier

Now, sticking your head down into a cannon which might go off any minute, just to be momentarily admired, is farther than most of us are willing to go. But everyone (man and woman, in the armed forces or not) goes through a soldier stage where the main objective and primary performance is to appear unafraid, in control, undaunted and possibly threatening, even when what you really want to do is cry and run home for a hug. During adolescence, a time when we can be easily hurt, it seems important to pretend that nothing can hurt. So we do a lot of one-upping, daredevil risktaking, obnoxious bragging. An overawareness of the audience produces some bad acting, stiff, self-conscious, and mannered.

While acting tough seems to be a crucial rite of passage into adulthood, not everyone makes it through the pass. Like the deceptive infant, some get caught up in this phase forever. A huge percentage of the population, largely male, linger in the land of swagger. Legions of movie careers and action flicks are reminiscent of Shakespeare's macho head-in-the-cannon stage. For some it is a harmless fantasy, for others it is a deadly way of life.

5   Saw-spouting justice

The well-fed people of this stage are always speaking as if what they say will be carved in granite somewhere. Everything has quotations around it. I find myself flirting dangerously with this phase, trying to skip it. Because I am in charge of an acting program, people are willing to listen to me and often even hover expectantly, pencil in hand. It is very easy to believe, for the moment, when someone gives you such authority, that Moses was not the only one to climb the mountain and chat with God. People who are used to being listened to, without having to fight for an audience, can pontificate to the point of self-parody.

Everyone gives in to the justice in himself, especially if you have just done something noteworthy. A student returning home as a member of the winning debate team or queen of a local beauty pageant may suddenly assume an exalted position as he or she passes on advice to mere mortals aspiring to the same glory.

6   Lean and slippered pantaloon

All of us have observed the elderly shriveling and experiencing surprise at how small their impact suddenly is. In this confused moment, some cling desperately to old casting and past power, exploding with rage when everything is no longer in place. Others begin to enjoy the freedom from responsibility, the lightness that comes with no longer being at the center of everything.

7   Second childishness and mere oblivion

Because Jaques is a melancholic, this final image is sad and desolate. Some very old people die long before their last breath. Others have a great final season. The key universal image is "second childishness." Some seniors return to a sense of childlike wonder and discovery, with no more complicated issues to deal with than being caught being naughty by *them,* or possibly not discovering enough things to do today to have fun. Even at this time of utter freedom, however, most opt to return to a distant, but familiar, performance mode, rather than striving for a new one. The memory brings forth a way of acting that is like their early days of discovery. Watching small children and old people discover themselves as kindred spirits, capable of complete sharing, is a great wonder, in those moments when they reach casually past all the generations between them.

All people, acting over a lifetime, fall into recognizable patterns and Shakespeare has powerfully written of seven. But this does not mean our acting is doomed to sameness. There are countless chances to vary each stage and countless persons defying the patterns. We all know geriatrics who remain lucid, mature, even brilliant and inspiring until the very end. Humans also tend never to completely leave an "age" behind, but rather to store it in their own increasingly complex repertoire. So we not only see mature statesmen suddenly mewling and puking unexpectedly, but also tired old men suddenly brave soldiers again, and bona fide cynics suddenly sighing like furnaces and writing eyebrow poems, completely in love. As you review your own ages, have you already found yourself returning to some for a visit?

Exercise 1.1

Ages Experienced, Ages Observed

Think of a one-sentence description of your most vivid performance in each of the first five of Shakespeare's seven modes:

1. infant
2. schoolboy
3. lover
4. soldier
5. justice

You may want to check your own memory with your parents' in the first three categories at least. Describe the most vivid example you have *observed* in each of the other ages:

6. pantaloon
7. second childhood

Exercise 1.2

Answering Ages

Pick a simple request like "What time is it?" and answer it in the voice of each of the seven ages. Take turns answering around the whole class, with other request lines. Be sure to respond in your own voice, remembered or foretold.

Seven Acts

In addition to passing through ages, we all perform "acts" or specialized performances in our lives outside the theater. Most have their roots in simple childhood Let's Pretend. Here are seven varieties:

1   Pageants

(Toto in a grade school *Oz?* Third Wiseperson, carrying myrrh, in a church nativity? Part of a Living Totem Pole in a scout jamboree? Ring Bearer at a wedding? Toastmaster at an anniversary? Homecoming Queen's court?)

You are dressed up, it is a very big occasion, the place is packed, in fact many of the essential ingredients for theater are present. You may be cast in a definite role, even though it might be an inanimate object, like a rock. Or, in public rituals, you may be cast as *you* without convenient camouflage. But this is a *transformed* you, amazingly cleaned up, polished off, and sanitized. The stakes here are very high, the price of doing something wrong is beyond your means, and you usually feel very proud.

2   Disguises

(A progression of ghosts and monsters for Halloween? A Disney or *Star Wars* character for a costume party? A sophisticated, world traveler for some bistro where you hope not to get carded?)

These performances are looser and more improvisational. Your intent is to *not* be recognized. You experiment endlessly with your costume pieces, you work on your walk, your gestures, you practice certain lines in order to get the voice, the timing, the inflection just right. Then you enter the world. Sometimes you only make it downstairs, before returning to your room for a few adjustments based on some early family reviews. But you get better and better as the evening progresses.

3   Alter egos

> (The "Muscle Bound You" who enters the playing field? The "Oxford Scholar You" who stands up to debate first affirmative? The "Vogue Cover Girl You" who glides onto the prom dance floor?)

Alter egos are second selves, often with improvements: You with "cheekbones" and a Ph.D. Some of us click into the alter ego as a way of upping courage. Seeing yourself slightly enhanced often has a startling effect on observers, who may see you that way too. Some people go so far as to name their other selves, which tend to be more assertive and colorful than the main self. They are used by many as a means of "rising to the occasion." Sometimes alter egos compete for your attention. Sometimes they even take on a life of their own.

Bette Midler *(discussing two of her alter egos): So eventually the big brassy broad beat the crap out of the little torch singer and took over.*[5]

---

4   Role models

> (You decide to lower your voice when angry, just like your father? To walk like a certain rock star? To emulate the unshakable dignity of your favorite teacher?)

Other human beings and literary figures serve as sources for the basic characterization you would like to present to the world. You may just want to shake your hair to the side like a certain actress; not necessarily to *be* her. You try on qualities like pieces of clothing, discarding one if it does not seem to fit. Borrowing may involve anything from a small mannerism to an entire outlook.

5   Understudying

> (Your folks are not home and someone tries to deliver a gross of electric can openers—what do you do? Your boss is gone and a

customer is getting unruly—what do you do? You are left entertaining your Great Aunt Helga who only speaks Swedish—what do you do?)

Standing in for someone who usually handles this situation and attempting to effectively trouble-shoot involves more than just trying to figure out how the other person would handle the situation. It may also involve trying to get their actions down pat, their manner of authority, their way of ending a sentence firmly. Even if lines of dialog come to you, you may find yourself struggling for the right word emphasis. You know the other (missing) person should be starring in this scene, and that you are merely an understudy. Like most understudies you try to give a pretty good imitation of the star.

6 Suppression

(Are you mortified beyond endurance, but determined not to appear upset? Flattered, but striving to appear as if compliments like this come hourly? Ecstatic over winning, but afraid the other competitors will not respond well to your leaping and shrieking?)

Cooling down your first response to something more manageable, less foolish or overbearing, is an acting challenge that may go on for hours before you can finally let it rip. If you win, you want to appear happy, even thrilled, just not obnoxious. If you lose, you want to appear transcendent, not devastated. Huge acting energy is invested in stifling emotional display.

7 Deception

("It wasn't really you who emptied out the cookie jar, was it?" "And the reason your jeans are torn and muddy is that you were attacked by a band of aliens?" "You've never tried smoking that awful stuff, have you?")

We all act, to some degree, less guilty than we are. It can run from a few harmless fibs to profoundly immoral lies. Feigned innocence is a universally acknowledged form of offstage acting. Even the most honest of us look back on a few occasions where we still cringe at not fessing up, but also feel some measure of pride in pulling it off. If the deception helps bring off a surprise party or visit, we feel triumphant and skillful when the amazed recipient gets the joyous news.

While serving jury duty during the writing of this book, I was stunned one day to hear the judge instruct us that it would be our duty to figure out who was acting and who was not. He later said to me, "If there weren't so many actors in the world, I'd be out of a job." Some cases and some careers are based on lies. But the vast majority of our performances, particularly in these last two categories, are humane, caring, even loving.

Imagine yourself getting up on any given day and following only "gut level" impulses, without any effort to please others. The damage done to furniture and egos could be enormous, even in your first hour of entry into the world. Daily acting involves sparing other people's feelings. You perform so as not to appear quite so bored, so offended, so amazed at their lack of sensitivity or tact, so appalled at the fact they missed the point or the appointment. If a friend is hurting, you and I try to figure out how to act so that she will feel supported and nurtured. We do not just figure out what to do, we figure out how to *act*. For many of us, even those of us who make our living in the theater, the finest performances of our lives are given offstage.

Exercise 1.3

Striking/Successful Acting

Keeping your description again to no more than one sentence, pull out the two most striking/successful performances you can recall in each of the seven offstage acting areas. They may have been striking but total flops and they may have been extremely successful but very low key. Or they may have been both.

1. pageants
2. disguises
3. alter egos
4. role models
5. understudying
6. suppression
7. deception

Optional additions (Those fortunate enough to have traditional onstage experience, see Appendix A):

8. media
   a. film
   b. television
   c. radio

9. theater
   a. productions
   b. showcases
   c. scene study

Exercise 1.4

Dueling Performances

The toughest moments in life can be when you are cast in two roles that you cannot play with equal grace and believability. Your role as Loyal, Respectful Daughter comes straight up against your role as Feminist if your father makes recurring sexist remarks. It is especially difficult if both roles are essential to your concept of self, way up near the top of those parts you fully intended to run for many seasons.

1. Try to identify five times in your life when you wanted to play two roles at odds with each other.
2. Which ones won?
3. Were you ever able to successfully blend the two? Is there a way the two women's roles in the previous paragraph could possibly be combined, without hurting either?

Exercise 1.5

Scripting and Improvising

A basic difference exists between offstage acting which has no script and onstage acting which does. Right? Not entirely. People who require risk as a constant in their lives will work a lot of *improvisation* into each day. Others, craving constancy, will nearly script themselves, with only the slightest variation in day-to-day dialog. Everyone scripts and carefully rehearses certain crucial life encounters (a seduction scene, a telling-off-the-boss scene, a finally-persuading-the-folks scene), hoping the other person(s) will pick up the right cues.

1. Recall two of your most carefully scripted or planned encounters.
2. Recall two of your least planned, most challenging, freewheeling improvisations.
3. Write four single sentence descriptions, beginning with "The time I

. . ." Keep these four memories in mind as you begin to explore other dimensions of your acting outside the theater.

(See Appendix A, "My Acting History," for an optional format for summarizing the acting you have experienced so far).

Why Study Acting?

So if all the world is acting, why is this something to study? Well, first of all, acting often does not necessarily mean acting well! Something this important to living fully is something we can all get better at.

A strong motive for acting is *l'Esprit de l'Escalier,* an evocative French term, which literally translates *The Spirit of the Stairs.* Imagine yourself at a party, where someone says something astonishingly rude to you. You are stunned and struck speechless. The evening goes on. You are leaving the party, descending the *stairs* and suddenly the *spirit* comes to you. You think of the most devastating, witty comeback line in the world, a perfect retort, very civilized, but sure to end all such rudeness forever. Unfortunately, the party is over, you are outside, your rude assailant is nowhere to be seen, and too much time has gone by for an effective retort anyway. You would love to rewind the tape of your life, but no such luck. Yet the line was perfect!

You arrive home and are sorely tempted to tell the story *as if* you did execute the key line at the key moment. Your ethics are strongly tested. If enough time goes by, you might start telling the story that way. You might even start *believing* it happened the way it should have—if there was real justice in the world. There *is* real justice in the theater. Characters often *do* think of the perfect comeback. It is glorious to have a script where someone has given you brilliant, or at least dynamic, responses. It can be deeply soothing and satisfying to take part in an art form where life is more the way it ought to be. And sometimes it rubs off. The more time you spend speaking the great lines of others, the better chance you have to think of them yourself. There is a bumper sticker that says "If all the world's a stage, I need better lines." Proximity to better lines can help. You may develop into someone who gets the spirit long before descending the stairs.

A Richer Life

Acting is a life-enhancing experience. Even if you never enter the door of a theater after the last day of class, you should have gained vivid personal awareness, higher communication skills, and a strong dose of compassion for your fellow humans. There are many ways of studying human behavior, but most disciplines do it from a distance, looking at large groups and leaving the student with far more theory than experience. I know of no better, more involving way to learn about yourself, and about the phenomenon of being alive, than acting.

You learn how to relax and focus your energy more efficiently. You find out about ways in which your own body, voice, and personality impact on other people. You get some tools for change if you do not like what you find out. You have a much stronger sense of the kind of figure you cut in the world. You get to free some dormant creative impulses, some unchanneled emotional expression, and some suppressed playfulness.

You gain much of the same insight regarding others as individuals and groups. You observe more carefully and you interact with greater sensitivity. You may start out studying acting as an atheist, a pacifist, and a political liberal. Before it is over, you may be cast as a fundamentalist preacher, a soldier, and a Birch Society member. You may even be in class with such people and form an ensemble with them. You will never be able to casually judge them or generalize about them again. You will never be able to think of them merely as members of their alienating groups.

You not only find out about you and about others, but the *connections* between you and others: making connections, avoiding them, solidifying them, breaking them, sensing hidden agendas, nuances, layers of interaction. There is a good chance of being able to "play" your own life more thoroughly and with greater detail, because you have studied acting.

The study of acting allows you to return to Let's Pretend. Making believe that you are someone else is a standard childhood pastime. In later years, you may replace playing Peter Pan with deciding to be French while you are in a restaurant, being stinking rich as you peruse the sapphires in a jewelry store, or giving yourself a made-up background to share with the stranger you are seated next to on the plane. Or you may have lost the urge. Perhaps your group of playmates and players has dwindled, your fantasy figures gotten more predictable, and a sense of childlike whimsy drifted out of your life. Most of us were much better at Let's Pretend in days of yore, than now. Acting class can get you back in touch with the child in yourself. Acting can unlock the you before the locks were put on your imagination, your capacity for delight, your sense of wonder. It can unlock your dormant ability to transform yourself and the world around you.

Bill Cosby: *"In America, the seven ages of man have become preschooler, Pepsi generation, baby boomer, mid-lifer, empty-nester, senior citizen, and organ donor."*[6]

Michael J. Fox: *Actors are people who were good at playing "Let's Pretend" as kids and now we're getting money to play house.*[7]

Actors versus Others

Human beings all act, but what about the actor as a recognized artist, a professional, someone *known* as an actor? What makes some get up and perform, even show off, where others fear to tread? The story of Og, the Caveperson, freely adapted here,[8] is a possible explanation:

> Imagine a society of prehistoric types where strength and courage are admired above all. Imagine a small male Caveperson, named Og, living in this group and not quite fitting in. All males supposedly like to hunt and all take their turns killing dinosaurs (I told you this was freely adapted). Og likes to carve on the walls, he likes to eat, talk, and mate. He is scared of hunting. But his day comes along like everyone else's.
>
> Og spends the whole day observing dinosaurs and other powerful creatures, having neither the heart nor the courage to kill anything. He drags his club home at sundown, only to encounter all the massive, powerful brutes standing around the entrance to the cave. "Hey, Og, where's dinner?" one asks menacingly. Og pauses nervously and considers trying to run away.

Suddenly he is inspired. "Wait 'til I tell you about it," he says. "There I was on the plain, the sun beating mercilessly down on my neck when suddenly this enormous green creature roars (he stops and roars) and rolls his head (he rolls) so fiercely that I got chills (his listeners get chills) and then . . ." (The details of his story can be omitted since, with some embellishment, he takes them through his day so vividly that they almost feel as if they were there in his place.) Og has his audience mesmerized. He imitates the dinosaur to perfection, he gets the sound of dinofeet on the sandy plain, all the details. Cheers follow the end of his story.

All is forgiven. There is ample leftover dinosaur around anyway. The group quickly agrees that Og should be excused from hunting from now on. Instead, he should follow the hunters and observe the hunt, recreating it for everyone at supper each evening, acting out all the parts. Well, *most* of the parts. Already others are volunteering to help out. He is happy to be excused and glad to have a function. As Og and his mate head off to their corner of the cave, she says to him, "Og, you've got it all over those dumb brutes. You're a real artist."

As another couple move to their corner, she says, "That Og. Isn't he amazing? The way he got just how the dinosaur's head swings back and forth. It was perfect." Her mate replies, "Well, alright it was pretty good. Personally I wouldn't have swung my head so far. It's more of a circle than a swing, actually."

And so the first actor is born. And minutes later, the first critic.

In every culture, someone finds he is better at showing society how it lives than in living at its center. Someone finds that her gifts are for *re*creating human experience so that it breathes again. She can literally give life back to an event from the past or give *form* to something in the mind. One of the questions you are probably at least exploring in taking an acting class is whether or not that sort of person is you.

Nearly everyone fantasizes at some time about an acting career and acting teachers are plagued by first-term students wanting to know if they have what it takes. This question is premature. No decent teacher will answer it until a student has studied the art for a few years. A teacher *will* tell you where your strong suits appear to lie, where you have made clear progress, what kinds of goals you should be setting, and what training you should be pursuing next. But no one should give you thumbs up or down but you. If you decide ultimately, down the road, to pursue the profession, it will be because you know you must! It will be because the art has chosen and possessed you and you have no choice. You may or may not be Og.

Bette Midler: *Everything else in my life receded, once I discovered theater.*[9]

That is all in the future. For now, growth will come by focusing squarely on the present.

Observing Yourself Act

What happens at the exact moment that an actor acts? There are several ingredients, which are present in any life encounter. Before you observe an actor performing, take a look at yourself. Any moment, involving someone else, will involve:

1. Some way of defining what you and this other person mean to each other (**relationship**)
2. Something you want (**objective**)
3. Something in the way (**obstacle**)
4. Your plan to get what you want (**strategy**)
5. Specific maneuvers within your overall plan (**tactics**)
6. Things said by you and the other person (**text**)
7. Things implied but not really said (**subtext**)
8. Times when you may not speak at all but are actively thinking (**interior monolog**)
9. Moments when the other person says or does something that makes you pause, consider, and *reject* several different answers before choosing a reply (**evaluation**)
10. Changes within the scene, signaling that some kind of transaction has been completed and a new one is starting (**beats**)

The terms that are in boldface are actor language for these ingredients. There is no simpler or more difficult lesson in acting than learning these ten items. They provide the basis of the Stanislavski System which will be covered later, but they are really the basis of human interaction. Almost all actors who perform well identify these ten ingredients in every scene they play. Almost all actors who fail, have forgotten this basic homework.

Imagine that you want to finish reading this chapter (only a few more pages), but your roommate's tape deck is blaring. You decide to get rid of her. You try mentioning her promise to call her folks tonight. You inquire if she shares your hunger for a pizza. She is not interested. She wants to sing along with the tape and to talk about how music has changed her life. Finally, you level with her that you cannot concentrate and ask her for 15 minutes of silence. She agrees. Curtain.

Active Ingredients

1. *Relationship:* newly assigned roommate; do not know each other well; seem to have differing tastes and lifestyles
2. *Objective:* to finish homework (chapter 1, *Acting: Onstage and Off*)
3. *Obstacle:* roommate's blaring stereo
4. *Strategy:* getting rid of roommate
5. *Tactics:* distractions (phone call, pizza); frankness (asking favor)
6. *Text* and
7. *Subtext* (possible sample: text in boldface type, subtext in parentheses):

> YOU: (Okay, here goes.) **Didn't you** . . . (God, I hope this isn't too pushy.) . . . **promise your folks to call home tonight?** (Good, sounded casual enough.)
>
> HER: (So who cares?) **Uh** . . . **yeah.** (None of your business, actually.) **So?** (Change the subject. Aha!) **I love this song.** (Let it go.) **[singing along and moving to the music] Your body, your body, your bodeeeee!!!!** (Can I shake it or what?)
>
> YOU: (I hope this isn't too pushy.) **Well, shouldn't you call them then?** (It was. I'm such a jerk.)
>
> HER: (One mother is enough, thanks.) **I already tried.** (Buzz off. . . . Oh, I guess she means well.) **They aren't home.** (Christ!) **I left a message on their machine.** (Satisfied????)

8. *Interior Monolog* (preceding the exchange above):

> (That machine of hers is driving me crazy. Alright now, what is this? Observe myself act? What is this guy talking about? How many more pages? "I wanna bang, I wanna clang." I can't get the stupid lyric out of my head. Please God, make the power go off. . . . I have to write out all this private stuff?! I wonder who's gonna see this.

"Clanga, banga, uh HUH!!!! Clanga, banga you-woo!!!" You-woo? What does that mean? Damn it all. I need quiet. I gotta get her outta here. What could I . . . Hey wait, what about her phone call home?)

Was some of this hard to follow? Reread it. Almost everyone's interior monolog will confuse someone else. References to previous pages in this chapter are overlapped with thoughts about the roommate.

9. *Evaluation* (possible alternatives later in the scene): She says, "Music makes me feel good," and you consider saying:

   1. "Shut that thing off or I'll kill you!"
   2. "Look, this is one half my space and I have some rights, so . . ."
   3. "I'm going to the library."
   4. "This book is too hard to deal with, combined with that music."
   5. (Alternative chosen after considering and rejecting the others) "Listen, I've got to get this reading done and I'm getting distracted. Could you do me a favor and let me have 15 minutes of quiet? I'll owe you."

10. *Beats:*

    1. Fuming by yourself until she enters
    2. Phone call home pitch, falls flat
    3. Pizza pitch, also flat
    4. Ode to music, pause
    5. Request for silence, acceptance.

The wonderful thing about this simple list is that if you are really thinking about each item, you are so involved that you do not have room in your consciousness for nervousness, awkward self-consciousness, or distractions. People who fail to get what they want are often failing to play their objectives strongly enough or to switch tactics, when one clearly is not going to work. Or even more often, they do not consider quite enough alternatives, during an evaluation, before choosing one.

Exercise 1.6

Playing Objectives

Improvise another scene with a different objective and conflict provided by the roommate character. Identify the ten ingredients.

Repeat the exercise trying to persuade:

1. your parent to let you take one of the family cars back to school for a few weeks
2. a policeman not to give you a speeding ticket
3. a salesperson to take an out-of-town personal check
4. a professor to accept a late paper
5. someone working registration to let you into an overcrowded acting class

Exercise 1.7

Real Life

The scenes above are just conjecture. Using the above format:

1. Find some real situations and jot down the ingredients before the encounters have passed from memory. Pick two scenes with different partners and quite different objectives.
2. Write down what happened in such a way that the outline or skeleton of each experience emerges. (See Appendix B, "Acting Observed," for an optional format for these observations.)
3. Identify:
   relationship
   setting
   other character
   basic situation
   objective
   obstacle
   strategy
   tactics
   text and subtext (at least four lines of dialogue)
   interior monolog (one or two paragaphs at a crucial moment)
   evaluation (at least four rejected alternatives plus the one chosen)
   beats
4. Repeat the process, for a third encounter, using the fewest possible words to describe the event. Do not let yourself get bogged down in description or detail. The result should scan easily. It should be clean and virtually free of verbiage.
5. Stop and notice during the next week when you shift beats, what range of tactics you employ, when you regret your choice during an evaluation and wish you had gone with the one rejected. You want to let the vocabulary become second nature and to heighten your own awareness of the theater present in each life.

A few guidelines before you go to a play and watch an actor using these ingredients onstage.

1. Objectives should be stated with the preposition "to" followed by an *active* verb. Never use the word "be" because it has no dynamics, unless it is all by itself ("to be or not to be"). Objectives like "to be happy" or "to be loved" are both so passive that they cannnot be actively enacted. So stated they give you nothing to *do*. "To find joy" and "to get a lover" are more actable.

2. Keep language simple and words to a minimum. Use down-to-earth unambiguous terms, which click quickly into the consciousness. Your analysis of a scene should read like a clear set of traffic signals, guiding you through the part.

3. The relationship between strategy and tactics is like that in sports between a game plan and plays. There is always a general plan of attack, but then there are a wide range of maneuvers *within* the plan.

4. Subtext may support the text, it may modify or qualify it, it may add dimensions that the text did not seem to imply by itself. It may actually contradict or work against the text as in the old vaudeville routine:

> STRAIGHT MAN: "Nervous?"
>
> COMIC: "NOOOPE!!!!!" *(second line given with so much terror and anxiety that it wipes out the word itself)*

    Subtext is an actor's food and air. Finding, changing, and shading subtext is what actors most love to do and what audiences most love to watch. Stanislavski says that subtext is what the audience comes to the theater to see, that if all they wanted was the text they could have stayed home and read the script. A firm, hard remark is modified with a gentle, warm tone and the most polite, civil response (words) can be filled with dangerous warning (delivery) not to tread further. Potential alteration of text, when spoken, is staggering. Subtext is a phenomenal source of power.

5. Do not be tempted to write out interior monologs like term papers with formal word choices and perfect sentences. These monologs are really jagged, full of incomplete and interrupted thoughts, sudden, illogical twists and turns. The language (because it goes on in your head and does not need censoring) is often rough, crude, irrational, profane, even silly. Your interior monolog is like a tape that runs continuously in your head day and night. When you are scattered or disorganized, it is doubly so. It is stream of consciousness, but this stream has a lot of

debris, driftwood, seaweed, and a few dead fish. No one's interior monolog is tidy.

Alternatives

What you consider, but reject, will vary from person to person and according to mood. If you are feeling ill and surly your evaluation may include several insulting retorts and at least one obscene howl. Most evaluations, however, include the following:

Response	*Sample Line*
complete rejection	"No way. Not in your lifetime. Not in this century. Eat garbage and die."
complete acceptance	"Whatever you say."
stalling	"I don't get it. Could you run that by again?"
guarded, ambiguous response	"Thanks for your frankness. I hear what you're saying."
logical, reasonable answer	"Let's go over each one of your points."
emotional, passionate answer	"Oh God! I love it!!!" or "X#&@!!!"
something threatening	"Go ahead. Make my day."
something charming	"You sure have a way with words."
any combination of the above	

Actors are tempted to leave out evaluations that people use in life. The result is bad acting. It is easy to omit evaluating because the lines are already there and the actor does not have to search for words. It is this *search*, however, that is compelling to watch. Great actors fill their evaluations with original, powerful alternatives. Whenever they are handed a difficult cue, we watch, intrigued by what they consider but choose not to unveil, enthralled, as they prepare to respond.

Exercise 1.8

Observing Alternatives

Take turns challenging others in the class with difficult questions (like pretending you hate the color of someone's sweater and how dare he wear it to class?), and listening carefully to the answer. Have the class identify alternatives they *saw* considered, but left unchosen, before the actual answer.

Exercise 1.9

Observing and Identifying

Sets of two volunteers get up, letting the class give them a simple relationship (such as brother and sister) and conflict (like disagreeing over the best Mother's Day gift). Have half the class "identify" with one person and half with the other. The first person to observe three complete beats stops the scene. Everyone should identify the ten basics for each brief encounter that has just occurred.

Exercise 1.10

Observing Class

Designate someone, at the beginning of the hour, to stop class at any given moment during the first half hour of the session. Then review the period so far, in terms of the ten basics. What were the shared objectives? What was the first noted obstacle? What was the most noteworthy evaluation? What general strategies and specific tactics have been employed? How has this class period divided into beats?

Exercise 1.11

Observing Offstage Acting

1. Observe and record an offstage encounter exactly as you did in class exercises 1.9 and 1.10. Be objective.
2. Now be subjective. Pick one of the people to side with, giving yourself a much stronger sense of one participant's subtext than the other's.

Exercise 1.12

Observing Onstage Acting

1. Attend a production and observe a single character with whom you feel some identification. Compare responses with your classmates.
2. Repeat the exercise with a character for whom you feel no identifica-

tion or sympathy, to experience some understanding and compassion from the perspective of a character who is so different from yourself.

Already an Actor

By now a profile of you as a performer should be emerging: the kinds of situations you thrive in; the fantasies and visions that inspire you; your own areas of vulnerability and of strength in public and in crises; the areas of childlike wonder that are still very much alive, and those that may need some resuscitation; where you script and where you wing it.

Many of these offstage experiences can be transferred to give you confidence and texture onstage. Most of your acting experience can be brought into the theater and used there. You have a giant resume of performances. Some were Oscar caliber triumphs. Others were such disasters you do not even like to think about them, unless enough time has passed to make them funny. All can be a source of learning. It would be a waste to start acting class convinced that you are an acting virgin. Your life is a fascinating fund that can be drawn on to help you become both a better actor and a more complete human being.

Now that your own acting past and present have been acknowledged, you are ready to learn an art form that can give you a future with:

A fascinating lifelong endeavor
A chance to utter great and just words
Increased insight and compassion
Stronger self-awareness
More successful human interactions
A reawakening of the child in you

Not bad for a single area of study. It is ironic that a portion of the population regards acting as frivolous and far from the fundamentals of life. What could be more fundamental than feeling full of possibility?

Jack Nicholson: *The actor is Camus's ideal existential hero, because if life is absurd and the idea is to live a more vital life, the man who lives more lives is in a better position than the guy who lives just one.*[10]

2

Relaxed
Readiness

(getting calm enough, yet
energized enough, to perform
fully)

William Hurt: *I'm not a talented man . . . I'm a focused
man.*[1]

Kathleen Turner: *A lot of it is awareness. I've learned to
use my eyes to focus attention. And I'm real good at concentrating.*[2]

Constantin Stanislavski: *The eye of a focused actor attracts
the spectator . . . . a blank eyed actor lets the attention of
the spectator wander.*[3]

Warming Up

Actors who are focused are fascinating. The best way to achieve
focus is to learn how to warm up. Because acting challenges the
body, the voice, and the spirit, all three deserve some attention. All
three can be eased into a higher state of alert responsiveness and
sharper focus. In the great offstage performances of your life so far,
focus came suddenly, perhaps accidentally. But this state can be
achieved deliberately.

An acting class or a cast is a group needing instant trust and
mutual acceptance. Everyone depends on everyone else. They have
no choice. Time cannot be wasted, while each individual frets over
when and how to open up to the others. Each person needs to

warm up his own instrument and he needs to warm up to those around him. This chapter will deal with preparing to act, as an individual and as a member of the group.

Balancing Opposing States

If you are too *relaxed,* you fall asleep. If you are too *ready,* you can explode. The actor seeks a balance between ease and eagerness, between indifference and anxiety. Someone heavily anesthetized is relaxed, but then so is a corpse. A guru of the past decade used to admonish his Quaalude-besotted disciples that they were aiming to become "laid back, not laid out." Concentrate only on relaxation and your performance is likely to come up short on energy, vitality, clarity, and power. At the other extreme is the player who works himself into a locker-room frenzy, overflowing with energy and anticipation, ready to explode. This works for sprinting and high decibel rock, but leads to acting that burns out quickly, to performance minus nuance, shading, and variety.

Images of cats permeate acting literature, because no other creature seems quite so loose, yet alert. Acting warm-ups shoot for *relaxed readiness* since actors are not automatically blessed with the cat's perfect energy state. As you learn the following sequence (or any other used by your class), keep yourself open and responsive. Avoid prejudging any exercise. Do not pick favorites; do not decide early which you do not like; do not decide at all yet. Just let go. It may seem for a while as if nothing is happening. When you finally get each exercise mastered and are free enough to allow it to work on you, you will begin to benefit.

Physical Warm-ups

While actors vary widely in their rituals of preparation, the following sequence of activities is probably the most commonly used:

Meditation
Tensing/Releasing
Alignment
Shaking
Stretching
Breathing
Aerobics

The warm-up that follows employs one or two exercises from each category, plus an optional return to a meditation wrap-up.

The sequence is important even if you vary the activity, since each phase prepares you for the next. Skipping steps in any designed exercise sequence could mean strain or even pain, since you may not be loose enough, yet, for whatever you have jumped to. Read through, stopping to try something if you feel like it. You will need unhampering clothing that lets you roll around on the floor and either very soft soled shoes or none at all.

Narrowing Your Circle

When it comes time to do the exercises in class, find a space for yourself and narrow your focus, so that you do not make eye contact with anyone. Listen to the instructions as side-coaching (you hear the words but do not look at the speaker), so you are alone, even though surrounded by others. Imagine that you have a circle surrounding your immediate territory, with no need to move outside it. Work in a state of public solitude, allowing the capacity to be comfortably alone, even in the midst of a large group. This is a state the actor often needs to enter in performance.

Modify any exercise if it appears to give you strain today. Feel free to drop out of the activity if you do not feel well. No need to explain your decision. Instead, just fade subtly out until you feel you can rejoin. Since all of these exercises are standard and tested, however, consistent problems with any of them means you should see a physician.

Breathe fully throughout each exercise, alternating a complete inhalation in one position with a generous exhalation as you move to the next. Do not concentrate so hard on getting the moves right that you forget to breathe. Let the air flow move you along, and help you loosen up.

Meditation

Even a few minutes spent silent, still, eyes closed, focus narrowed can be calming. Meditation is usually done sitting or lying on the floor and involves repetition of a sound silently to yourself. Breathing tends to get more and more shallow as concentration turns inward.

Exercise 2.1

Here and Now

The time devoted to this exercise will vary depending on the need of the group. If everyone seems high-strung today, this may be extended. Everyone should find "their own space." If there is a sense of calm unity already in the room, even two minutes may be enough:

1. Let go of responsibilities carried from the past and expected in the future. Past and future are like heavy, cumbersome layers of clothing you let drop aside so you can breathe. Give yourself permission to be in no time or place but right this moment, in this room, surrounded by these other actors. Feel the earlier part of the day, and the later part ahead, drift away, so you feel completely here, in this moment.

2. Help yourself focus here and now, by picking out small physical sensations: feelings of jewelry against your skin, places where clothes feel loose and draped, a radiator humming, your own shallow breathing, the places your body makes contact with the floor. Nothing is too tiny or trivial to notice if it is immediate.

3. Choose a word or sound that pleases you: a suggestive verb like "soothe," "ease," "release," "complete," "renew"; or something purely sensual and abstract like "velvet," "music," "embrace," or "dawn"; the name of a favorite object, place, or a nonsense syllable that makes you feel good. Repeat the word silently to yourself, continuously, without any effort, letting the qualities of the word wash over you and allowing your mind to wander where it will.

Tensing/Releasing

The principle of adding *some* tension to an area of the body just prior to letting that area unwind or fall free is widely accepted as a means of producing greater release. A moderately tensed muscle relaxes more when let go than it would from a neutral state, and the immediate contrast produces, for most people, a pleasurable, easy feeling.

Exercise 2.2

The Prune

Lie on your back with arms and legs uncrossed and loose. As each area of the body is called, tense it up, keeping everything lower on your body loose and relaxed. The tension will accumulate, moving from head to toes, before you finally let everything go and float from the release. Each tensing is more effective if you imagine you are making that area of the body taut, in order to protect yourself against some shock.

1. First tense all your facial muscles inward toward the center of the face, as if it were rapidly withering and drying up into a prune.
2. Tighten the surrounding skull as if it were suddenly locked in a vise.
3. Shoot the tension into the neck as if it were in a brace and frozen in place.
4. Shoot it across the shoulders, locking at the shoulder joints (remember everything below the shoulders is still loose).
5. Tighten the upper arms, both sets of biceps and triceps.
6. Tense at the elbows, locking the elbow joints . . .
7. into the lower arms . . .
8. locking the wrists as if they were tightly bound . . .
9. tightening the palms of the hands as if catching a ball . . .
10. drawing the fingers halfway into a fist that will not complete itself but remains suspended and partly closed.
11. Tighten upper chest and back . . .
12. stomach and lower back as if protecting against a blow.
13. Tense hip joints, which are then locked.
14. Tense the groin area and the buttocks . . .
15. stiffen upper legs . . .
16. lock the knee joints . . .
17. draw lower legs taut . . .
18. lock ankles . . .
19. stiffen feet, extending toes.
20. Point toes finally at the wall opposite you.
21. Final position: pull upward towards the ceiling at the center of your body, so that your torso is lifted up off the ground and your body is supported only by the back of the head, the shoulder blades, and your heels, as if the whole body was drying up like a prune. Hold.
22. Release, letting it all go, feeling almost as if you are sinking into the floor or floating in the air, but in no way confined anymore by gravity. Relax and savor the sensation of easy, released floating.

Figure 2-1 The Prune
Full tension just before final release. Body supported in just three places.

23. Repeat more quickly, remembering to keep everything loose until it is called: tighten face, head, neck, shoulders, upper arms, elbows, lower arms, wrists, hands, fingers halfway into fist, upper chest and back, stomach and lower back, hip joints, groin and buttocks, upper legs, knee joints, lower legs, ankles, feet, toes pointed, body pulled up towards ceiling and release. And savor.

Alignment

The spinal column has become universally recognized as a primary center for the body—a center of energy and also, unfortunately, tension. The vertebrae tend to literally close off in a way that shortens the spine and blocks your physical and emotional responsiveness. Fortunately the column can be returned to a relatively open state by beginning on the floor and allowing the space between each vertebra to return as the back stretches toward an aligned state and the rest of the body follows.

Exercise 2.3

The Accordion

1. Still on your back and without pushing to achieve it, simply allow your spine to stretch out along the floor. Imagine your body is like thick syrup that has splashed on the floor and slowly, easily spreads in every direction.
2. The back should be absolutely flat against the floor. For many, this feeling will be achieved more easily by raising the knees slowly and/or extending the elbows slightly to the side. Shift around until you find your own flattest, easiest position.
3. Imagine the spine as a hand accordion stretching to its full length but still undulating gently and feeling no pressure.
4. Imagine air whirling gently around each vertebra, as they all ease apart. Imagine that your head is several miles away from your tailbone, as these two ease gently in opposite directions.
5. Roll over on your side into a curled position and slowly move to a standing position by uncoiling, with the head the very last part to reach the top and the column returning to the same aligned, stretched sensation that it had when pressed against the floor.

6. Think of your head now as a balloon floating high above the rest of the body, which hangs comfortably from the balloon. Plant your feet firmly and imagine them many, many miles away from your head-balloon. You should feel as if your posture is excellent, but that it was achieved without effort and maintained without strain.
7. Sense your accordion spine moving imperceptibly, comfortably stretching.

Exercise 2.4

The Puppet

1. Drop the entire upper body forward like a puppet, breaking at the waist so that your hands almost brush the floor.
2. Let the knees bend slightly and use the lower body only for balance and support, ignoring it otherwise and letting the entire upper body hang loose and limp.
3. Test your own looseness by swinging arms and head apelike back and forth until you are really limp.
4. Imagine a string connected to your tailbone which begins to tug you up as if a puppeteer is pulling you into action. Imagine similar strings connected to each of the thirty-plus vertebrae all the way up into the back of your skull.
5. Allow yourself to rise very slowly, string by string, untensing slightly with each tug. Avoid any temptation to pull upper back, neck, and

Figure 2-2 The Puppet
Note that the head is the very last part to rise, even after the entire torso is erect.

head up too early. They are the very last strings. You will reach a
completely erect position before your neck even begins to rise.
6. Collapse again and repeat.

Shaking

At any of the joints (wrists, elbows, shoulders, and so on), stiffness
or the false sensation of cramp in a nearby muscle may be relieved
by spinning the appendage in a circle or just shaking it out. The
sudden rush of activity tends to awaken that area of the body, so it
joins the rest of you and takes part again.

Exercise 2.5

Rag Doll

1. Imagine yourself as loose as a rag doll or scarecrow and simply shake
   out, standing in place, wherever you feel a little tight.
2. Spend some time on just the wrists, then elbows, then the whole arm
   from the shoulder joint, then alternating legs, finally all of these going
   at random.

Return to shaking at any point in the exercise sequence when you
feel like it. Do not isolate it at this point, but return to it regularly,
as a constant way of loosening and of filling time while you may be
waiting for others to complete an exercise.

Stretching

In physical conditioning, stretching is an effective counterbalance
to muscle-building activity. The muscles narrow and contract as
they build, restricting flexibility, as in "muscle bound." Stretching
gives pliability and helps add grace to strength. More than any single activity, stretching serves to prevent injury, keeps muscles sup-
ple, and the body flexible. It can be profoundly healing. Oddly
enough, while animals seem to know instinctively how to stretch,
humans have largely forgotten. The upper back and neck area tends
to gather tension and benefits particularly from stretching. The following exercise may be the one most widely used by actors.

Exercise 2.6

Head Rolls

1. Standing tall, with feet firmly planted, let your head drop forward into the chest, chin landing gently on your clavicle.
2. Begin slowly rolling head in either direction in a moderate circle that grows in size with each repetition.
3. Change direction after you work your way to a wide circle.
4. Keep the rest of the body upright and isolate the action to the head and neck so the shoulders and chest are in no way active. Make no effort to keep your mouth closed or eyes shut, but let them drop if you feel the impulse. Make no effort for any sort of regularity of rhythm; if you feel like lingering briefly as the head is over the right shoulder in order to relish the stretch there, go ahead. Let yourself sense where you *need* to linger. If you feel like it, increase the speed of the circles, but only if that feels good today.
5. It may help to think of the neck as a ball bearing at the connection between torso and head, a ball bearing firmly placed but capable of a large range of safe motion.

A stretched body is capable of reaching farther without strain. Physical stretching can make you feel more capable of emotional, creative stretching as well.

Exercise 2.7

The Sun

This is one of many variations of a popular, Yoga-based exercise that not only stretches the whole body, but can be infused with optional spiritual connotations as you worship the sun, salute it, or (if the day is overcast) try to will it into appearing. There are eleven stages: 1 and 11 are the same. So are 2 and 10, 5 and 7. This will be more complicated than anything so far, but the stretch is worth it:

1. Stand tall, hands clasped, palms together, as in prayer or traditional Oriental greeting.
2. Explode into a giant X figure, arms and legs wide and open, leaning back slightly in order to face the sun.
3. Legs together and straight, bend upper body over (as in toe touches), but with hands grasping ankles, getting a full stretch along the back of the legs.

Figure 2-3 The Sun

Coding these eleven moves into simple calls:

1. hands   2. salute   3. ankles

4. side stretch   5. V

6. cobra   7. V

8. side stretch   9. fetus

10. salute   11. hands

4. Hands out on floor, support the body (as at the beginning of a push-up), but with only one leg extended behind, while the other is bent beneath the upper body, stretching the extended side of the body. The overall position is similar to a sprinter about to take off. (In each of these full body stretches, the head is tilted slightly back so that the line from head to foot is a very moderate C curve.)

5. Extend the leg that was bent to join the other and move the body into an upside down V with your buttocks the point of the V and high in the air.

6. Lower upper body as if to do a push-up, but as the face nears the floor, curve the torso around into a cobra position, providing a gentle stretch along the lower back and upper legs.

7. Repeat the upside down V.

8. Repeat the stretch in step 4, reversing extended and bent legs so that the stretch is on the other side of the body.

9. Feet together and supporting your weight, curl the body into the smallest possible position (approximately fetal), head against knees and arms wrapped around lower legs. Squeeze yourself inward in preparation to explode out.

10. Repeat the X full salute of step 2.

11. Repeat the hands-clasped stillness of step 1.

Eventually, when all moves are second nature, aim to perform the Sun as one continuous, flowing action. Pulse slightly in each location, but imagine a floating, unbroken, easy dance, with all moves having the fluid, spineless quality of the cobra for whom position 6 is named.

   Alternative: If time and space make it difficult to do the Sun, just taking a few minutes to stretch anywhere *you* feel tight, working your way gradually through the body is a simple substitute.

Breathing

The term "breath support" means more than having enough air to speak. The manner and depth of breathing you choose can produce differing energy states. Research shows that changing breathing patterns can change the way you feel. The act "supports" you in varying ways: from the calm stillness of shallow meditation breathing to the highly energized, almost juiced sensation of full diaphragmatic breathing and the stamina of lower back breathing. The actor needs at different moments to call on a whole range of support. The following exercise touches on the *deepest* breathing, because most of us need to be reminded of the reserves of breath storage. Also, in this warm-up sequence, it is time for something energizing.

Exercise 2.8

Lung Vacuum

This exercise literally cleans out stale air and replaces it forcibly. Some dizziness is natural, particularly for smokers, at the very beginning.

1. Collapse exactly as in the Puppet, simultaneously blowing air out vigorously (and audibly) through the mouth.
2. In the collapsed position, continue to blow out air in short, powerful spurts until you feel completely emptied of air. Imagine that you need to get rid of harmful fumes and replace them with clean air, but that it will only work if you are totally empty. Proceed at your own rate with no need for group coordination.
3. Rise slowly, keeping air out, making sure your footing is secure and solid. Keep air out as long as you can manage it. (NOTE: Do not try to do this in sync with others in the group. This is not a competition and lung capacity varies between people who are identically fit.)
4. When you feel you *must* breathe, allow air to sweep in, feeling it pour almost to the end of your fingertips and toes. You should feel much like Woody Allen looked in his balloon suit in *Sleeper.* Notice the rush of air to the small of the back. You should feel an intense rush as the new air sucks in with a vacuum force.
5. Repeat sequence at your own rate.

Good actors always work to inhale faster (so they do not waste valuable time) and to exhale slower (so they can speak longer and more confidently). This exercise is an intensification of that sensation with exhalation extended for quite a while, and inhalation happening in an instant.

NOTE: The following two sequences should be considered optional, depending on the needs of the group. If the vocal warm-up is being included, it should be inserted at this point.

Aerobics (Optional)

The value of a regularly raised, sustained heartbeat has been established for cardiovascular fitness and health fringe benefits. Some kind of aerobic activity is standard for anyone pursuing fitness, and the payoff is especially strong for actors who need endurance and controlled breathing.

Long-term benefits are not the reason for aerobic exercise in this warm-up, however. A minimum of fifteen minutes three times a week is needed for that. The following activity is designed to get the heart pumping and the blood flowing after the calmer earlier exercises.

Exercise 2.9

The Blender

This sequence is performed as fast as the group can manage it and, unlike earlier activities, usually done watching someone lead the movement. The leader calls moves with a definite, clear beat. Everyone bounces lightly on the balls of the feet throughout.

1. Two jumping jacks—familiar exercise with leader setting time.
2. Two elbow to knees—elbow touches opposite knee, as the other arm swings high in the air; then other elbow touches other knee.
3. Two touch feet in back—hand slaps shoe in opposition as above (left hand to right foot, right hand to left foot) as foot is raised in back. Again, unused arm swings high in air.
4. Two side jacks—same as jumping jacks, except body is turned sideways each time with one arm to the front and the other back; one leg bent to one side and the other leg straight and extended to other side.
5. Two kicks—one leg up and forward with both arms extended out to the sides.
6. Two starbursts—similar to positions 2 and 10 in the Sun. Dip with hands just above knees, then leap off the ground into a big open X in the air.

Exercise 2.10

Here and Now II

Return to a sitting or lying position, close your eyes, and renew your sense of here and now, with the added stimuli of the preceding exercises. Drop away any lingering past or future distractions; touch on some immediate physical sensations; repeat a word or sound that makes you feel good. Allow yourself to feel a part of the group around you with whom you have shared the activity. Let yourself be the same as those around you, still *you,* but even and comfortable with others.

Figure 2-4 The Blender

1. jumping jacks

2. elbows to knees

3. touch feet in back

4. side jacks

5. kicks

6. starbursts

Figure 2-4 The Blender (continued)

Changing Images (Optional)

Countless exercises could be substituted for any above. Do not give in to the temptation, however, to want new exercises every day. If you are bored with a warm-up, it is because you are not yet giving yourself up to it. Acting warm-ups do not work until you can do them mindlessly, without struggling to remember what is next. The variety and enhancement can come with the *images* you change in your head. Here are some possibilities:

Prune: You age radically with each tensing. You are a hideous crone (like the picture of Dorian Gray) by the last "pruning." Youth and vigor all return as you release. You are rejuvenated and renewed.

Accordion: As your spine lengthens, so do you. You are Gulliver being tugged at gently by the Lilliputians or Paul Bunyan napping luxuriously over acres of timberland. When you stand you can see across continents.

Head Rolls: You are Samson or Rapunzel. You have an amazing mane of hair that whirls in slow motion around you like a cloud. Each roll of the head increases your own power, beauty, pride in your mane.

Puppet: You are an ape when you collapse. At each tug along the spine you move through an evolutionary cycle from primitive to a fully formed human of the future (passing through Og about one third of the way up), bright, complete, and ready to conquer new worlds.

Sun: You are a much-revered priestess/dancer or medicine man. Your people have pinned all their hopes for survival on you. Each move is a supplication to nature for Spring to arrive and save your people from the cold. You literally *will* the sun to come out and warm those under your care.

Lung Vacuum: You are saving the world. At great peril to yourself you have breathed in toxic fumes, which you now blow out of your body and off the planet. You are successful and when you inhale, you are cleansed and safe.

The Blender: It is an Olympics far into the future and you have been chosen healthiest and most beautiful human in the world. You are dancing for a throng of people who wish to emulate you. Each move has them gasping with wonder. Each move fills you with power, which those who watch share because your energy is contagious.

It helps warm up the mind, if the physical maneuvers are accompanied by a rigorous workout of the imagination. You might pick a theme for a given session (the examples above are all about *power* and *heroism*), depending on your interests or needs that day. If you are warming up for a character, you might direct images to the character's background/perspective, so you are entering her world through each exercise.

Vocal Warm-ups

This sequence should take about five minutes, once mastered, and is more effective if it follows a complete physical warm-up (see suggested point of insertion in preceding sequence). When the body has been relaxed, aligned, and stretched, when breath has been tapped, then the voice can be freed. A vocal warm-up that is not preceded by a physical one is like building without a foundation. A standard progression involves the following stages:

Releasing
Breathing
Rooting Sound
Shaping Sound
Precision

Releasing

The muscles of the face and throat need to be allowed to relax so breath and sound are not constricted. It is as if a free, open passage needs to be created, before the voice can pass untroubled. Some moderate tensing will be introduced again so the relaxation is fuller when it follows.

Exercise 2.11

Letting Go

1. *The Lion:* Stretch your face open and out in all directions, bug-eyed, like a Kabuki lion or like the Munch painting *The Cry.* It is as if you are executing a silent scream. Your mouth is wide open, tongue extended downward. Imagine a silent scream with full desperation but no sound.
2. *Skin Slide:* Let the scream disappear. Allow all the facial muscles to collapse slowly, including the jaw which drops open. Imagine the skin almost sliding off the skeletal structure of the face, because it is that relaxed. Your eyelids may drop half-shut. Let them.
3. *Jaw Drop:* Open and close your mouth several times, effortlessly allowing the opening to increase slightly each time. Test to see if you can easily get two fingers into the opening, without strain. From now on, let the jaw drop open or closed, with no effort to control it, unless an exercise calls for it.
4. *Full-Body Yawn:* Let your whole self participate, the body doing a big stretch, forming a loose X, with a full, audible, lengthy sighing sound released as your arms drop to your sides again.
5. *Shoulder Drops:* Raise your shoulders very high, then let them drop. Repeat twice more, raising the shoulders slightly less each time.
6. *Inclines:* Incline head to right and left back and forth, in a gently rocking motion, feeling a light, soothing sensation in the throat with each move.

7. *Nods:* Do the same movement to the front and back as if you are agreeing with someone. Allow head to fall back as far as it falls forward. Remember, let the jaw hang loose.

Breathing

Now that the path is clear, breath is needed to help reach for sound and carry it forth. This sequence also works breath storage to the small of the back, more gradually than in the Lung Vacuum.

Exercise 2.12

Respirating

Consciously record air passing through each of the following areas:

1. *Nose and Throat:* deeply inhaling.
2. *Upper Chest:* letting air pass *through* without any expansion in this area.
3. *Floating Ribs:* Three sets of lower ribs are unattached at the front, so when they part, air flows fully. Feel them open like a double door of welcome for the air.
4. *Diaphragm:* Normally in an arched and raised position (figure 2-5), it both lowers and flattens as deep breathing occurs. Feel the area in the lower torso expand to its fullest as the diaphragm descends.
5. *Lower Back:* Finally the air reaches deeply into this most efficient, often unused, storage room.
6. Now sigh out in exhalation, recording the *reversal* of the process, as the air moves out and past the lower back, diaphragm, floating ribs, upper chest, and mouth.
7. Repeat the process a few times, then follow with another Full-Body Yawn.

Rooting Sound

With air to ride, sound can be strongly summoned from deep in the torso, where your fullest, most resonant music lives. The specific physiological location is less important than what it feels like. Sound that feels rooted, like a firm, proud tree, will fill a space and vary itself with little deliberate effort.

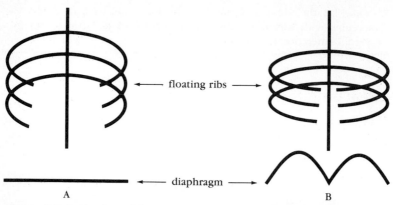

floating ribs

diaphragm

A   B

Figure 2-5 Active Breathing
Whereas much of the breathing process is passive, two distinct and
striking activities occur within the torso when deep, full respiration takes
place. First visualize air causing the three sets of floating ribs to expand
and the diaphragm to lower and flatten as you inhale (A). Then visualize
the diaphragm returning to its double-arched, humped position and the
floating ribs returning to a more closed position as you exhale (B).

Exercise 2.13

Sounding

1. *Planting:* Plant feet firmly and imagine voice planted way down in
   your tailbone, with roots passing down through you, through your legs
   and into the ground beneath you.
2. *Humming:* Reach down for sound on inhalation and hum on exhalation. Explore the tones and colors available. Let sounds resonate in the
   facial mask.
3. *Roller Coaster:* Work the hum up and down your register from lower
   to higher pitches and back, like a roller coaster, rooting deeper each
   time sounds descends. Note the sensation of vibrating sound along the
   front of your torso as you resonate. Note all the places the sound *can*
   vibrate if it needs to.
4. *String:* Imagine a string pulling sound louder as it tugs away, then
   softer as it returns to your mouth. Hum, then evolve into an
   AAAHHHH sound. Let the volume increase and decrease, without
   pitch going up, tension in the throat, or stridency in the sound, but by
   confidently rooting. As it gets louder, feel the string confidently extending to some great distance. As it gets softer, the sound is no more
   comfortable, but capable of greater subtlety.

Shaping Sound

Parts of the body may be exercised separately, for particular attention. Organs for shaping sound into words can benefit from individual exercises. Just as some parts of your body tend to add fat or lose flexibility more easily than others, if not worked, your organs of articulation may need degrees of attention to keep them in shape. The consonants and vowels used in the drill sections are those that give most people difficulty. These exercises can all be performed quite rapidly (not tensely, but quickly, for dexterity), once they are mastered. Most consonants (except *f, v, s, z,* and *th*) can be struck more cleanly, quickly, and simply than is often done. They need to be tapped, not bludgeoned.

While the animal images are evocative, the consonant and vowel drills are helped by making up specific occasions, messages, languages, or attitudes as you speak them ("Pay, Pay, Pay," cries the cossack to the Czar; "Kay, Kay, Kay," orders the galactic ship captain to his staff; and so forth), filling the exercises with both imagination and purpose.

Exercise 2.14

Isolations

The Lips

1. *Fish:* Isolate and expand lips as if moving through water, stretching them like you are a guppy, as if you have fish lips.
2. *Horse:* Make an unvoiced P sound which expodes like a horse when it shakes its head. Work for maximum vibration of the lips.
3. *Motor Boat:* A VVVVVV sound, slowly starting the motor, taking off, changing gears, choking the engine, dying out.
4. *Lip Drill:*
   PAYPAYPAY   PAYPAYPAY   PAYPAYPAY   PAH
   BAYBAYBAY   BAYBAYBAY   BAYBAYBAY   BAH
   MAYMAYMAY   MAYMAYMAY   MAYMAYMAY   MAH

The Hard Palate

5. *The Fly:* ZZZZZZZZ sound varying pitch and volume
6. *Snake:* SSSSS sound threatening prey, varying intensity
7. *Hard Palate Drill:*
   ZAYZAYZAY   ZAYZAYZAY   ZAYZAYZAY   ZAH
   SAYSAYSAY   SAYSAYSAY   SAYSAYSAY   SAH

The Tongue Tip

8. *Cat Lap:* Lap at imaginary milk all different directions and distances as rapidly as possible.
9. *Tongue Tip Drill:*
   LAYLAYLAY   LAYLAYLAY   LAYLAYLAY   LAH
   TAYTAYTAY   TAYTAYTAY   TAYTAYTAY   TAH
   DAYDAYDAY   DAYDAYDAY   DAYDAYDAY   DAH
   NAYNAYNAY   NAYNAYNAY   NAYNAYNAY   NAH

The Back Tongue

10. *Jungle Heartbeat:* Repeat the NG sound several times through an extended sigh.
11. *Tongue Back Drill:*
    KAYKAYKAY   KAYKAYKAY   KAYKAYKAY   KAAAAAH
    GAYGAYGAY   GAYGAYGAY   GAYGAYGAY   GAAAAAH

Precision

Articulation drills can increase the crispness and clarity of sound, but should be preceded by full warming and releasing so that they do not add unneeded tension. Because of the challenge, some actors, even warmed up, drop the benefits they have just acquired. They get tight in anticipation. It is important to keep a sense of loosenesss and enjoyment, which is why this next exercise is designed to play off of a partner. (NOTE: This exercise does not have to be done with a partner. It is just more fun that way.)

Exercise 2.15

Lip Reading

1. Pick a partner and lock eyes with him.
2. Repeat together very slowly and precisely the following simple list of articulatory organs:
   THE TIP OF THE TONGUE
   THE ROOF OF THE MOUTH
   THE LIPS AND THE TEETH

3. Gradually speed up your delivery and mutual lip synching of these lines to the point where delivery is rapid-fire, highly crisp, but with no increase in tension, tightness in the throat, volume, or rise in pitch.

4. When your eyes tell each other you have gone as fast as possible, slow down gradually again, step by step, to a very measured, leisurely pace, and then stop.

5. Mirror each other on one last Full-Body Yawn.

Alternative Exercise 2.16

Twisters

Substitute or add the following tongue twisters to the corresponding consonant drills above.

p — "Pulchritudinous Paula provided poor, parched Paul a passionate passage through puberty."

b — "Bitter bitch Bette bested bastard Blake by buying back Boston for big bucks."

m — "Marvin's mogul mother might make many more mongrel monster movies, Marilyn."

z — "Zany, zealot Zelda's zenith was Xeroxing zinc zodiac zippers."

s — "Sarcastic Sheila slowly sashayed South, Sunday, spouting sleazy, sharp, sick satires."

l — "Loathesome leech Louie lazed listlessly around Loretta's, lapping liquor like a lounge lizard."

t — "Due to too much testosterone, Todd tended to tirelessly tackle two ton tyrants."

d — "Divinely decadent Dorothy delightedly destroyed downtown Dallas, daily. "

n — "No new naked nervous nerd knows near enough novelties, Norm."

k — "Carpingly critical Carrol called Carl's Caliban a crude caricature."

g — "Go grab Grant's grandma's grotesque green garters, Gloria."

Vocal Progression

Because there are so many short exercises in a vocal warm-up, take time now to review all those just covered. If you can't recall any single one, go back until you can float through the sequence quickly:

Letting Go
The Lion
Skin Slide
Jaw Drop
Full-Body Yawn
Shoulder Drops
Inclines
Nods

Respirating

Inhaling
Nose and Throat
Upper Chest
Floating Ribs
Diaphragm
Lower Back

Exhaling
Reverse
Full-Body Yawn

Sounding
Planting
Humming
Roller Coaster
String

Shaping
Fish
Horse
Motor Boat
Lip Drill
The Fly
Snake
Hard Palate Drill
Cat Lap
Tongue Tip Drill
Jungle Heartbeat
Tongue Back Drill
Lip Reading
Twisting

Mental Warm-ups

The body and voice are worth little if the mind fails to respond to the call for adventure. The mind can free your spirit, which is an elusive combination of imagination, energy, and openness to experience. We all recognize the spirit of, say, Christmas or brotherhood, without being able to trap and keep it. Your acting spirit is strongly connected to the child in you. If you have begun to play with images and fantasies while moving through physical and vocal warm-ups, you are already well on your way to tapping your inner willingness. The next step comes from those around you, letting them give you courage and conquering your own fear of unmasking.

You do not act alone. Everything covered so far in this book could be done without coming to class. The old actor cliche goes: "I don't know what happened. It was *great* when I did it at home in front of the mirror." I often joke with casts, as we approach opening night, about the fact that the audience will soon come and interfere with everything we have done, audaciously interrupting us with their laughter and applause. But communion with other actors and the audience is the whole *point*. It just takes adjustment. The others often do not respond the way they did in your head (or your mirror) at home. You need to allow others to become your mirrors and your guides.

Demons

The first step is to exorcise yourself from demons that follow all actors around. These are some of the things they whisper in your ear, so that it sounds like *you* speaking:

"These people are all much more talented than I am."
"They've all acted a lot already. I'm the only baby here."
"I'm the only one who looks bad in *tights*." (Substitute any clothing worn so far.)
"They're all so colorful. They'll think I'm too straight."
"They're all so normal looking. They'll think I'm too weird."
"Everybody remembers the *warm-ups* but me." (Substitute any topic covered so far.)
"They all know each other already. I'll bet they all signed up as a group."
"Maybe I should have taken *Art History* instead" (or any other subject offered in the world).

This list and this paranoia are boring. And a waste of time. All of the things on the list are false and you know it. And most of the fears are *shared* fears. Yet nearly everyone gives in to some demons. Promise yourself not to.

Exercise 2.17

Dumping the Demons

1. Write out the list above.
2. Cross out those items you actually have not succumbed to yet.
3. Add your own demons. The possibilities ("The teacher already hates me," "They'll never cast me here") are endless.
4. Scrawl something colorful over each item ("B.S." "Hogwash," your own favorite retaliation).
5. Have a private exorcism, where you dramatically shred the paper, toss it out to sea, burn it, or all of the above.
6. Get on with your acting.

Class Commitment

If you will decide today that you have an emotional investment in these people, there will be dividends that few stockbrokers ever dreamed of. The dividends are intangible, inspirational, and impossible to exchange on any market. When you are invested in someone, you want that person to do well and you project your hope onto her, you bend a little when she disappoints you, you always look ahead to what this person might become with a little support. Instead of seeing this person as competition, you actually equate your own progress with hers. You want to be part of a group of actors who are, without exception, exceptional. You want your teacher to find the task of making qualitative distinctions impossible.

Laurence Olivier: *The actors must understand each other, help each other, absolutely love each other. They absolutely must.*[4]

Acting classes are rarely graded on any kind of scale, so everyone in the class could get an A (or, of course, possibly an F). But with this fellowship comes mutual responsibility. If you are absent one day in your psychology lecture of 300 students, it matters to no one but you. In acting class, you may be partnered with different people to lead warm-ups, to perform someone's offstage memory, to (coming in subsequent chapters) imitate, to explore subtext, to perform a scene. If class time is devoted to these activities, you could leave a virtual platoon of partners in the lurch by not being there on any given day. If you are late for some other classes it does not really matter. If you are late for Acting 1, someone probably may be off in the corner by himself, because you were his partner for the activity that started the day.

Even if you have been a flake all your life, this is the time to feel responsible for others in the group, to move beyond your own habitual self-indulgence to a sense of community. Once you do, it will feel so good!

Stage Fright Substitutes

The term *stage fright* has largely dropped out of use, because we now know that dwelling on something this malevolent gives it power. If I tell you not to be afraid, you will dwell on your fear. If I say, "Do not think of fast food burgers under any circumstances," an assembly line of them will parade in your mind. The key to most fears is substitution. On the simplest level, you replace the ogre with something less menacing, to fill your consciousness.

A great actor is like a great host. His concern is for the comfort and well-being of his partner and his audience. Great hosts ease you into a feeling that everything will be fine. They soothe you and make you feel effortlessly open to the next course. They never force you with overwhelming offers of "More dip???!!!" placing the green stuff millimeters from your mouth. For the hosts themselves, once they have concentrated fully on their guests, there is no room, in their consciousness, to be worried about whether the baseboards were dusted or if the stain on the rug will show. There is no room in the head for such monsters. If you will project your concern to your listeners, really thinking more of their comfort than their verdicts, everything will fall in place.

The best advice I ever received from a veteran actor was, "Step out of the center of the universe." Once you do that, your perspective and your humanity are both back in place.

Accepting the Audience

An audience is an audience, whether it is one friend, a handful of classmates, or thousands of paying customers.

Harrison Ford: *I don't think of the audience as someone separate from me. You have to seduce an audience. You can't beat 'em and you can't kiss their asses.*[5]

Here are some other hints for allowing those *out there* to be with you, instead of assuming they're against you:

1. No matter who is really out in the audience, place a familiar, nurturing, warm somebody out there. Place the spirit of someone who supports you.

2. Make friends with a piece of furniture, a window, a radiator, a blackboard, any object that seems comfortable and familiar, perhaps reminiscent of some place you like. Connect back with it occasionally for assurance.

3. Remind yourself that at the same moment you are walking up front to tell your little joke in acting class, millions are being born and dying, a crucial piece of heart surgery is being performed, a couple is making love on some secluded Bahaman beach, a cure is being discovered in the lab for some crippling illness, a plane is being treacherously landed with all on board grateful that only a few have been killed or injured. What you are doing is not the beginning and not the end of life. You are a grain of sand (albeit a great grain) and this moment is not even a semi-finalist among the big triumphs and traumas going on right now in this world.

4. Tell yourself those people out there are potential best friends. In acting class, this is definitely true. In a peformance hall, it is potentially true. You go out in front of a crowd. They are not merely a crowd. They are 1,200 of your best friends, or at least *potential* best friends. What you want with your audience (especially if you address them directly) is a sense of confiding in someone you trust. If you will project that trust out into the house, the audience will lovingly receive it.

5. No one sits in the audience hoping to be bored and disappointed. In fact empirical studies have shown that when mistakes (line drops, fumbling pieces of business) have been deliberately inserted in performances, to test audience response, almost no one could recall these errors later, because they had cheerfully edited them at the time. That is how much each of the people watching are on your side. If the audience happens to be a camera lens, instead of people, you can still give it a friendly, unthreatening identity.

Kathleen Turner: *The camera is just like this adoring dog; it just looks at you all the time. It's so flattering, it's ridiculous.*[6]

Group Warm-ups

Sharing

While trust can be projected onto strangers, it helps a lot if you can simply stop being strangers. It is worth taking time, the first weeks of acting class, for people to get to know each other. I believe it is worth a *lot* of time. Here are some of the things others usually want to know. Sharing this information will help you skip steps and drop barriers.

In the following exercises, think about what you would like to say or show in each category. Have an answer even if it is only a conjecture, your best guess at the moment.

Exercise 2.18

Shared Pasts

1. Your Acting History

As much ONstage, as much OFF as you want to share. Only a summary, to give others a *feel* for what you have done. A paragraph tops. Do not *dare* say you do not have any. Reread chapter 1.

2. Your First Role, Your Favorite Role

Two highlights out of the general pattern above. If you have not yet done a play, you must have done a pageant. No one totally escapes these things. We are talking about your debut here. The occasion you choose to think of as launching you, as a potential ham.

Your favorite may or may not be the same as your first. It may be one you have actually never played but dream of playing. It may be ON or OFF. Try to identify, in no more than a sentence, *why* it is your favorite, what delights or thrills you when you think about it even now.

3. Why You Are Here

The Truth. If this was the only open time slot in your schedule, fess up, so others will know you do not worship daily at the altar of Dionysus. If you have already decided to pursue a professional acting career, have the courage to say so in the open air. The real reason you happened to end up in this class, at this school, at this time. The more straightforward you are, the more you will get from all this.

Exercise 2.19

Shared Opinions

4. How You Would Be Type Cast

Whether you choose to accept your type, fight it, change it, or *expand* it is something to determine later. Now is the time to *acknowledge* it. You need to know how others perceive you, even if you elect to alter that perception. How would a casting director place you? What sorts of parts would she be likely to send you out for? How do most strangers perceive you? This question requires some self-awareness.

Remember, type has little to do with the way you are deep down. It is the impression you leave. It may also have little to do with your chronological age. Audrey Hepburn was the screen's reigning ingenue for many years, playing innocent young girls well into middle age, because her essential quality was "young love." Margot Fonteyn and Roberta Peters were the same in ballet and opera.

It may also not relate to the parts you have played so far. You may have done roles, in your hometown, because you were the only one around with the size or the voice to pull it off. In a larger casting pool, this may not be your perceived type at all. Offstage, you may have been cast as a leader, heading student governments, fund raisers, you name it. But you may not look and sound like a leader at all.

Are you cringing at the whole idea of having to be any type when you want to be a great, versatile, limitless actor? Of course, you are. But you must know how you are viewed *now* in order to do that. If you are uncertain, your friends will be glad to help you. Your best information will come from new friends, who do not have unfair information. Ask others:

What sorts of roles on TV they feel you could fit in (if the current actor disappeared)?
What celebrities you remind them of (if even just slightly)?
Which people in the dorm or in this class you are most like (and least like)?

This information can really be eye opening.

5. Your Favorite Actor

"Oh, I don't really have a favorite. There are so many wonderful ones." Come on. Pick one. This is not engraved in stone. You may change your mind next week. But right now, who is someone you really admire? And why?

Pick an actor, not just a star. *Just* a star, you say? There are actors who are stars, but there are stars who are not actors. If you are serious enough about the art to study it, you're ready to make that distinction. Pick people whose artistry, skill, or versatility you admire at *least* as much their charisma, size, or sex appeal. When you think of an actor, you think of quality work, not just a great set of eyes, biceps, or breasts (not that there is anything wrong with *those*). Pick someone whose art you admire at least as much as anything else about him.

Paul Newman: *I picture my epitaph: Here lies Paul Newman who died a failure because his eyes turned brown.*[7]

---

6. Performance That Impressed You Most

Sometimes, watching an actor at work just fills you with awe. You are vividly aware that this is art of the highest order. You get chills, the works. What is the closest you have come to feeling that way?

Exercise 2.20

Shared Performances

7. Offstage Performance You Would Most Like to Share

You reviewed these as you went through chapter 1 exercises. Which, out of your vast repertoire, would you enjoy telling about? Or demonstrating? Which would be most likely to help these classmates feel they know you? To get a sense of you, acting in the world?

8. Offstage Performance of the Week

If a vivid one has not been thrust upon you, by an unexpected visit, Rush Week, or new living arrangements, you may want to stage one, armed with all the information you now have. If you had to recreate this moment for the class, how would you cast it from among your classmates?

9. Favorite Story Joke

A story joke takes a minute or two to tell. You need to establish characters and circumstances that involve change, so that there is quite a bit more than a setup and punch line. Again, imagine it two ways: one with you just telling it, the other with the story staged and featuring you and some of the other actors in class. If you do not have one you like, this is a great time to ask everyone you know to tell you theirs, until you find one you would like to tell.

10. Character Identification Monolog

You have probably noticed that this list moves gradually from simple information sharing, to opinions and thought questions, to recreated events or small performances. This last item is the closest to traditional theater, since it is a written speech, which you memorize and present. Something one to two minutes in length is best. It does not have to be from a play. It could be from an interview, magazine article, essay, someone's advice column, your favorite novel, or even some john wall, as long as the character speaking is not *you,* but rather someone with whom you identify.

    Your reason for identifying with the material could be that the humor clearly matches your own, the political/moral position is one you feel strongly, the pain of the speaker deeply moves you, or this is the kind of situation you could see yourself getting caught in. Try to share, in a sentence, *why* you identify with this speech.

    "But I don't read plays and have nothing in mind. I don't even know where to start." Not so. On this earth, and probably on your bookshelf at home, there must be some speech that speaks to you and for you. You cannot possibly be that unformed. Give yourself credit. This is a chance to share something you love.

Too Much, Too Soon?

How will you ever share all this? You probably will not have to. Your teacher might elect to go through the whole sequence, but will more likely pick and choose and skip some items, as the sense of the group becomes evident. Whether it gets done in class or out, this gives you good stuff to talk about with your classmates as you get to know each other outside of class. These questions, incidentally, are fairly standard at an audition or actor interview, so many actors spend their lives refining and changing their answers as *they* change. I suggest the following ground rules:

1. As others share, go ahead, stop, and ask them for clarification of anything said. Question each other if curious. But try to stay with curiosity that is likely to be *universal.* If you wonder if someone had the same home-room teacher you did, find out outside of class.
2. Everybody learn the line "Just the high points." Chant it to the occasional motor mouth, who goes through everything he has ever done, a book of reasons for taking the class, or needs to pick ten favorite actors, with an ode to each. This can be done good-naturedly. Anyone can forget and rattle on.
3. If someone is genuinely drawing a blank, others might offer their impressions. If others in the group disagree with the actor's own perception of herself (this happens often with "type"), everyone should feel free to speak up. All here are in the process of defining the self and can use help.
4. This is nonjudgmental sharing. There are no right answers. There are no preferred responses. The whole idea is just to get to know others, so the work that follows will be grounded on awareness.
5. You should not ask to have your answers, offstage performance, and monologs critiqued by the teacher or others. Critical response is not the point here. The whole experience should be completely free of evaluation. You want to share who you are, without others telling you, in any way, if that meets with their approval. Not every theatrical act needs reviews. The sharing is enough.

Exercise 2.21

Shared Viewing

As a group, decide on one or more audience experiences that everyone will experience this term. If a play is being performed by your theater, everyone should try to read the script, attend the performance, agree on what acting elements will be observed, and use this show as the basis of discussions for the rest of the term. If everyone agrees to watch several episodes of the same TV series, another, different kind of basis for discussion and improvisation is possible. Acting concepts are much easier to understand if you have all experienced the same performances. Also, the act itself eases informal, offstage discussions among members of the group.

Names

Try to get everyone's name down the first week. Have pencil and paper nearby as these exercises progress. If you are terrible at names, draw cartoons of people, pick animals or old acquaintances they remind you of, words that rhyme with their names, particularly memorable things they have said about themselves, whatever it takes. Just as it is important to get past a stiff formality early in acting class, it is vital to know who your peers are. When people start to speak, say their names to yourself beforehand, then check to see if you are right. If there are lulls in class, look around the room and try to identify everyone in it. Remember, you are investing in these people and the first step is knowing who they are.

Exercise 2.22

Name Trunk

1. Imagine an enormous trunk in the middle of the room, which will be packed with something belonging to each person in class.
2. The first person pantomimes putting in an imaginary possession that starts with the first letter of his or her name (Terry's trapeze, Gloria's guitar, Sandy's skateboard).
3. Pick something that might actually express you, or at least your own sense of humor, not just because it is alliterative.
4. Each person repeats both the packing motion and the naming of items of everyone who went before. Once the trunk is packed, the names should also be firmly in place.

When and Where to Warm Up

Should you do this standard sequence in every single performance situation? No. That will not be possible. But all these exercises have been tested repeatedly. There is nothing kinky here. These are classics used in many acting programs, so you will start with a sound, basic pattern and sense of progression. If you will persevere, warming up can free your own instrument to respond fully.

> **Vanessa Redgrave:** *I know that when I feel strong and my back is the source of strength, I feel the earth beneath my feet, I feel something going right up through me, very strong, clean and washed all the way through. It is of the utmost importance for one's body to be so obedient to the impulses that come, that they obey you.*[8]

Members of class should take turns leading the warm-ups here, possibly working in pairs. You do not really know it until you can *speak* it and guide others through it. The ability to lead this activity is also a skill that every performer wants. Any director should be able to turn to you and say, "Could you lead us in a warm-up?" without you dissolving into Jell-O. Work briefly from this book, then from note cards with exercise names, then from memory. The time when you will most want to get a group warmed up will probably not be when you have your books or notes with you.

Edit, vary, or expand an exercise according to the occasion and your own needs. If you are in a crowded room, a quick Prune is not possible, physically or emotionally. If you have two minutes, a complete Here and Now cannot be done. But you *can* tense and release along the spine and both sides of the torso, even sitting in a chair if you work with modifications. And you *can* think of soothing images, focus on something in this strange room that is *not* strange, but comforting. You can repeat a sound that settles you, even for just a few moments. The secret of warm-ups is in adapting them, but not neglecting them.

Offstage Adaptations

Every situation you encounter in the theater has some parallel outside. Every activity in this chapter has potential offstage use. The Prune is a great muscle relaxer, if you are having trouble sleeping (and if we did not move immediately on in class, many actors would doze off). Rooting Sound may be just what you need, prior to a difficult conversation with your parents, especially if your objective is to be viewed as an adult. If you still suffer from "baby voice," it is hard for anyone to seriously listen to you as a grown-up, no matter what the other facts of your life may say about you. A Here and Now may help you enjoy the family reunion at hand, and stop dwelling on the fight you *had* with your girlfriend before vacation, and the paper that *will be* due (but you know you will not write until) the week after next. It may help you *be* with your family, so you do not miss the moment. Actors are hardly the only people tempted to get so caught up in their pasts and futures that they seem to overlook their presents altogether.

Exercise 2.23

Warm-ups in Real Life

1. Try to remember at least three major encounters within the last year where it would have helped you perform more effectively if you had been able to warm up beforehand.
2. Identify three or more regular situations, ones that are constant, predictable parts of your life, where you could warm up to function better.
3. Project into the future for occasions similar to those in item 1, where you could plan now to give yourself more of a feeling of control by planning a warm-up as part of your preparation.

The body, the voice, and the spirit can all be helped become ready to respond, with warmth, to all the potential goodwill waiting for you when you perform, as an actor or as yourself.

Shirley Maclaine: *All of us seem to be playing roles in real-life dramas that we are not only starring in but have been scripting too. We are each the author and leading player in the entertainment called "my life."*[9]

3

Individual Inventory

(knowing enough about yourself
and your equipment to use
everything you have)

Richard Dreyfuss: *The actor's instrument is only himself
and the more interesting your instrument is, not only are
you going to be remembered, but the more use you can
be put to.*[1]

Taking Stock

Actors need to take inventory like stores. They need to know their
own merchandise. And no matter how similar an actor may be to
others in small ways, the sum total is individual. No other creature
has been put together just like you. So your Hamlet, your Blanche
Du Bois, your Tinker Bell will not be quite like any other actor's.
As comforting as that is, it helps if you have some idea *how* yours
will be different. This chapter is about checking and counting you.

You will not like all information you uncover. You may be
carrying a self-image that needs to adjust, maybe even collapse. But
you will get to know yourself better and then feel more as if you
live inside your own body. As long as you do not have an inflexible
vision of what you *should* be, there can be wonderful revelations.
If you have picked some god or goddess as the *only* image you can
accept, you will be devastated. But if you want to act well, you can
only kid yourself for so long anyway. There is no point in doing
inventory, if you do not want to know what is really on the shelves.

Knowing Your Instrument

Taking your individual inventory is challenging because you cannot stand back and look objectively at the product. The violin player can reverently place his Stradivarius in the case and look at it. The master mechanic can clean up and then go back out to look over his masterpiece motor. The writer can flip through the pages and see the product. You *are* the product.

I once worked as an assistant to a brilliant, eccentric, somewhat out-of-touch professor, who worked herself into a frenzy, trying to get students to experiment with new vocal and physical techniques. She would shout during a lecture, "You each need to go out and play with yourself!" The whole group would fall apart laughing, and she would mutter, confused, "I mean play with your . . . (interminable pause here) . . . instrument!" And the class would again collapse. This communication breakdown was a perfect example of the actor's dilemma. The very stuff you need to work with is tied to matters private. So the most innocent suggestion can seem suggestive. And the most professional advice can sound personal.

Your body, your voice, your mind are your materials for acting effectively offstage and on. Your inventory will be helped if you allow yourself the same measured objectivity any craftsman would give to examining tools of his craft, even when you are examining your own thighs. Knowing about your performance history (Acting Acknowledged) and about focus (Relaxed Readiness) will help in understanding your particular equipment. Time to take stock.

Body Awareness

Public interest in the body as a machine is at an all-time high. Never have so many studied so much about diet and exercise. This awareness is good for an actor, but he needs to move beyond the body as machine, to body as interpretive instrument. Our focus, here, will be on the constant interpretive choices you make by just standing, sitting, walking, or gesturing. And on your own particular mannerisms.

There is nothing inherently wrong with a mannerism. The acting profession is packed with successful and mannered artists. People like Katharine Hepburn and James Stewart are almost too easy to imitate, their quirks are so pronounced. But you want to be *aware* that you have them and that sometimes they are distracting to the observer. No one wants to lose a role (a client, a scholarship, an interview, a job, a date) because of a nervous gesture or because of the way you shift your weight. These are tiny things, but they may be getting in the way of an audience's capacity to believe you. And they can be modified.

Check your own body in four overlapping categories: habits, adaptations, cultural binding, and isolations.

Habits

When you are in no particular mood, simply passing through the world, what choices are you most likely to make? No matter how these personal tendencies first came about, they are now habitual. They happen without thought or effort. They are automatic. Habits can be subdivided into *still* (you caught in repose, in a photograph) and *active* (you caught in motion, on film).

Adaptations

When you add stress or stimuli to an otherwise average day, how does your body respond? As you are alone or in a group, as you are touching someone or being touched, as your mood changes, how do your neutral responses change? Note yourself adjusting to *space invasions.* You have an amount of space that you like to keep between you and others. It is as if you carry an invisible bubble around you. It may be larger or smaller (or more or less flexible) than someone else's bubble. Except for intimate relationships, it is your desired distance for most interaction. If you are alone on a mountaintop or aboard a crowded elevator, your bubble adjusts in size because you know what to expect. But your bubble bursts and you are unhinged when someone unexpectedly *invades* what you regard as personal space.

"Space invasions" sounds like a science fiction horror title, and some people do respond, with genuine horror, to the most accidental violation of their own bubble, forgetting that it is invisible. Others are mindless invaders, forgetting that just because *they* like bear hugs and pats on the fanny does not mean everyone they meet craves that kind of contact. You can invade another's space by moving very close without touching (as in certain South American cultures where people like only three or four inches between them for conversation), by enveloping or trapping, by grabbing hold, by gentle touching in an area the recipient considers off limits, or by simply staring so that your eyes invade. Omitting overtly violent or sexual moves (in our culture someone a mere three or four inches away may indeed have one or both of these in mind), there are still a wide range of invasions. So it is understandably easy not to share the same covert limits as someone else.

Cultural Binding

Any group whose members share the same behavior is called a culture. Behavioral scientists call it *binding* when you are tied so strongly to the group that you have trouble breaking away from group limitations, even when you need to. You can be bound to a culture like a prisoner bound to a stake. All of us are group members. Membership not only helps define who you are, but can give you a sense of *pride,* especially in your heritage. You may be bound emotionally, even spiritually, but you may also be unaware of binding by geography, conditioning, age, sex, family, and personal interests. Binding becomes a problem when you want to be believably cast as a member of another group.

Isolations

Any single part of the anatomy may acquire a life of its own. From foot tapping to knuckle cracking to teeth grinding to shoulder shrugging, an *isolated* movement may be a response to stress or it may just be an unconscious, acquired taste. Some heads may lean in all of a sudden on every key word spoken ("chicken neck" as many actors call it), others tilt to one side when listening, toss hair back suddenly, nod repeatedly, or sink down so far in the torso that the neck almost disappears. And this is just the start of a "head" list. Studying an individual body part can reveal mannerisms somehow overlooked in the categories above. It is a way of double checking.

Go through the list of questions on the following pages. When the question makes no sense or you draw a blank, get up and move around. Take a look in a full-length mirror. Skip over questions that are still puzzling, but jot down responses when you think you know how you fit into the category. Study yourself. Ask people who have been around you for a while. If you have not got a clue now, give yourself permission to start noticing. It is time to do some research and what could be a more interesting research topic than yourself? You do not even have to go to the library. You *are* the library. Start watching other people in repose and in action to see ways in which others use their bodies like or unlike you.

Expect to be overwhelmed by more questions than you can answer and more categories than you can immediately comprehend; but also expect everything to get easier and clearer, the more accustomed you get to studying you. (The Body Awareness Checklist that follows the next series of exercises can help you keep track of your observations.)

Exercise 3.1

Habits

Answer as many as possible of the following questions about you still and you active.

Still

1. *Standing*

Where is your weight placed in your typical silhouette?
Can you sense which part of your body really *carries* the load?
Where are you *centered*?
Does energy start from one spot on the torso in particular?
How close to *aligned* are you?
Without warming up?
Where does the biggest change take place when it happens?
How close to *symmetrical*?
Any tendencies to lean or cross yourself or favor one side?
What is your *posture* like?
If you do not tend to "stand tall," what is your specific variation?
Is any part still moving even when the rest is still?
Does any part *seem* active or dominant, even when still, so the *focus* is
   clearly on one area of the body?

2. *Sitting*

How collapsed or erect are you when sitting or reclining?
How much do you appear to have sunk or *released* into the chair or floor?

Which parts of your body, if any, remain upright or rigid?
Is there any *contrast* between areas of the body?
Are you often *leaning* towards or away from anything around you?
In what direction?
Is your body *crossed* in one or more places?
How tightly crossed?
Do you appear to be covering yourself anywhere?
How open and expansive is the spread of your arms and legs?
How much *space* are you taking?
Do you appear to be thrusting any part into view?
To be exhibiting any part of yourself?
What *curves* are present?
In the spine? The appendages? The tilt of the head?
Are you curving in more than one direction?
Are you sitting on any part of yourself? Your own leg? A hand?

Figure 3-1 Habits (Sitting)
What information do you convey simply sitting still?

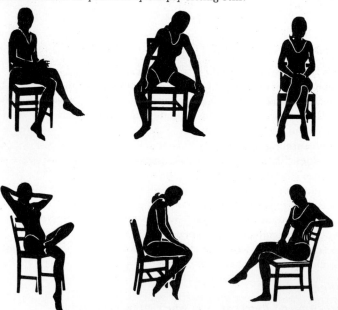

3. *Expression*

What is the *typical* look you tend to have on your face?
How would you describe it?
What are the three or four runners-up for most typical?
What *range* of facial change do you habitually go through?
Is your eye *contact* with others usually direct or not?
How intensely do you look?
How long before looking away?
Do you squint or narrow your eyes when you look? Do you droop your
    lids?
Do your eyes open wider or alter otherwise when you make contact?
Do your eyebrows move at all? If so, how?
Do you wiggle your nose? Purse your lips?
Any regular changes in other *parts* of the face?
Does your smile come suddenly or does it very slowly and gradually ex-
    pand?
Do expressions generally tend to linger or to disappear abruptly?
How are they *timed*?
Are you easy to read or somewhat "poker faced"?
Are your expressions pronounced or more subtle and muted?
How much *energy* is present in the face?
How lively and open is it?
(To what extent is stillness an easy category to think of you in? Are you
    so mobile that you are rarely caught in repose? Do you *appear*
    active even when you are not moving? Or do you really seem at
    rest?)

Active

4. *Tempo/Rhythm*

Are your movements generally fast, slow, medium?
What is your basic *rate*?
How *constant* is your tempo?
Are you fairly predictable or do you change radically?
Are your steps heavy or light?
Do you really land with full *weight* or glide, making only minimal contact
    with the ground?
Do you tend to *punctuate* or stress each move with any part of the body
    as you make your way along?
Could someone tap your movement patterns like playing a drum?
How *regular* or varied are they?

What is the *relationship* between your speed and your rhythms? To what extent do they affect each other?

5. *Motion*

When walking, taking a seat, or leaning, where is the exact point you make *contact* with the surface below?

Is the contact flat and solid or gradual and curved?

Do you *prepare* to move by shifting your weight, adjusting clothing, swaying slightly, or do you just take off?

When you stop, is there a *recovery* period of similar realignments?

Do you settle, even squirm into a stillness, or do you just land and stop moving?

What kind of *support* do you give yourself?

Do you reach out with your hands to furniture before you sit, lean on walls or corners as you round them, grab railings on stairways?

Do you get swinging motions, going for momentum, when walking?

Is the general pattern of your movement *fluid*, smooth, effortless or is it jerky and labored?

How obvious is the changing of gears as you accelerate or change direction?

Do the moves tend to be *direct* and assertive?

Do you face your target straight on and shoot for it?

Or do you tend to ease into furniture sideways, to sidle up to people, to curve across a room, to insinuate yourself into a space?

6. *Gestures*

Are the movements of your arms and hands *expansive,* wide, covering a lot of space and air?

Or do you work tighter to the torso and more economically?

Do you change according to the subject under discussion?

How *frequently* do you gesture?

Can you sit on your hands without going crazy with the need to use them?

Or are your gestures fairly infrequent and selective?

Do you have moves that are *predictable* and repetitive?

That are employed nearly all the time?

How standard are your gestures? The same ones shared by many, or unique to you?

Do you have certain props that you always seem to be playing with?

Do you literally *demonstrate* your feelings/experience physically?

Could someone who does not speak English figure out, from your gestures, what you are saying because of the pictures you are drawing?

Or are your hands more likely to move in abstract, less literal ways?

Do your gestures cause the rest of your body to move too?

Do the shoulders get engaged, do you lean in to make points, does the head join in?

How *connected* are they to the torso?

How free or independent from the rest?

Where is the *focus*?

Do you tend to be pointing to and making references towards your listener? To yourself? Towards the universe around you?

Where are the gestures headed most often?

Or is there no identifiable pattern?

Exercise 3.2

Adaptations

Identify how you react when external elements change.

1. Public versus Private Behavior

Do you react differently when the crowds come?

When the focus of a large group of people turns to you?

Do you find yourself shifting posture, relating to furniture in a different way, walking more or less lightly, changing your timing?

Are you more consistently yourself in intimate groups, or are you one of those people who only really come alive when there *is* an audience?

Do you register uncomfortably when forced to deal one-to-one with someone?

How do your comfort and behavior change as the numbers around you change?

2. Space Invasions (Initiating and Receiving)

What if actual physical contact with others is involved?

What kind of an invader and receiver are you?

Are you more likely to be one than the other?

How likely are you to *initiate* physical contact?

What is your own desired distance?

How unsettled are you when others close in?

When they touch you while speaking?

Do you adapt well?

Are you good at reading intentions?

And are you more likely to touch a particular place on another person?

How sensitive are you to clues about others' preferences?

3. Mood Shifts (Up and Down)

To what extent does your physical life express your emotional one?

Is the receipt of good or bad news likely to show in your body language, while you adjust to what you have heard?

Even if you do not leap in the air continuously for good news or punch your fist through walls for bad, do you use space somehow to express what you feel?

Does the kind of day you are having affect your posture, your eye contact, the freedom and expressiveness of your gestures?

Does intense feeling explode into movement of some kind?

Or are you unlikely to change at all? To *mask* shifts in feelings?

Do you compensate with movement that actually runs contrary to what you feel?

Do you pick up mood signals, from others, and tend to mirror their physical change with your own?

Exercise 3.3

Cultural Binding

Try to identify these influences on your physical life.

1. Geography

Does everyone guess where you were born? Even if they do not hear you speak?

Can others tell every place you have lived, because you have picked up so many giveaway regional signals?

Do people know you are from the city or the country or various terrains and climates without having to ask?

Does body language reveal not only where you have been, but where you have *not* been?

2. Family

To what extent is your ancestry obvious?

Do you share a whole set of moves with other people whose parents were the same nationality, religion, or any other dominant affiliation?

Would many items on the "habits" list be the same for your large groups, and not unique to you at all?

Is your birthline clear, in even simple gestures?

3. Conditioning

Do you send strong information that you have been told for years not to
assert yourself in groups, lest you be thought overbearing?

Or that you were told to push, shove, shout, get seen, grab attention,
whatever it takes to get what you deserve?

Is your bubble the same as others in the family, even though you are very
different people inside?

How evident is the rewarded behavior and the punished behavior that
was part of your home, school, or church?

To what extent is your presentation of yourself based on areas of the
body that you have somehow been conditioned to think of as un-
acceptable? Consider this list:

facial complexion	breasts
nose	stomach
teeth	genitals
ears	hips
hands	thighs
nails	feet

Everybody is different, but these are the places people are likely to make
some unconscious effort to conceal or negate, moving so as to call attention away from an area of the anatomy. Ironically, the habit may linger
long after you have actually altogether changed your *feelings* about that
area of your anatomy.

4. Interests

Can others tell where your special skills lie?

Can they determine which of your abilities are most developed and what
you like to do just by watching you?

Is it obvious from movement patterns that you are a dancer, an athlete, a
pianist, a body builder, a scholar?

Have you picked up all the trademarks, along with the love of the activity?

5. Age

Do they get your age right no matter how worldly you try to look? Or no
matter how fresh and innocent?

Or worse, do they always get the age wrong, because your body action
is so completely locked at a certain age that you are always pegged
younger or older than your chronological years?

How aware are you of the subtle alterations in movement that come with
age?

Not just the extremes of babyhood and ancientness, but the slight tendencies to economize and modulate that increase every few years?

6. Sex

From early childhood images of traditional males and females (crass generalizations about puppy dog tails at one continuum end and sugar and spice at the other) still permeate our culture.

On a scale of extreme sexual stereotypes, where are you?
Somewhere in between, right? But where on the scale?
More important, how flexible and changeable are you?
Do you fall into a relatively traditional sexual image?
Do you have an androgynous mix of characteristics?
Or is your behavior largely neutral?

Exercise 3.4

Isolations

Which of your body parts have developed distinct and potentially distracting tendencies?
Consider particularly: head, torso, arms, hands, feet.
Which of these isolated mannerisms is most, which least, pronounced; which most and least variable?

I Am What I Am

If your emotional response is like mine, you may look at a list like this and say, "I am what I am!" and reject the idea of changing. But remember that adjusting and changing are not the same thing. The truth is cultural binding limits your casting. If you are "a nice Jewish girl from the Bronx," you are three wonderful things to be. But imagine yourself cast as Antigone, one of the great tragic heroines. She is "a nice Greek girl from Thebes." The actor cast in the role must achieve a classic, universal quality. Too much Bronx in stance, gesture, eye contact and there is no way on earth the audience will successfully place her in the ancient world. You cannot get in the way of the audience's imagination. You want to *unleash* its imagination.

So how can you win? Learn to recognize your own binding, modify it when appropriate, but do not lose it! First, you never want to lose your own heritage, because it is precious and important. Few things are worse than going home and finding you have forgotten *how* to be at home there. Second, the minute you virtually wipe out all the Bronx from your body and voice, guess what the next part to come along will require? Guess what kind of accent and physical life? And guess who will have conditioned herself out of consideration? What you want is control and flexibility. Being other people does not need to mean losing who you are.

Exercise 3.5

Using the Body Awareness Checklist

Make a copy of the worksheet on pages 72–73 and jot notes to help remember information gathered about your physical life. If terms are unclear go back over that section in this or earlier chapters. There are far more categories than you can probably handle. Just fill in what you can. See if a clear physical profile emerges. If there are a lot of empty spaces, promise yourself to start observing yourself closer in those areas.

So far you have looked at your offstage life and to your potential casting. Take another look at the list, imagining that you have already been cast and are beginning to put together a characterization. Pick any role you have ever wanted to play. Ask yourself about the *character*'s center, gestural range, personal bubble, adaptations, and all the rest. These are concrete ways of building a full performance. Consider the range of options open to you. These categories offer the actor ways of building on pure intuition, by making tangible technical choices.

> **Laurence Olivier:** *I usually collect a lot of details or characteristics, and then I find a creature swimming about in the middle of them.*[2]

Imitation for Double Awareness

Actors are observers. They ride the bus or wait in line and watch, noting a walk, a nervous gesture, a set of eyebrows knitting close together. They use the people they see as a limitless encyclopedia.

(continued on page 74)

Body Awareness Checklist

HABITS (STILL)

Standing

Carriage _____

Center _____

Alignment _____

Symmetry _____

Posture _____

Focus _____

Sitting

Release _____

Contrast _____

Leaning _____

Crossing _____

Space _____

Curves _____

Expression

Typical _____

Range _____

Contact _____

Parts _____

Timing _____

Energy _____

HABITS (ACTIVE)

Tempo/Rhythm

Rate _____

Constancy _____

Weight _____

Punctuation _____

Motion

Contact _____

Preparation _____

Recovery _____

Support _____

Gestures

Expansiveness _____

Frequency _____

Predictability _____

Demonstration _____

Regularity _____

Relationship _____

Directness _____

Connection _____

Focus _____

ADAPTATIONS

Groups

Public Behavior _____

Private Behavior _____

Contact

Receiving Invasion _____ Up _____

Initiating Invasion _____ Down _____

Mood

CULTURAL BINDING

Geography   **Family**   **Conditioning**

_____   _____   _____

Interests   **Age**   **Sex**

_____   _____   _____

ISOLATIONS

Head   **Torso**   **Hands**

_____   _____   _____

Arms   **Feet**   **Others**

_____   _____   _____

73

They store away, imitate, translate, and interpret what they have seen. And often they learn more about themselves in the process. Actors develop that highest form of flattery, imitation, to an art form.

Dustin Hoffman: *If an actor can find the personal rhythm of the character, he's home free. And one of the best ways to do that is to follow a person down the street, unbeknownst to him. Pick up his walk, IMITATE it and continue it, even after he's out of sight. As you're doing it, observe what's happening to you. By zeroing in a guy's personal rhythm, you'll find that you've become a different person.*[3]

Physical-Life Project

Everyone will be a spy in this next assignment. It is vital to do this research without consulting anyone. You will be observing, on the sly, two other actors in class, for about two weeks, while actual class time is devoted to other activities. You are trying to capture the physical life of two other people. At a later point, when the physical is mastered, the vocal will be layered on, but for now the work is silent.

Your mission is to observe these two performers in as many different contexts as you can: officially "acting," just "being," in groups, alone, one to one, calm, excited, going through their behavioral repertoire.

Step 1 You draw a slip of paper that will have on it two names (these same two names will have been drawn by another classmate, but for a while you are on your own) which you will show only to the teacher. Your espionage career is launched.

Step 2 Everyone comes to class prepared to complete the following "self-imitation" exercise designed to help the people who are observing you.

Exercise 3.6

Self-Imitation

Only two chairs will be placed at the front of the room with some space between them. Both chairs face the audience. Everything else you fill in, from your past or your imagination. Carry your usual life props: book bag, jacket, notebook, purse, whatever.

1. Enter imaginary classroom.
2. Look for a place to sit.
3. Move past imaginary others to sit down.
4. Once seated, change your mind and move to the *other* chair.
5. Interact with an imagined classmate.
6. Take notes on a lecture or demonstration going on.
7. Attempt to get the teacher's attention but fail.
8. Do something interesting!
9. Let something in your circumstances make you angry.
10. Leave imaginary classroom.

You will wish to run through this sequence a few times, before doing it in class, so that it comes easily and believably. Use a situation drawn mostly from your own life. If the class is not made up primarily of under-graduates, any shared activity (grocery store trip, sale at the mall, some kind of registration hassle) can be substituted.

Remember, you are completely yourself in a typical but *intensified* situation. Make no effort to entertain or charm the audience. In fact, let yourself be boring. If your concentration is complete, even in this simple set of tasks, you will probably be fascinating. Questions to consider:

1. Enter Classroom

How large?
How light or dark?
Cold or warm?
How many people in here?
Where are the authority figures located?
How closely are the authority figures observing?
What time of day is it?
Are you late or on time?
Where have you been just before this?
What is your attitude towards this class?
What do you expect to happen here today?
What are your plans once the period is over?

2. Look for Place to Sit

How crowded is it already?
Is your favorite place gone?
Do you hope to sit next to someone in particular?
How close to or past starting is the lecture?
Was there a crowd jammed up at the door?
How easygoing or rude were they?
How relieved or indifferent are you to have just arrived?

3. Move Past Others to Sit Down

How difficult is this task?
How narrow are the aisles?
How cooperative are those you need to pass?
Do you have to ask anyone to clear your path?
How self-conscious are you?
How likely is it that you are being observed?

4. Once Seated, Change Mind, Move Someplace Else

What is your motive for moving?
Something puts you off where you are?
Something attracts you over there?
Something beyond your control?
How much of an endeavor is this going to be?

5. Interact with Another Classmate

Do you need this person's help?
Does he/she need/want yours?
Is it related to class or personal?
How much do you enjoy this interaction?
How well do you know this person?

(Remember this is silent. Say real words and hear real words but *silently,* so that, to the audience, it looks like the sound had been turned off, but everything else is realistic. Make us have to read your lips, if we want to know exactly what is being said.)

6. Take Notes on Lecture/Demonstration

How do you go about getting out notebook and something to write with?
Do you need any other supplies?
What is your attitude towards material presented?
Is it clear, fascinating, obscure, boring?

How much do you need to understand this stuff?
How crucial is this class to your survival?

7. Attempt to Get Teacher's Attention and Fail

Why do you make the effort?
What exactly do you do?
What is going on up there that makes the professor ignore you?
How aggressively do you pursue this objective before giving up?
How devastating or inconsequential is being ignored to you?
How often does this happen to you?

8. Do Something Interesting!

This is the part that is up to you. The part where you can have some fun
with it, or you can agonize over it. Try to find the something interesting
from the body of the scene you have created, so that it moves organically
out of the situation. It may be an extreme reaction to being ignored, a
mischievous impulse from you, or it may be motivated by someone else
in the imaginary room. Infinite possibilities.

Actors are always being given seemingly impossible tasks like "do
something interesting," especially at auditions. The best solution is always
to go back *into the situation,* instead of worrying about imposing something clever from the outside. These challenges are chances to explore
your own creativity and capacity to discover everything a situation has to
offer.

9. Let Something Make You Angry

The teacher?
The person next to you?
The chair?
Your broken pencil?
Your frustration at what just happened?
An entirely new atrocity?

10. Leave Classroom

(Let us assume the bell has not rung so class is not over. You *decide* to
leave.)

How has your life changed since you came in here?
What do you know now that you did not before?
What do you care more or less about?
How much of what you hoped for has happened?

How much do you care who notices you leave?
How much do you *want* to make a disturbance?
What is the next objective you are shooting for?

Interlude   Now, while the class officially turns its attention to other matters, you embark on your spy mission. You might start by making comparisons between your two subjects and yourself, especially since you were your own first subject. Use the Body Awareness Checklist to help you organize your observations.

Step 3   After you have been working alone for a while, your teacher will reveal the name of the other student who is spying on the same twosome you are. Meet your partner and compare notes. Begin working together, checking in with each other daily, alerting each other to new developments in the case. ("Did you notice how he stands when he's coming on to somebody?" "Look at how her expressions change when she talks to the teacher." "I think he's going to be at _____'s party tonight. See if you notice anything different when he's just hanging out, having a few beers.") The research should be enjoyable, even addicting.

Interlude   As the time approaches to present your findings in class, you may have reservations about "doing" another actor. Will it seem cruel or condescending? No. When the time comes, everyone enjoys this activity. The observees get so much new information (remember all the blank spots on your self-observation sheet?) that they are actually grateful. Why not just videotape actors and have them watch themselves? Because they do not *see* what you see. Early in their training, actors watch videos of themselves, focus on their noses, moan at the size of their hips, and discover resemblances to Aunt Harriet they never noticed before. Their vision is scattered and personal. (Video can be a great tool later on, once some self-awareness sinks in.) The real, valuable lessons for your subjects will come from seeing *their* physical tendencies through *you*. It helps objectify the experience and systematize the information. The habits themselves are what come to the foreground.

Remember to identify what you *see,* without passing judgments. You will not go into class and say, "You have this weird walk and this bizarre gesture you do"; but rather something like, "You land heavily with the full foot, especially when you're preoccupied. And your right fist sometimes opens and closes when you grasp for ideas or words." No mannerisms are inherently positive or negative. They just are.

It helps if some written report is turned in and eventually read by the observees. (See Appendix C, "Physical Life Observation," an optional, more streamlined version of the checklist, with more room to write.) When words fail you, you may wish to use drawings (stick figures sitting, a facial expression sketched, a diagram of a series of gestures) to help clarify points you want to make.

At some point in the work with your partner, you will decide which of you is going to be the primary presenter of which observee, probably because you have more of a knack for one subject than the other. In other words, you and your partner (A and B) have drawn names of two other actors (C and D), but even though you are both working on both, each of you will gradually take more of the responsibility for one of them. The primary presenter will be the first one up to demonstrate what he has discovered.

Step 4 Results are due and this is what happens:

Exercise 3.7

Imitation Sequence

Let us say A is specializing on C and B is specializing on D.

1. A gets up and walks through a silent imitation while the class calls out their guesses. A ignores the guesses until someone gets it right (and shouts "C!!!!"). A nods to show that the guess was correct but continues until the planned imitation is completed.
2. A then restarts the imitation, this time adding narration ("When you walk into a room you always look around and then down at the floor. You tug your book bag back up onto one shoulder and walk in, putting your weight on the balls of your feet and bouncing slightly, keeping your eyes on the floor . . ."). The execution of the imitation is exactly the same, but this time A is telling C the details while doing them.
3. B now joins A up front and adds any pertinent details A may have left out ("I also notice that you often swallow just before starting to move into a room and you place both hands around the handle of the book

bag when you tug at it . . .”). B may also share an area of disagreement or a different observation (“I really think you put your weight more on the outside of both feet, not towards the front.”).

4. A and B now talk their way through the list on the observation sheet, making sure each relevant category is covered, if possible, through both demonstration and description.
5. Once the work on C is completed, A and B reverse roles and cover D. B first does the imitation once, then with narration. A adds details for D, then the partners once again work their way through the list. It is the same exact procedure with B leading the way this time.
6. The class may wish to add the occasional two cents, and C and D may have a few questions based on the information they have gotten.

After enough imitations have been completed for the class to be very clear on the procedure, it is possible that only parts 1 through 3 may be done in front of the whole class. Breaking into smaller groups to go through the checklist can save a lot of time and still give both observers and observees the benefit of the experience.

NOTE TO TEACHERS: After watching a few complete demonstrations all together, the class can benefit from working in smaller groups, although, for this to work, it will take some figuring on your part pairing up partners. Actors rarely shortchange each other on this assignment. They feel a strong responsibility for a complete and systematic observation. Your only real monitoring need will be to check extremely subjective or naive observation and to suggest other alternatives.

Exercise 3.8

Alternative Imitations

If time does not allow the full spy exercise, any number of reduced versions are possible where both the act and the observation are abbreviated. Classmates might be imitated:

1. walking to the front of the room and writing names on the board.
2. raising a hand and participating in class discussion in a typical manner.
3. performing in any other assignment presented in class so far.
4. sharing brief examples of the biggest differences between their on-stage and offstage personas.

5. doing just a few assigned categories from the checklist, instead of the whole thing.

    Smaller imitations can also be used by way of warming up for the big one. While some of the suspense is lost, it can help actors check in with the class at various stages in their observations. If the class stays together for a year or more, additional imitations can be blended in, adding layers of sophistication.

Imitation Payoffs

What has all this accomplished?

1. You have looked at yourself in quite a few physical categories, in order to begin to get a sense of the kind of figure you cut in space and how you use the space around you.
2. You have presented yourself in an everyday situation to the class, demonstrating basic acting principles firsthand. You have performed realistically with a heightened reality.
3. You have observed other actors (and others have observed you) going through self-imitation in order to get precise information and personal insight.
4. You have spied on your subjects in every possible situation in order to sharpen your sense of detail, your eye for nuance of movement, and your sophistication regarding the body.
5. You have partnered with someone, making all the negotiations and compromises that always need to happen between sets of actors.
6. Two people closely watching you have helped you recognize, for better or worse, many of your own tendencies.
7. You have been able not only to watch, but to *organize* what you see, so that a system of physical characterization is available to you.
8. You have given a gift to other actors, by mirroring them, so they experience a friendly but revealing reflection.
9. You have experienced the sensation of performing with both involvement *and* objectivity, of becoming someone else, but then removing yourself and describing the event. You have maintained that balance, essential for an actor, between being onstage and out front at the same time.
10. An exchange of mutual benefit has happened between a group of actors starting to trust and support one another.

Applying Body Awareness

What do you do with this information now? It depends on how close or distant your "mirror" was to what you had expected, how pleased or distressed you are by what has just been reflected to you. A beginning acting class aims to enlighten, not necessarily change. Ask yourself if any of your mannerisms interfere with the effectiveness of your communication. Do not do anything without reflecting. What you communicate may be just fine and you now have self-awareness to add to self-acceptance. Or you may choose, gradually, to proceed with some changes. If you want to change, you can apply some of the skills you developed in imitating others.

Vocal Awareness

Body work comes before voice work, because it is easier. You know your body better. You can see it and feel it. You can look at most of it, even while you read this page. The rest you can see in the mirror. The family album is full of you in various sizes and shapes. Imagine the family *voice* album. You can examine the body, because it is out there to be counted. You have known your body for years; you may not like it, but you know it. The voice cannot be seen or touched. It is hiding. You own voice may, in fact, still be a stranger to you.

The result? A whole society of people who have no idea how they sound. The world is full of women who spend many daily hours, working to look breathtaking, but they sound like Bambi. Of men who pump enough iron to look like warrior chiefs, but talk like Thumper. They do not seem to notice. It is almost as if they *think* like a silent film.

Kathleen Turner: *You see women who are absolutely stunning, in $10,000 worth of clothes and jewelry. And there they are at Spago (an exclusive L.A. restaurant) and they say 'Well, I'd like a prosoota peetsa' (said in a Minnie Mouse voice) and you think, Oh shit, what did they waste their money on* this *for (pointing at some imaginary Balenciaga gown)? I think it's very ugly. I mind it very much.*[4]

Yet, countless crucial moments depend on the voice. Onstage, the action of the play stops, an actor sits on the edge of the stage, and with the slightest movement, beautifully speaks a soliloquy that may be the heart of the whole evening. Offstage, speaking on the phone, reading aloud to any group, talking with a lover in the dark of the night, encouraging hope in a friend whose eyes are closed in anguish, over and over again, the full expressiveness of the voice is essential to acting your own life.

Body work also tends to precede voice work because the body *houses* the voice. If the body is free and aware, the chances are good for the voice to follow. The good news is that much body awareness is transferable. The bad news is that you probably have a lot of catching up to do. You may be starting with 20 years of voice habits and no voice *thought*. But you can work on your voice in the grocery store, the car, the shower, wherever you have the inclination. First some basic terms.

Quality

Your voice has a tone and texture unlike any other. Quality is the *feeling* of the sound you produce. It is determined largely by a combination of surfaces inside you (facial bones, nose, sinus cavities, mouth, pharynx, chest) where sound resonates. Voices are traditionally described as harsh, mellow, thin, full, light, dark, husky, nasal, strident, resonant, large, small, breathy, hoarse, or in more metaphoric terms like silk or velvet.

Tempo/Rhythm

The relationship between speed and emphasis has been explored in the body section of this chapter. The tempo/rhythm of the voice uses the same principle, frequently with surprisingly little connection to the timing of physical movement.

Articulation

How crisp or precise is the way you form sounds? Precision of speech is determined by how your consonants are completed; where the articulation organs are put (placement); how long the contact is sustained (extent); how much force is behind it (pressure); and whether or not your vocal folds are engaged (vibration). When someone says he cannot hear you, most of the time what he actually means is that he cannot *understand* you, because of poor articulation.

Pronunciation

How close to standard is the way you speak? To the speech heard most often in performance, which does not seem to come from a particular, recognizable region or group? Some confuse this category with the one above. Pronunciation has nothing to do with how precisely you say something, but with how close you say it to the way most *other* people say it. The standard pronunciation of a word can actually be quite slurred.

Pitch

Your speech could be written out on sheet music identifying the various notes employed, from the top to the bottom of your own register. Your tendency to repeat certain pitch patterns is like having your own theme song. While research shows that people respond more positively to the lower pitches, most speakers actually restrict themselves to the upper half of their range.

Volume

Most of us are aware of tendencies towards loudness or softness in our speech (Are you someone who is always being asked to speak up? Are you someone who is always being shushed?), but it takes a sophisticated understanding of projection to adjust to varying listeners and spaces.

Word Choice

Do you tend to choose primarily complex, four-syllable words? Or explicit four-letter ones? Or both, depending on the occasion? Since the same event can be described with infinite variety, the choices you make strongly define you.

Nonverbals

No one utters just words. There are countless noises or spurts of sound, beyond recognizable language. These express emotion beyond words. Nonverbals add color and interest to vocal life. Oddly enough, beginning actors frequently fail to use them in scene work, in part because the playwright usually leaves it up to you to add them. A scene will often seem too *clean* to be real, but once sprinkled with nonverbals it will breathe with a whole new believability. Nonverbals are used heavily offstage, especially when we are surprised and thrown off by the cue we have just received. They help fill our evaluation period while we recover. ("Hmmmm . . . I . . . uhhh . . . think we . . . ummmm . . . need to talk about this.")

Influences

You can look at your vocal life from the same perspectives we used for your physical life.

Habits: What are the characteristics of your voice in standard, low-key, daily circumstances?

Adaptations: How does it change in public, when your bubble alters, when your mood swings?

Cultural Binding: Which of the influences of geography, family, conditioning, interest, age, and sex figure strongest in what other people hear from you?

Isolations: Are there singular tendencies that defy rational explanation but still contribute to your sound?

(The Voice Awareness Checklist that follows the next set of exercises will help you remember all these terms and categories.)

Exercise 3.9

Basic Parts of a Vocal Life

Unlike the body, the simplest vocabulary regarding voice may be unfamiliar or unsteady to you. You may need to track down some of the terms below in the dictionary. In each of the following categories, jot down one or two word responses as they come to mind.

1. Quality

What is the basic tone or texture of your voice?
How constant or variable is your sound?
What *adjectives* best describe the feeling of your voice?
Are there abstract or metaphoric words to identify your quality?
Is it reminiscent of someone else's quality or altogether your own?
Where do you primarily *resonate?*

2. Tempo

Do you speak *quickly, slowly, medium,* or somewhere in between?
What is your standard *rate?*
How does your vocal tempo compare with your *physical* movement tendencies?
Do you sustain speech or always deal in short spurts? What is your typical *duration?*
Are you constant or do you use different, *varying* tempos?

3. Rhythm

Do you really *stress* certain words in each statement or give all words relatively equal value?
What is the *weight* of your stress?
What does it sound like if you try to capture your own timing by tapping out what you consider typical?
How light or heavy is your touch?
What kinds of *phrasing* patterns do you use to separate parts of your statements? Do you take pauses after a predictable number of words or syllables?
Where do you tend to break up speech for breath, evaluations, suspense, or lapses in thought?
Is the overall impression smooth or jerky and eratic? How *fluid* is your speech?

4. Articulation

Are you ever accused of mumbling? Of having lazy speech?
How *crisply* do you shape each sound?
How many consonants do you actually say completely, how many skip over, and how many only half say or *slur?*
If you are precise, is it effortless or is it *labored,* so you seem to be working hard?
Are there particular words and sounds that always give you trouble, or are all *easy* to pronounce?

Are you aware of some words that others find difficult to speak, but are simple for you?

Are you *inconsistent,* finding it sometimes more trouble to articulate well than others?

5. Pronunciation

Is your way of saying words *standard* or if not, how far off?

Does your speech reflect the *region* of the country you are from?

Do you have any eccentric tendencies that are yours alone? *Idiosyncratic* pronunciations?

How easy is it for you to slide in and out of various accents and dialects? How sharp is your *ear?*

Do you reveal your ethnic heritage through speech?

Are you aware of *substituting* one sound for another?

6. Pitch

Is your voice *higher or lower* than most people's in terms of the notes used in everyday speech?

Borrowing music terms, would people dub your speech as tenor, alto, bass, soprano?

How much variation do you use and how predictable is it?

Do you have a regular *melody pattern* so that graphing your pitch would show repetitons?

Or does your pitch change radically? Do you *inflect* frequently, moving from pitch to pitch?

Within your range, how much pitch do you use?

How close to the top and bottom do you venture? What *restrictions* do you place on pitch?

Do you lock your voice in the top half or in the very bottom few notes?

Do you roll up and down the bottom half like some FM announcers?

Are you able to comfortably explore widely varying pitches without strain? What is your *range?*

7. Volume

Are you basically *loud, soft,* where on the continuum?

Do you project or fill a room effortlessly?

Does your voice seem to have *power* or are you aware of needing to push in large spaces?

Do you move quickly between whispers and shouts, or stay largely in a modulated middle projection? How *varied* is your volume control?

If there was a volume knob on you, how much does it get adjusted and under what circumstances?

Are you sensitive to being too loud or soft for others' comfort?
How predictable, adaptable, and *adjustable* are you?

8. Word Choice

Do you pick mainly slang to communicate with?
Is your language more *formal or casual?*
Are you often asked to explain the meaning of the big word you just
    dropped?
How do you arrange your words in sentences or thought clusters? Your
    typical *syntax?*
Do you have an identifiable *idiom?*
Are you always using the latest jargon and changing like you change
    clothes? *Fad* words?
Do you stick with certain words and phrases that are definitely yours?
    Favorites?
Do you have meaningless phrases that permeate your speech like dust?
Do you use a specific vocabulary, such as computer language or theater
    terms, no matter what the circumstances?
Do you favor certain kinds of images?
Is your speech sprinkled with regional or ethnic terms or largely main-
    stream?
Do you arrange your sentences in a recognizable way in terms of word
    order or syntax?
Is your working vocabulary relatively large?
Do you make an effort to adjust word choices in various groups or do
    you use the same language no matter what?

9. Nonverbals

Do you have quite a few sounds mixed in with words?
Noises that may have clear meaning, but do not show up in dictionaries?
Squeals of delight?
Laughter that gurgles up like a pot boiling over? Or bursts suddenly and
    briefly, then stops?
How many *stalling* sounds do you make when you are pondering a ques-
    tion?
How likely are you to sigh, groan, growl, moan, chuckle, pop your lips,
    or yawn audibly?
How *dominant* are these sounds in your communication?
How likely are you to *explode* into a nonverbal as a *reaction* to what
    someone has said/done?
Do you hum or whistle little snatches of tunes all the time or make per-
    cussive sounds?
Do you have any sounds that are absolutely your own?

Exercise 3.10

Using the Voice Awareness Checklist

Use this worksheet (pages 90–91) exactly as the body chart. Start analyzing yourself, then listen to others, using what you hear (and what you imagine) when putting together a character so that you hear the character speak. Sharpen your skills with imitation each time you recognize a new vocal twist.

Noticing voices starts for almost all of us much later than noticing bodies. Try these small awareness exercises before moving on to full-scale imitations.

Exercise 3.11

Resonators

Produce the sound for the following lines from the designated location. Make no effort to avoid cliches or stereotypes. Just find the resonator.

Head: "Heidi's head voice gives me heartburn and a headache."
Mask: "Max's mask makes for major magnification."
Nose: "Norm's nasality and neckties are noticeably nerdish."
Sinuses: "Selma's sound search settles sharply in her sinuses."
Mouth: "Thelma's throat thrashes, throttles, and throbs."
Pharynx: "Phil's FM fullness comes from his pharynx."
Chest: "Charles' chest sound challenges, charms, and takes charge."

Exercise 3.12

Classic Voices

Use the same approach to this list of standard voice descriptions. Start as close to the stereotype that the line suggests, then move away to imagine subtle variations. There will be some inevitable overlap with the resonator list.

Harsh: "Hey, Harry, how's come Helga hates your hide huh?"
Mellow: "May tomorrow mean more music and magical memories."
Thin: "Think thankful thoughts throughout your thrashing, Theodore."
(continued on page 92)

Voice Awareness Checklist

HABITS

Quality

5 Adjectives _____

_____

_____

Resonance _____

_____

Tempo

Fast, Slow, Medium _____

Compared to Body _____

Duration _____

Variety _____

Rhythm

Stress _____

Weight _____

Pausing _____

Fluidity _____

Articulation

Crisp _____

Slurred _____

Labored _____

Easy _____

Inconsistent _____

Pronunciation

Standard _____

Regional _____

Idiosyncratic _____

Ear _____

Substitution _____

Pitch

High, Low, Middle _____

Inflection _____

Restrictions _____

Melody Pattern _____

Range _____

Volume

Loud, Soft, Medium _____

Power _____

Variety _____

Adjustment _____

_____

_____

Word Choice

Formal, Casual _____

Syntax _____

Idiom/Fads _____

Favorites _____

_____

_____

Nonverbals

Laugh _____

Stalling _____

Reactions/Explosions _____

Dominant sounds _____

_____

_____

_____

ADAPTATIONS

Contact _____

Mood _____

CULTURAL BINDING

Family _____

Conditioning _____

Age _____

Sex _____

Geography _____

Interests _____

ISOLATIONS

_____

_____

Full: "Ferdinand's final fanfare filled and overflowed the farthest foothills."

Light: "Lovely Lili looks luminous in lace and lurid in lamé."

Dark: "Don't dare doublecross Delores or you die."

Husky: "Hey, hot stuff, how's about holding hands?"

Nasal: "Nadine is nowhere near normal."

Strident: "So far season sales simply suck, Sam."

Resonant: "Raoul reveled in Rio with the ravishing Ramona."

Large: "Laurence loves to laugh, longs to live, and lives to love."

Small: "Silly, shy Suzy sat stiffly at sorority sing-along."

Breathy: "Baby wants a big blue Buick, boys."

Hoarse: "Watching Harry's horrible Hamlet hurt. It gave me a hernia."

Exercise 3.13

Around Town

Find examples of extremes on each list and each item on the chart: on trips to the bank, the grocery store, a restaurant, or bar. Ascertain when you are hearing a really low voice or a distinct regional pattern.

Exercise 3.14

Sizing Up the Class

Debate who in class has the highest and lowest voices, who is loudest and softest, work your way through the list. If there are disagreements, discuss differences in the way you hear people.

Exercise 3.15

Do the Teacher

You observe the teacher (and any teaching assistants) long and hard day after day. Try to capture their vocal lives. Work as a class trying to top or outdo each other, referring back to the list so you do not just mimic, but identify what you have done. Try to do other members of the faculty as well.

Exercise 3.16

Celebrities

Who in the class does a celebrity voice? Everyone try your best one and let the natural mimics do several. Then go through the chart and state what happened when the new voice was created. Identify the physiological changes that created the new voice.

Exercise 3.17

Voice-overs

The following are standard voices, used by people who work in commercials and narration. The list represents our own cultural stereotypes. We recognize each one after a few words of dialog. Immediate recognition is essential, since radio spots are brief. The more of these and other voices you have, the more usable you are to a recording studio or agency. Try each. Consider taping them.

You do have a number of voices in you and can probably radically change your sound without even thinking about it. Now is the time to think about it. Try to identify, with the basic voice vocabulary, what you *did* to achieve any of these sounds:

tough guy (detective, sergeant)
starlet
sick person (cold, sore throat, fever,
   headache)
cowboy
snob
wimp
executive
secretary
homemaker
high brow
sex symbol
greaser
airhead
AM frantic announcer
FM mellow announcer
farmer

deity
lover
enthusiast
little kid
adolescent
grandparent
old geezer
animals
Santa Claus
Disney characters
fairytale characters
Dracula
witches
impersonations:
   movie stars
   comics
   politicians

dialects:	European
regional American	Slavic
British Isles	Asian
Middle Eastern	

Vocal-Life Project

This time you are not a spy, you are an investigative reporter. Your subjects know you are after them. You might draw new names or keep the old ones, depending on time factors. If you keep the old subjects, you can build on your previous efforts. If you get new subjects, you need to do a physical observation on them, as the basis for the vocal.

Because you know the class much better by now and hear them regularly, you do not need to have a self-imitation to launch the assignment. If time allows, everyone in class might read the same paragraph aloud and describe the same event, so you have a ready comparison of the group's different vocal lives. Like any good reporter, you will uncover and even invent ways of studying these voices, but here are some standards:

1. Call them on the phone and experience the voices in isolation.
2. Interview both of them on tape and study their interaction later, replaying each phrase until it is in your ear.
3. Tape them in other circumstances, particularly when they officially perform in class, so you can hear the differences from regular conversation.
4. Determine other voices that are similar, both among classmates and celebrities.
5. If possible, listen to someone from these actors' families, hometowns, any groups you suspect may have a binding influence.

The rehearsal process should be the same as the physical life assignment, only this time you are putting together a scene, in which both your observees appear. Where might these two meet? What would they be likely to talk about? What kinds of conflicts might be present? Use everything learned about basic acting encounters to set up one between your subjects. Cast yourselves according to your aptitude for imitating one of the subjects. Be sure to switch roles sometime in your rehearsal to experience what your partner does. Pick a scene that is physically varied, so you have a chance to base your vocal work firmly in their physical lives. The less you choose to do with your bodies in the scene, the less chance you have for capturing the home where their voices live. Your bodies will reveal vocal choices once you are carrying yourself the way your subject does. It is also more fun to explore the space between these two people. Each person wants a clear objective in the scene. Do not just feature them sitting around, shooting the breeze. Idle chitchat can be part of the scene, but for dynamic acting, each person is there for a reason and with a strategy.

Exercise 3.18

Voice Imitation Sequence

Since everyone knows the subjects this time, the game is not one of who is it, but *what* is it. There is still a strong sense of recognition, this time of vocal tendencies heard all term, but never really recognized, until they come from another actor.

1. Perform the entire scene first.
2. Go back over the checklist. Walking through a narrative is not really possible, but do get up and move around and stop to demonstrate every chance you get.
3. The class will want to view at least one complete scene and checklist combination, plus all the other complete scenes, even though breaking down into groups will again be helpful, in taking subsequent subjects through the lists.

Applying Vocal Awareness

It is important to leave this class understanding the vocal instrument you have, and what you do with it. It is far beyond the capacity of this class to bring about sweeping vocal changes. Be patient with yourself. You are already far more vocally sophisticated than you were a few weeks ago. All the material following the body section can be applied here as well. For now be content to listen more carefully and to master even small changes. And begin to recognize elements of the voice as ingredients for character recipes. ("If I lower my pitch and use a slightly more nasal quality, then slow down and smooth out my delivery, the character can express . . .")

Personal Awareness

You enter the stage with your body and voice as your primary tangible equipment. They are what you use to communicate in the offstage world too. But you are obviously no robot, with mere machinery. There is a whole complex personality, with a fascinating history, some of which you have already explored. There are dreams, memories, and textured experience, which the finest actors and most fascinating people manage to bring into their performances. Your personality allows your own spirit onstage, just as it allows it to be shared off. However, if the voice is less tangible than the body, then the spirit is even more elusive than the voice.

Molly Ringwald: *One of the most important things about being an actress is to have a strong sense of your own experience, emotions, and style.*[5]

Peggy Ashcroft: *You have to live in order to act and what you put into your performance is what you've learned from life.*[6]

Examine the following incomplete statements. Some you could fill in now. Other statements you will just want to think about for a while. These are all questions you will be asking later, about a character in a play, when you prepare a standard character analysis. Some you have already considered. The best answer to each question is usually the first one that comes to mind.

Exercise 3.19

Your Past

Complete these basic statements, making no effort for answers to make sense to anyone but you:

I come from . . .
My childhood was . . .
Family conditions were . . .
Major influences on me include . . .
Experiences making the most lasting impression on me were . . .
Strongest cultural binding involves . . .
Ten most important facts about me are . . .
Five people whose opinions are most important to me . . .
Crucial events prior to this moment in my life were . . .
My outlook on life was primarily determined by . . .

Areas to consider in answering each of the above:

Hometown: (influence? roots? memories? sense of connection?)

Parents: (living? married? rich? poor? happy? successful?)

Brothers, Sisters, Caregivers, Companions: (bonds? influence? significance?)

Early Years: (happy? forgettable? terrifying? ideal?)

Family Offerings: (affection? rejection? overprotection? drive? discipline?)

Home Conditions: (divorce? alcoholism? religion? illness? wealth? poverty?)

Education: (level? specializations? skills developed? areas omitted? subjects hated?)

External Influences: (war? travel? political climate? exposure to other worlds and perspectives?)

Lingering Forces: (image of God? role models or idols? best friend and worst enemy? important fantasy or literary figures? chief nurturers/authority figures?)

Exercise 3.20

Your Present

At the exact moment you are reading this and jotting down responses, the past, while influential, is not immediate. What is going on in your life right now?

Factors influencing how I feel at this moment . . .
Other people tend to describe me as . . .
I often use these terms to describe others . . .
In groups I . . .

I am basically . . .
My physical appearance is . . .
My physical life involves . . .
My usual style of clothing and type of accessories include . . .
My vocal life can be outlined as . . .
My most distinguishing characteristics are . . .
My favorites would have to include . . .
My temperament could be described as . . .
My lifestyle involves . . .
I am most and least interested in . . .
If an actor were playing me, he/she would have the greatest challenge in
    capturing my . . .
Three objects surrounding me that mean a great deal emotionally are . . .
They are important because . . .
My interior monologs often sound like . . .
Three evaluations I have to do most often . . .
The scenes of my life tend to have beats that are . . .
The tiniest struggles of my life include . . .
Above all else I believe . . .

Suggestions for identifying your present:

Self-Descriptions: (healthy? ill? bright? rich? independent? thoughtful?
    cute? confident? troubled? powerful?)
Choices: (foods? music? pastimes? people? places to go?)
Body: (basic physique? muscle tone? health/conditioning level? co-
    ordination? center(s)? distribution of weight? habitual expres-
    sions? silhouettes? postures? sense of space? isolation of parts? eye
    contact?)
Moves: (walk? gestural patterns? use of props? space invasions and adjust-
    ments? energy fields?)
Voice: (quality? pitch? volume? tempo? rhythm? breathing patterns? dy-
    namics?)
Speech: (word choice? nonverbals? articulation? pronunciation? favored
    images? topics?)
Appearance: (style choices? way of wearing/handling clothing? hair?
    amount of artifice? neatness? colors? degree of awareness?)
Grouping: (manners? joining? conformity? alignments? friends? social
    tendencies? leadership potential? adjustments to pressure?)
Daily Life: (work/play priorities? career decisions? relationships? degree
    of privacy? schedules/patterns?)
Adjustment: (personal satisfaction? reactions to stress or conflict? sense
    of guilt? feeling of responsibility for others? defense mechanisms?
    vision of reality? humor? degree of self-awareness?)

Exercise 3.21

Your Future

A large amount of anyone's time is spent planning things to come. Or daydreaming about things you *hope* will come. With the world waiting before you, what do you see now?

My main objective or what I want most to achieve in life is . . .
Other important objectives would include . . .
Obstacles I face are . . .
My strategy for the near future could be described as . . .
Specific tactics I am most likely to use in my life are . . .
Clues I tend to look for from other people to gauge my success with them
    include . . .
Clues I'm always looking for, but never seem to get, include . . .
If I have a life plan, it would be . . .
In five years, I see myself . . .
In ten years, I see myself . . .
In twenty years, I see myself . . .
If I work hard, I believe I can have a future where . . .
If I am remembered it will be for . . .
In my darkest fears, I'm terrified that I end up . . .
In my wildest fantasies, I . . .
If all my dreams come true, I will . . .

(This future list will need more contemplation and imagination. You are not just trying to figure out information. Here you are dealing with dreams.)

Bringing Yourself Onstage

Consider the list above for things you are ready to share with new friends and with the audience, if the role warrants it. Note, but file away, experiences too raw, new, or uncertain to comfortably use. Later this checklist will be helpful to compare yourself with a character you play. It will give you a clearer idea of where you stop and the character begins.

Bob Hoskins: *Whoever I play, whoever I become, I must have a starting off point. I must be sure of who I am, so sure it doesn't worry me, before I become someone else.*[7]

One of the biggest problems any actor faces is acting more onstage the way she does off. Actors are always being critiqued, by those who know them, with lines like:

"I've heard you do very forceful things with your voice. Why are you whining so much in this scene?"
"You personally have a wonderful stillness, but you're too busy in the part."
"Why isn't any of your joy and vivacity in the scene? No one is more fun than you, but this character is stiff right now."
"You're so bright. Please don't deny the character's intelligence."
"Get some of that urgency you've just shown me discussing politics, into the character discussing her marriage."

Undeniably some of your own qualities will work for a given role, and some could use alterations, to suit the needs of the character. But edit only those parts of yourself that would be *imposing* your own experience and vision of reality on that of the character. Find as much of yourself in the role as you can. Offer as much of yourself to any important life encounter as you can. Do not edit at random. Make the performance yours, not someone else's.

Exercise 3.22

Acting Journal

One of the most effective ways of recording and keeping your individual inventory is an *acting journal*. Sometimes this is a class requirement, sometimes an option. It is always useful in later years to look back on, and it feels good to have a place to "store" your acting experiences. Having been recorded, they seem much more concrete. I suggest you find something small enough to carry around with you all the time, but sturdy enough to hold up to being banged around.

The following is a standard format, which may work for you. Consider dividing your journal into three parts:

1. Acting Class

How are you feeling about it?
How is class going for you?

How are you enlightened? How confused? Any suggestions?
Are you getting enough (or the right kind) of attention?
What is helping you most? What least?
What would you like to share with your teacher that is somehow easier
   to write about than talk about?

2. Acting Observed

What are you noticing about actors you see in live theater, film, or TV?
What do you see occurring at auditions you watch?
How are your critical responses changing as you see more?
What do you notice about people in the world that might help your
   acting?
What do you see when you visit a rehearsal?
What are you discovering about yourself, both in assigned projects and
   your own imagination?

3. Acting

What are the circumstances of each of your rehearsals this term? What
   happened at each session and how did you feel about it?
When did you audition and what occurred? What did you find out that
   you can take to the next audition?
Which of your offstage performances might apply directly to your work
   onstage?
Which of your life experiences would you "play" differently, given the
   chance to repeat? What have you learned from them to prepare you
   for the future?
When did you meet to work with a partner? How did you use each seg-
   ment? When did you work most and least productively?

Within any structured journal format, try to personalize the
whole document, so it becomes a real tool for your growth and a
reflection of you. If your journal is turned in for class, but there are
entries that you wish not read, indicate that, and trust that your
privacy will not be violated.

A journal has a very simple purpose. It helps you *capture*
what you live and act. Theater is the most ephemeral of arts. You
invest months of your life in a show, then one day it is over and
this big piece of you is just a newspaper clipping, a telegram, some
opening-night good luck notes, maybe a pressed dead flower, all in

a drawer. The journal gets memories tangible and it revives them. Actors have a tendency to repeat the same old bad habits. Some always get paranoid the second week of rehearsal, some always get morose once the show opens. If you have a record of your acting experiences to read over, you can better catch yourself falling into old patterns, and even stop yourself before you sabotage yourself one more time. The journal helps you trap moments. It gives you a better chance of not repeating the bad moments. It gives you a shot at repeating good ones.

Choosing for Yourself

By now you have a clearer idea of how others see you, whether that is the person inside or not. You are foolish to fight your type, and you are foolish to accept it. Work towards a never-ending expansion of your range and power. But work in a way that lets you grow step by step.

Paul Newman: *I was always a character actor. I just looked like Little Red Riding Hood.*[8]

The best scenes and monologs for Acting 1 are those that allow you to focus on the truth of the moment, to concentrate fully, to commit with all your energy to what the character wants. If you have to keep *remembering* to be anorexic and 62, you are unlikely to accomplish the more important objectives above. That is why your first choices in acting class should be close to type and why you should not let type upset you, or in any way stop your desire to change and grow.

Getting yourself onstage, just the right amount, so the performance has a sense of sharing and intimacy, without self-indulgence, is an important accomplishment. Once you have been completely who you *are* onstage, who you are can be limitless. The very best means of being yourself in front of an audience has been designed by Stanislavski. Ironically, it involves finding yourself . . . by forgetting yourself.

Shirley Maclaine: *I'm interested in getting out of my own way and letting the character happen.*[9]

Meryl Streep *(before starting work on* Sophie's Choice*): First I'll learn Polish. Then I'll forget me. Then I'll get to her. That's my plan of action.*[10]

4

Stanislavski's System

(understanding the only complete
process by which actors build
characters)

Vanessa Redgrave: *I think a lot more attention could be
paid to Stanislavski as there is still a great deal of very
messy acting.*[1]

"I really don't believe in all that Stanislavski stuff."

One hears this statement often. The person who says it does
not *know* the Stanislavski stuff. The speaker has picked up some
distorted version, indirectly, from someone who did not know what
he was talking about in the first place. The speaker has not read
Stanislavski's works, nor studied his actual precepts. No one has
contributed more to our progress as actors, and no one has been
more misunderstood for it, than Stanislavski.

Stanislavski created the only known complete system for putting together a character, and it is used to some degree by every
reputable acting program. Programs often expand and *vary* the System, but always acknowledge the sound principles this man gave
us. So why all the bad-mouthing?

104

Myth and Reality

Information about the System came to Americans in scattered doses. Just as you can quote one piece of scripture and distort the Bible, people have been quoting this particular genius, out of context, for decades. He suffered from unclear translations of his works reaching these shores out of sequence and decades apart. His complete vision took quite a while to get here. (In fact, we still do not have many of the 12,000 documents found at his death,[2] and there are major differences between Soviet and English language editions of works.[3] Stanislavski's ideas suffered at the hands of American studios, which took bits and pieces of his work, presented something called the "Method" (a bastardized conception bearing only marginal resemblance to Stanislavski's "method of physical actions"), and watered down his vision. The Method was nothing more than shorthand to the System.

Even digested versions of Stanislavski, however, worked well for certain scripts, particularly for film, where sustaining, repeating, and projecting performances were not always necessary. Even Stanislavski in shorthand can have merit. But after a while, people began to realize that the Method could lead to the worst kind of self-indulgence, self-absorption, muddy, mumbled communication, and a general confusion of the *actor's* feelings for those of the character. Guess who got the blame?

In more recent years, the full range of Stanislavski's contribution has been acknowleged. But there are still quite a few people who have not gotten the message.

Who Was Stanislavski?

Constantin Stanislavski (1863–1938) was a brilliant actor, director, and teacher who co-founded the Moscow Art Theater in 1898 and changed the way actors worked forever. He did as much for performance as Darwin, Marx, and Freud (his contemporary) did for biological science, political science, and psychology. In fact there are similarities in the way these four helped open new ways of understanding human behavior. Stanislavski wrote four famous books *(An Actor Prepares, Building a Character, Creating a Role,* and *My Life in Art)* which eventually make their way into the personal library of almost any serious student of acting. In the first three of these books, he uses a brilliant device: a master teacher, called Tortsov, takes a group of acting students, including the book's eager narrator, Kostya, through several years of classes. Both Tortsov and Kostya are really Stanislavski at different points in his life (Kostya is, in fact, the common nickname for Constantin). So the elderly Stanislavski meets the young actor he once was and the books distill his own learning process.[4] There is no relaxation, concentration, imagination exercise, no warm-up, no improv, no script experiment currently practiced, for which the basic principle and at least the germ of the exercise itself do not appear in these works.

Fortunately for us, when Stanislavski started acting, he was not a "natural." He was awkward, ungainly, and ill at ease; so he was motivated to study what all the great performers did to calm and focus themselves, and to report the results in a systematic way. He later found himself working with new plays (by writers like Chekhov and Gorki) that cried out for truth in acting, instead of the more extravagant and bombastic attacks many actors had been using. He found a system to achieve this calm and truth, now taught all over the world. Since organized classes and degrees in acting were unknown when Stanislavski started working, it might be argued that without his contribution, your class might not even exist today. Many of the spiritual gifts you receive, as you train as an actor, come, indirectly, from him.

Basic Ingredients

You have already experienced the basic Stanislavski System back in chapter 1 when you identified these ten crucial ingredients:

1. Relationship
2. Objective
3. Obstacle
4. Strategy
5. Tactics
6. Text
7. Subtext
8. Interior Monolog
9. Evaluations
10. Beats

Go back and review anything that fails to come immediately to mind. This is the actor's fundamental vocabulary. You want it secure

Figure 4-1 Stanislavski: Offstage and On
At right, Constantin Stanislavski in some of his memorable characterizations for the Moscow Art Theater. From top right: Dr. Astrov in Chekhov's *Uncle Vanya*, Prince Abrezkov in Tolstoy's *The Living Corpse*, Famusov in Griboyedov's *Woe to Wit*, Vershinin in Chekhov's *The Three Sisters*. (Photos courtesy of Sovfoto and TASS from Sovfoto)

and working for you. (For simplicity and clarity, terms on this list are those most widely used now by actors, whether they were part of Stanislavski's original working vocabulary or not.)

Stanislavski perceived that in any life situation (or theatrical encounter), the person (or character) always determines her choices based on her feelings about others around her. She has something she wants, something in the way, and a constantly changing plan to get what she wants. She experiences words spoken, but also other meanings implied, in fact a constant series of words going on in her head. She and her partner each *consider* saying a number of things that they actually end up rejecting along the way. He recognized that any encounter, between humans, could be broken down into units, when changes occurred. Therefore, instead of being one long, confusing blur, the encounter could be seen in easily manageable parts. (The acting terms have been deliberately avoided in this paragraph. Can you substitute acting words for the ones used?)

The Legacy

What is so magical about all this? Well, like most brilliant discoveries, it seems like common sense once you think about it. If an actor really does each of these things, his attention will be fully engaged, his instrument will respond honestly, and he will be *compelling* to watch. Certain actor blocks, like tension, stiffness, and self-consciousness, tend to fall away, because the mind can only hold so much (researchers say seven separate categories are the maximum, at any moment, for most people). If "I don't know what to do with my hands" or "I hope the critique isn't devastating" enter your head, you are not concentrating in the mode above, so you are not using the System.

The elements above identify only a single interlude in the whole major event that is a play or a life. They help you enter an isolated encounter, while the total Stanislavski System helps you put yourself in a character's complete world. The list above addresses only those facts of which each person is consciously aware. The System involves the subconscious as well. The System embraces a larger picture and multiple levels. Stanislavski has summarized his vision into three overall ideas he calls "propositions," paraphrased here:

Proposition 1 The actor needs to achieve a state that is like a normal person in life. In order to do this, he must be:

1. *Physically Free and Controlled:* His instrument needs to be free enough for him to control it with ease.

2. *Alert and Attentive:* Combined with his freedom, this amounts to the state of relaxed readiness.
3. *Listening and Observing:* He must be in genuine contact with actors who play opposite him.
4. *Believing:* He must accept and live inside the reality of the character.

Proposition 2   If the actor puts himself in the place of the character, he will then be able to achieve honest action onstage by combining:

1. *Psychological Action:* Strong motives drive the character forward towards his objectives. An involved, feeling actor automatically executes organic physical actions.
2. *Physical Action:* Feelings are powerfully sustained and expressed through movement. Physical actions support psychological states.

(The beauty of the "method of physical actions" is the way the ingredients sustain each other. You see the symbiotic relationship between elements. On a very simple level, let us say you achieve a state of anger and forcefully grab the back of a chair. The movement is just right, and you may never have discovered it without immersing yourself in the character's perspective. In performance, even if you are not always fully angry, the power of the move as the body remembers it and anticipates it is likely to help you generate anger and consistently communicate it to an audience. Stanislavski understood very clearly that the body was more directly reliable and available than the emotions, which "run through your fingers like water" and that the body should therefore be used as a pathway to elusive feelings. Of course, your likelihood of discovering both physical and the psychological actions is stronger if you are truly sharing in the character's own perspective.)

Proposition 3   The organic action that results from the combination above will give rise to sincere, believable feelings on the part of the actor, but only if he has thoroughly researched and analyzed the role. The actor's meticulous preparation ensures he is in the play, not some fantasy of his own, and his homework frees him to experience "metamorphosis."[5]

Most Misunderstood

In all fairness, Stanislavski's writing style is dense and florid by today's standards: His sentences are intricate and complex; he does not always name each concept; and sometimes he appears to call the same idea by different names. He also changed his mind continuously as his system evolved and much information has been passed on by various disciples, who happened to be working with him at one point in his life, went their own ways, and did not develop as he did. As one of his most celebrated spiritual descendants, Jerzy Grotowski, has said, "Stanislavski's method evolved, but not his disciples. Each disciple is limited to his particular period."[6] Yet there are five widely accepted myths for which there is no sustained support in his work:

1. Since truth is what it is all about, you do not need to bother with technical work.
2. You should be yourself, instead of bothering to develop a characterization.
3. You should use all your own memories and feelings onstage and think about your past.
4. You should forget the audience altogether.
5. You should wait until you really feel it, before you do it or say it.

You can probably see why lazy, narcissistic actors would grab at these half-truths, and why conscientious artists would be appalled. The fallacious five constitute a license to follow your whims, without work. You can also see why even these System distortions might succeed in isolated contexts. In filming, all you need is one good take. There is an old Hollywood story about a ruthless director who, supposedly, would walk up to his little child star just before a shot, and say something mind-boggling like, "Someone just killed your little dog"; then to the crew, "Okay, roll 'em!!!!" Let us hope it is just a sick, funny story, but what *is* true is that, regardless of how he got the tears he wanted, he did get them. Once. The audience, seeing the film, would never know the child was crying about something unrelated to the movie. And there would be no need to repeat the scene on Thursday, as there is in the theater. All five myths are false.

1. No Need for Technique? Stanislavski was so convinced of the need for painful, meticulous technical work that, paradoxically, he often did not write about it. You know how you assume certain truths to be self-evident? He was working in a culture and for a company where discipline and daily, lengthy classes were so standard that he probably never dreamed that some jerk would presume to walk in front of an audience raw and untrained. The actors described in his books are, in addition to their sessions on the System, taking classes in dancing, gymnastics, fencing, other swordplay, tumbling, voice placement, diction, movement "plasticity," boxing, and mask work! There are constant references to daily "drill sessions." He maintained consistently that the actor needed to be *tuned,* in order to induce the desired automatic responses. Otherwise it just would not work. The vessel would be too weak to carry the water.

2. Yourself Instead of Characterization?   Where does the actor stop and the character start? Stanislavski's concept of the *magic If* suggests that the actor imagine herself in the character's place. Note: There is a crucial difference. The charge is not to imagine yourself there, instead of the character. The character's place is her whole life. It is all her training, all her fears and prejudices, all her habits. You do not ask, "What would I do *if I* were there?" but "What would I do *if* I had experienced *this person's* entire life up to this moment?" If anything, this technique assures that you will *not* impose who you are on the character's life. This concept is often not just misunderstood, but entirely reversed.

3. All Your Own Memories?   Perhaps the most controversial technique in the whole System is called "emotional memory," where actors summon up feelings from their own pasts in order to achieve emotion onstage. It is, however, recommended as a rehearsal rather than a performance device and then only with experiences that are not so raw that they threaten your sanity and control. Actors should use everything they have got, but only when they are masters of the emotions instead of vice versa. Everything onstage is under control. Or as Stanislavski puts it, "It is only permissible for an actor to weep his heart out at home or in rehearsals."[7] What the actor uses in performance are simply triggering impulses and images discovered in rehearsal, not detailed summonings of his own past.

Dwelling on the past? The System asks the actor to dig deeply into the character's past to determine reasons for his behavior and help clarify motives. But Stanislavski never suggests that any of this is what the actor thinks about onstage. It is part of the *process.* The

System demands enough present and future thinking to occupy the actor. But without the past research, the future thinking might be empty. You have been asked to dig back, quite a bit so far in this book, into your own history. But that is to give you self-awareness and a sense of all you have to work with. You do not think about those things at the moment of performance, but they help clarify the thinking you do.

4. Forget the Audience?   Stanislavski helps the actor keep the audience from *invading* the actor's work. He never suggested the audience be excluded. He suggested that you keep yourself busy and focused enough that the audience could not inhibit you. His operative word is *concerned*. ("As soon as the actor stops being *concerned* with his audience, the latter begins to watch the actor."[8])

His tool called "circles of concentration" identifies a way of working the audience in and out of your consciousness as necessary. You focus on a specific task right in front of you whenever you feel your concentration or involvement wavering. The smaller and more physical the task, the better (sort of a tiny Here and Now). You spiral out your circle to include your acting partner, when the two of you need to interact. You spiral out further to include the entire stage at the appropriate moment and further to take in the audience, when there is a specific audience response to deal with, or when you know there is a difficult moment of projection. A state of *public solitude* is achieved.

Basically, these circles keep widening and narrowing according to the needs of the moment. Stanislavski has described them as "elastic," letting the actor's awareness stretch, expand, and contract with minimal effort as is necessary. Clearly, the actor does not wish to be preoccupied or obsessed with the audience. But he wishes to have at his disposal the means of widening and narrowing his perception because "the audience constitute the spiritual acoustics for us. They give back what they receive from us as living, human emotions."[9]

5. Wait Until You Feel It?   Not on your life. Stanislavski suggests taking action aggressively onstage because it is likely (although not certain) that feeling will follow. His writings are filled with concern for maintaining the right tempo/rhythm; and he would probably have wanted to assassinate contemporary actors who indulge themselves by taking huge amounts of time to summon up feelings from some dark hiding place, while everyone else waits. The investment of time, for the System, is in actor homework and careful rehearsal, all geared towards making it unnecessary for the actor to stumble around in front of an audience searching for his lost emotions.

Leaving behind the five fallacies, let us consider the fundamental truths of the System.

Empathy

If one had to summarize the whole Stanislavski approach in one word, I think the best choice would be *empathy*. You empathize with someone when you so completely comprehend what that person is going through that you share his feelings, thoughts, and motives. Empathy is a far more powerful connection than sympathy or pity. It generates an involuntary physical response, beyond an intellectual/emotional one. You may watch a fight and actually feel a blow being struck with your whole being. Depending on which fighter you identify with, you may feel the blow received or the one given. This is empathy on the simplest level. You may also empathize to the degree that you can comprehend actions that most observers would find inhuman and beyond justification.

Exercise 4.1

Comprehending

What would it take to get you to empathize with the following people:

1. A woman who would steal another's child?
2. A terrorist who would try to assassinate the Pope?
3. A dictator who would order an entire race of people terminated?
4. A mother who would murder her own two children?
5. A spy who would betray his country and family for money?

When, in your own life, have you found an act or a person beyond your comprehension, but then something happened that made you empathic with the person you used to despise? On a personal level, developing empathy is a profound, troubling, deeply humanizing experience. It feels wonderful to be able to stop judging others, but disturbing to find your crisp black/white world turning muddy and full of maybes. On an acting level, empathic response is essential. You may be cast as any of the five people in the list above. Those parts are all written and waiting.

Stanislavski showed us that actors are nonjudgmental, totally compassionate artists. You play any role, saint or demon, with an equal amount of involvement. You play Hitler or Gandhi with empathy. It prevents you from presenting a generalized performance, full of vague attitudes. You play everyone as the everyday hero of his own life. You play everyone as just some guy doing the best he can with what he has, since that is the way most "guys" see themselves. Gandhi did not view himself in a celestial glow. He was just getting on with life, doing what he had to.

If there is any part of the System that might be said to possess magic, it is that point where you immerse yourself so thoroughly that appropriate, involuntary actions occur. This is empathy. And if it is a miracle, it is also, as Stanislavski was the first to point out, simply a law of nature and an everyday experience. Humane, loving people experience empathy all the time. As do sensitive, responsive actors.

Richard Dreyfuss: *You've got to find out how to love her, because you can't play a character that you don't love.*[10]

Once you understand your character, not just intellectually but deep within, you are not just on your way to a decent performance, you are also freed from your own prejudices. And, in the vivid words of Stanislavski, "Prejudices block up the soul like a cork in the neck of a bottle."[11] How do these responses get started, when you have a role where you feel you hardly know the character, much less function deep within his being?

Ten System Steps

To add to the ten basic ingredients you experienced in chapter 1, here are ten more that embrace the entire System. If you wish to inhabit someone else, you:

1. Learn all the relevant facts that influence this person's behavior (**given circumstances**).

2. Use these facts to place yourself inside his life perspective (**magic If**).
3. From his point of view, determine what he wants most in life (**super objective**) and his range of lesser but still important goals, both conscious and unconscious (**objective hierarchy**).
4. Experience his particular way of dealing with a variety of obstacles and setbacks. Find the *connection* between all the moments when a psychological motive prompts a physical impulse, through rehearsal experimentation, until a pattern emerges (**through-line of actions**).
5. Write down the results in manuscript form and mark the script into workable units (**score**).
6. Project onto people and objects, real and imagined, qualities from your imagination and experience that bring them to life (**endowment**).
7. Use your five senses to awaken memories of both physical sensations and emotions that can be filtered into the character's feelings (**recall**).
8. Add to your constantly playing interior monolog a film of the mind, then speak, not to the ears of your partner, but to her eyes, trying to get her to see what you see (**images**).
9. Alter your own tendencies to suit those of the character, particularly your sense of time and intensity of experience (**tempo/ rhythm**) so none of your inappropriate mannerisms are imposed on the role (**external adjustments**).
10. Allow yourself to use all the previous research to free your entry into the heightened reality that allows you to both discover and control simultaneously (**creative state**).

The ten steps enter the concern of the actor in the order above, but one step does not stop while another takes over; each is layered in, as the others continue to be actively engaged. Take a look at each of them as they operate in your own life:

Step 1: Given Circumstances

Those details you considered in the last chapter regarding your own past and present are your own *given circumstances*. They are life factors that influence how you now behave. Relationships, training, conditioning, social life, financial status, age, period of history are all part of the picture. Your life has provided you with these circumstances, for better or worse. The playwright gives some of them to a character to help you inhabit that character's world. You fill in the others. You ask all the basic journalist's questions that begin with *who, what, when, where, why,* and *how.* Then you put together a list, trying to determine which of a multitude of circumstances are most important. Look at both the external as well as the internal circumstances these outer conditions have created. Almost always there are a few given circumstances that are breakthroughs in your understanding. Start by looking at situations and characters instead of moods.

Exercise 4.2

Others' Givens

1. What are the ten most important given circumstances of one of the actors you imitated for class?
2. Of your best friend?
3. Of the person you most admire?
4. Of someone you dislike intensely?
5. Of the historical figure you find most fascinating?

Step 2: The Magic If

Next you take the given circumstances and ask yourself how you would respond if you were in his shoes. The legendary American Indian adage to hot-headed young warriors—"Do not judge another brave, my son, until you have walked in his moccasins"—is probably repeated in some fashion in all cultures by the wise, experienced, and forgiving to those too ready to fight. It is the capsule *magic If.* You step into the other brave's moccasins and try to walk around for a time. The If is the means of entering the character's givens.

You particularly employ the magic If in those areas where you have the least in common with your character: If you are an agnostic cast as a Bible-thumping revival tent preacher, you engage that character's early literal visions of God the Father; the prayer meetings that were the source of great thrills and visions; the time he was literally spoken to by Jehovah and told to spread the word; the triumphant cleansing he feels every time he leads another sheep back to the flock. You leave behind your own experiences of disillusionment and scientific perspective. You do this, as much as is necessary, to stop feeling superior or judgmental, and to play the character from a full heart, in his own vision of reality. You end up feeling that in his place (his *total* place) you would be bound to act as he did.

Jane Alexander: *I think all* good *actors use the Magic If.*[12]

Exercise 4.3

Planting

1. Pick anyone from the last exercise and "plant" his given circumstances on yourself, replacing your own when they are incompatible.
2. Spend a half hour giving yourself over to the magic If.
3. Perform any simple physical task (sweeping? setting the table?) entirely from the character's perspective.
4. Observe an event (a TV show? a ball game?) and see it from his eyes.

Exercise 4.4

Class Ifs

1. Imagine three separate classmates, each cast as you. Where would each of these actors need to use the magic If to play you fully?
2. Reverse the process for three other classmates, imagining yourself being cast as them and playing them well.
3. Pick the one of the three most removed from you. Use the magic If to act out any event that would be more comfortable for the person you are playing than it would be for you.

Step 3: Super Objective

We have already examined the objective involved in each encounter, but everyone has something she wants more out of life (or in the course of the play) than anything else. For most of us this is the driving force, the cause we would go to the mat or even to war for. By moving through the character's given circumstances and immersing yourself in the magic If, the super objective may come clear. It is usually actor-detective work, because playwrights rarely come out and state it. It should always be emotional rather than intellectual and strong enough to involve "our whole physical and spiritual being."[13] It should be stated in the simplest, most active terms. The super objective unifies all the tiny objectives that occupy moment-to-moment living.

Objective Hierarchy   From the super down to the smallest, our lives are full of objectives pursued. Some objectives you consider for super, but do not choose. These go right near the top of the list as finalists, because they are still very important. There may be some that are not conscious, but are very strong, motivating forces. Strong subconscious objectives should be considered as well as conscious ones. A character often has a dominant objective for each act, and always for each scene, in the play.

Exercise 4.5

Hierarchies

1. Try to put into simple phrases what you a) want most of out life; b) want very strongly but not quite most; c) wanted most during each of the past four weeks; d) wanted most during each of the past four hours; e) wanted most (if your objectives changed) during the last four minutes.
2. Try to review and uncover several moments in your life when you thought you were pursuing one objective (conscious), but then suddenly realized you were unconsciously pursuing another.
3. Recreate one of these scenes. Have classmates act other participants, based on your description of the rough scenario. Hierarchize the objectives you had and let them all work to motivate you.

Exercise 4.6

Class Objectives

Discuss as a group, with someone writing choices on the board, the shared class super objective for the term, other contenders, the class hierarchy for the term. Do the same for each week so far and for today's class meeting up to this moment. Conjecture about hidden or subconscious objectives that may also be shared by more than one person in the class.

Step 4: Through-Line of Actions

Each isolated action you perform in life has an inward (the *need* to do) and an outward (what is *done*) dimension. Whether you need to quench your thirst so you get a glass of juice or you need to validate yourself as a student so you get a Fulbright, large or small actions all combine the psychological impulse with the physical attack. The actor needs to discover both elements for a character.

The physical action, discovered through rehearsal experimentation, is "the bait for the emotion,"[14] aiming to "rouse your subconscious."[15] While emotions cannot be directly summoned (and trying to do so is usually disastrous), the body can plant *conditions* and open doors in the hope that "the spirit cannot but respond to the actions of the body."[16] This physical action may be overt, violent, extravagant, or it may involve no discernible movement at all. "Action, motion, is the basis of the art followed by the actor," writes Stanislavski, but "External immobility does not necessarily imply passiveness. You may sit without a motion and at the same time be in full action."[17] In such a case, the tension in the body, the light in the eyes, the *commitment* to stillness are likely to communicate at least as strongly as a large sweeping movement.

Over an entire play or life, patterns occur as the character keeps running into various obstacles, which Stanislavski calls "counteractions." People tend to repeat choices. When confronted with obstacles, some people give in all the time and even change their objectives rather than fight. Others employ threat tactics, rarely seducing or gently luring, in order to get what they want. Some always work indirectly and never say what they really have in mind. Some stick relentlessly to the same strategy, while others change easily, making adaptations as they go along. Look for patterns of behavior through the role that tie the whole together just as your life patterns begin to define your own through-line of behavior. The through-line ends up like the spinal column with each action finally connecting to its neighbor in one continuous, fluctuating organ, which is why the through-line is often called the spine of the role. No action is too small to contribute.

The very smallest actions are often called *bits*.* Not to be confused with "doing a bit" or piece of stage business of some kind, the bit is like the smallest piece of information (byte) that can be contained in a computer. To illustrate, I am returning home from a walk: the first bit would be I hope I have remembered my keys. I hear them jingling, so that first objective is achieved. I next reach into the right pocket of my jacket, hoping the keys are there, but they are not; so that second bit did not end with an achieved objective. I reach into the left. They are there. Achieved. I hope the house key is easily accessible on the ring. It is not. It is not even close to the top. Not achieved. I get the key after sorting through several, and, because I am entering a door I do not usually use, I hope I have it inserted at the right angle, and I do! The door opens and life goes on! These silly, tiny little triumphs (sometimes called moment-to-moment victories) are the way we get through life.

Actors often fail to break the role down into nearly enough bits (which are also called *units)*, resulting in a performance that is too general. Stanislavski says that "in general" is the worst enemy of the actor. Most people playing the admittedly less-than-riveting scene I starred in above would do a very general looking-for-the-keys thing (one muddy bit tops) without getting to it *bit by bit* (there are six separate ones described) the way we actually do in our lives.

If you are cast as Hamlet, you can be overwhelmed by the size, the grandeur of the role, by all the great "others" who have played it. Or you can break it down from his super objective to each small victory. In your first scene, all you have to do for a while is successfully avoid your uncle Claudius. Then your mother approaches you, and you just have to hide how distraught you are from her. She speaks to you, and all you have to do is think of the briefest possible answer to get the conversation over. And before you know it, you are dead and someone else is saying, "Good night, sweet Prince." You work your way bit by bit, objective by objective, and the role is not frightening, because each unit in it is manageable, and then you move on to the next. "Proceed," says Stanislavski, "bit by bit, helping yourself along by small truths."[18]

---

*There is some controversy over Stanislavski's use of "beat" and "bit," partially due to translation confusion and partly to the fact that they were pronounced the same by Europeans teaching Americans. For our purposes, bits are always smaller and it takes a number of them to consitute a beat or a complete transaction.

Exercise 4.7

Tiny Triumphs

Break down the following experiences into the smallest bits possible:

1. The next time you arrive home.
2. The next time you arrive for acting class, the period from entering the building to taking a seat.
3. The first two minutes after you wake up in the morning.
4. The last two minutes before you go to bed.
5. Any short excerpt from a rehearsal with a partner where text is not involved.

Exercise 4.8

Triumphant Entries

Volunteers enter the room in one of the situations above. Class members call out identifications of each attempted small triumph, then "yes" or "no" if it was successful or not. Cheer the actor each time one is achieved.

Variation: Act is performed silently with each observer jotting down victories. See if all agree on total tried, lost, and won.

Remember that all objectives from super to bit are *positive*. Even characters who appear bent on self-destruction are usually acting in order to still some demons inside themselves. A pathetic, diseased wino lying in the gutter, reaching out to the bottle on the curb for one last swig of rotgut, is not trying to make himself sick; he is trying to *achieve* peace, to sleep, to settle nagging self-doubts, at least for tonight.

As his work progressed through the years, Stanislavski preferred attempting to define the role in larger units and breaking the performance into bits only when a section was not *working*. The through-line of actions represents the total effort at achieving objectives, the various sections of the character's struggle.

Step 5: Scoring the Role

Stanislavski recommends that you *score* your script and accompanying notebook much like a musician sits down and notates a musical score. You have important things like the super objective at the front, probably in big letters. Then each scene has its own means of being highlighted. You take each of the ingredients listed in this chapter and find a way of notating them, perhaps drawing a line where each beat begins and ends for you, so that what emerges is like "a long catalogue of minor and major objectives, units, scenes, acts"[19] designed to "draw the actor as a human being closer to the real life of his character or role."[20] Many actors end up doing a great deal of scoring in their heads, but I recommend that you do it on paper at least a few times, to lock it in place for yourself. It also takes a while to work out your own codes, to determine how best to lay out information for yourself.

The score has an obvious relationship to the acting journal and may be combined with it. While no one else should tell you how to prepare a document this personal, and a great deal of what you write may be virtually incomprehensible to others, there is enormous value in the process of writing (sketching, drawing, coding) it down. Actors who score, go back over and over for help and inspiration from the document. And, of course, it is one more way of making a very elusive art form recorded and concrete.

Jack Nicholson: *The first thing I do with a script is divide it up into beats and measures—a measure being a sequence of beats—to get at the fundamental rhythm of the part before playing it in rehearsals.*[21]

Sigourney Weaver (*on her role in* Aliens): *I secretly structured myself to play Ripley like (Shakespeare's) Henry V and like the women warriors of classic Chinese literature.*

From her director: *Her copy of the script was marked with 17 different colors of ink. In her margin notes, she got the dramatic significance of almost every line of dialogue and how each one might tie in with a later scene.*[22]

The score is not completed before rehearsals begin and then kept perfect like scripture. It is revised and altered throughout the whole rehearsal process and even during the run of the show. It is usually messy looking, with lots of erasing and crossing out. It is a dynamic, ever-changing work, always in progress.

Step 6: Endowment

You had no problem, as a child, making a stick into a magic wand or into Excalibur, with taking an old sheet and *endowing* it with great beauty, weight, and even ermine trim as it became your cape. Onstage you endow plastic swords and capes trimmed in rabbit fur or cotton batten. Props and set pieces tend to be lightweight, cheaply made, and somehow unconnected with reality. You endow a glass of tea, which is supposed to be bourbon, with aroma, a burning sensation as you sip, a rush of lightheadedness as a possible aftermath. You endow some stiff plastic flowers with invigorating scent, softness, freshness, and the cheap plastic vase you are putting them in, with the weight, coldness, and smoothness of porcelain or crystal. You endow a partner with great beauty in order to find him irresistible.

Endowing something or someone requires a clear knowledge and memory of the original. If it is not in your experience, you do research. Actors need to keep all the senses awake with each new experience, for the possibility of having to recreate the sensation. They also need to go beyond the obvious, into creative conjecture. The bourbon may be a rare vintage given to you for your 21st birthday and sipped on the rarest of occasions. The flowers may be a hybrid developed by a gardener who worshiped you and was sent away by your snobbish parents. The vase might be something your mother brought back from a trip to China, quite expensive, but a color you abhor and she *knows* it. The cape may have been sewn by angels before history.

Some endowment will be suggested by the script but the vast majority is up to you, full of creative possibility. The audience will never know the details as you are sipping or arranging flowers, but there will be a sense of depth, texture; you will look as if you really *live* in that space and the performance can take on the qualities of a tapestry.

Stanislavski divided endowment into *external,* where feelings are used to give imaginary life to tangible existing objects, and *in-*

ternal, where your own memory is used to create altogether imaginary objects, such as those that might appear on the fourth wall or in the character's offstage life.

Exercise 4.9

Adding Consequence

1. Try wandering around the house and endowing objects that are of no consequence to you. Stop and note those that have giant sentimental value and study what happens to you as you contemplate, savor their history, flash on the relationships they symbolize. Go back and endow one to which you have been largely indifferent.
2. Pick some objects that are available in large enough numbers so that everyone in the group can endow them (empty Styrofoam cups, coins, notebooks, and so on). Work on adding physical properties and then layering in emotional ones.
3. Each person bring an object to class. Work with a partner, first taking the other person's object and endowing it from your own imagination. Compare your own addition of consequence to that of the person who brought in the object.

Step 7: Recall

Repeated feelings, according to Stanislavski, "are the only means by which you can, to any degree, influence inspiration." He also warns that "the moment you *lose* yourself on the stage marks the departure from truly living your part."[23] The primary tool for untapping controlled, repeatable emotion is the memory of the senses. While sight is probably the most powerful, all five (sight, sound, smell, taste, touch) have the capacity to release with great strength. Obviously you need to use, with great care, any untapping of your own life that might intrude on the character's experience rather than help you connect to it.

On a simpler level, each of the actual five senses are used onstage to assist in endowment where the theatrical object lacks the fullness of the real thing or where the real thing (an actual blow fully struck, a genuinely repulsive smell) would be dangerous to the actor or beyond the tolerance of the audience.

Exercise 4.10

Bringing It Back

Let each of the suggestive phrases below hit you in the appropriate sense, with the first memory to come along. Let the image expand to include the given circumstances and allow the feelings to return.

1. a landscape where you felt small and lost
2. a song that used to get to you
3. the voice of a lost loved one, soothing you
4. something baking at your grandmother's home
5. the perfume/cologne of someone with whom you were infatuated
6. your father's handshake or hug, your mother's embrace
7. your first taste of an "adult" beverage
8. the taste of your favorite birthday cake

Release Pictures When calling on emotional memory, there is often a single lingering image, like a photograph in the mind, that summons back all the feelings in a rush, that releases that emotional vein. Finding these images (once the experience is repeatable) can be far more effective than trying to recall the entire lengthy experience, which can get muddied by sheer overload of material. You may recall an entire romantic summer affair by the image of one sunset, watched seated quietly behind your lover. The tanned back of your lover and the colors in the sky, reflected on the loved one's skin, can be so vividly etched that the rest unlocks. You may recall your attachment to a favored grandparent by the image of a rocker with an afghan thrown over it. The icons of our times (a flag, a cross, a swastika) serve as *release images* for many, every time they are viewed.

Sometimes, when you look through a photo album, you stumble across a release shot, unexpectedly, after pages and pages of photos that were enjoyable, but did not unlock emotional memory. And suddenly you are flooded with feelings.

Exercise 4.11

Release Album

Identify a release photo for an emotional memory for each of the following. Experiment with variations of long shots, close-ups, slow motion, and other visual alterations to make the image even more evocative for you.

childhood delight	heartbreak	feeling utterly
awakening sexuality	triumphant	insignificant
inspiration	accomplishment	complete freedom
romantic love	humiliation	selfless compassion

Step 8: Images

If you have a definite picture in your own head as you speak a phrase and if you try to get your listener to see the same picture, your words are likely to be more vividly expressive and your connection with your partner more intense. It is almost as if you were plugging your energy into your listener and causing him to catch your vision. Thinking in images, instead of just words, is exciting and evocative. You have a film of the imagination for which your interior monolog is the sound track. Here are some examples of the way Stanislavski uses images himself, describing actor problems:[24]

Excessive gestures: "trash, dirt, spots on a performance"
Involuntary, nervous movements: "convulsive cramps" causing "blotches on a part"
Sloppy pronunciation of a word's beginning: "a face with a bashed in nose"
Swallowing a word's ending: "a man minus a limb"
Dropped letters or syllables: "a missing eye or tooth"
Actor who speaks well: "a phonetics gourmet, savoring the aroma of each syllable and sound"
A comma: "the warning lift of a hand, making others wait for you"
An unfilled pause: "a blank hole in the fabric of artistic creation"
Accenting a word: "a pointing finger singling out"
Use of an adjective: "to color a noun and set off this particular 'individual' from others"

You see how much more exciting these standard suggestions for stage movement and speech become when a picture is painted?

The capacity for rich speech and intense partner connection is strong.

Exercise 4.12

Imaging

1. Working with a partner, speak the following lines with Stanislavski's images in mind:
   "You need to get rid of all those extra gestures."
   "I don't think you mean to make all those nervous little movements, but they are really distracting."
   "I can't understand the beginning of your first three words."
   "What happened to the last part of what you were saying?"
   "You're just not saying everything, so I can't get what you mean."
   "You really speak well. I love to listen to you."
   "You made it clear to me where the punctuation, especially the comma, was."
   "You took pauses, but I couldn't figure out why or what for."
   "You need to show which words and phrases are important, which need to stand out for attention."
   "Those adjectives are there to help you. Try to alert the dark, shadowy, reticent recesses of my sluggish, tired imagination by the way you use descriptive words."
2. Describe any brief experience you have had in the past few days, once with just the words, then with the movie of the experience (and occasional striking still photographs) in mind, trying to get your partner to see the same movie and notice the same still shots. Discuss the comparative "look" of your film and his.

Step 9: External Adjustments

No matter how much of yourself you find in the character, some altering of your own habits is going to be needed to portray this other human being. Some adjustments will have occurred automatically in setting up each of the previous conditions, but others can be layered in from the outside. These externals may involve any of the physical or vocal tendencies explored in earlier chapters, but Stanislavski believes, above all else, in experimenting with various *tempo rhythms*. The character "in time" is crucial to untapping who he really is. Character detail is liberating. "A characterization," says Stanislavski, "is the mask which hides the actor-individual. Protected by it he can lay bare his soul down to the last intimate detail."[25]

Step 10: The Creative State

When an actor is able to pull together all the elements above, he has an excellent chance to enter a state in which he is open to inspiration. Stanislavski compares the *creative state* to "the feelings of a prisoner when the chains that had interfered with all his movements for years have at last been removed."[26] In this state of metamorphosis, he is able to think as the actor *and* as the character, without either interfering with the other. The performer functions simultaneously on two planes, with actor perspective running parallel to role perspective "as a foot path may stretch along beside a highway."[27]

Far from naive or mystical about the state, Stanislavski is quick to point out that you only have a shot at achieving it *if:*

> . . . you have understood the play correctly, analyzed the character accurately, have a good appearance, clear and energetic diction, plastic movement, a sense of rhythm, temperament, taste, and the infectious quality we often call charm.[28]

Nor does he claim that the mood will come whenever called, but rather emerge between stretches of struggle. Much of the time an actor onstage is not functioning in "a second state of reality," but wavers back and forth between actor and character awareness. The creative state is always worth pursuing. The careful preparation involved will ensure that decisions made will be honest ones. "Plan your role consciously at first, then play it truthfully."[29] If the internal and external work are both "based on truth, they will inevitably merge and create a living image."[30]

Open Scenes

One of the best ways of applying the basics of the System is the *open* scene. It is called "open" because the lines of dialog are essentially nothing, waiting to be filled. Here is a sample.

Exercise 4.13

Open Dialog

This dialog is so open that the characters are called One and Two:

ONE: Ah.
TWO: So?
ONE: All set?
TWO: No.
ONE: Well.
TWO: Yes.

Stage it in class or simply imagine it with the following contexts:

1. Leaving home for a very long time (parent and child)
2. A drug bust (dealer and narc)
3. Revealing notice of academic probation (parent and child)
4. Picking out a new outfit (two friends)
5. Answering an ad in the classified section (advertiser and customer)

Repeat with the class suggesting more specific given circumstances to alter the scene.

Open scenes provide a comfortable introduction to the System because you are allowed to make up things. You get to be a little bit of a playwright, as you master the basic terms. Then later, when you approach a work scripted in greater detail, you will be able to respond more sensitively to the playwright's vision as you *investigate* the same elements you *created* for your open scene.

Closing Scenes

You can tell already that no scene is completely open. Even in one this simple, one character is obviously more aggressive, the other more defensive or indecisive, one is inquiring, the other responding. This and every scene is to some degree closed by information implied. Some open scenes are put together by a random computer search of short lines of dialog. No matter how objectified the process, an implied relationship always emerges in the resulting text. There is also no such thing as a closed scene where everything is defined. No matter how simple-minded or explicit the material, there is still a dimension left to the performers. All scenes are only *relatively* open or closed, but it is useful to look at any script, asking yourself right away *how* open the material is: How much information has the playwright provided or closed for you; how much needs to be inferred; how much invented by you?

The following open-scene script is a favorite because it is so potentially complex in its twists and turns. It is a classic used in many theater classes, for both directing and acting projects:

ONE: Oh.
TWO: Yes.
ONE: Why are you doing this?
TWO: It's the best thing.
ONE: You can't mean it?
TWO: No, I'm serious.
ONE: Please . . .
TWO: What?
ONE: What does this mean?
TWO: Nothing.
ONE: Listen . . .
TWO: No.
ONE: So different.
TWO: Not really.
ONE: Oh.
TWO: You're good.
ONE: Forget it.
TWO: What?
ONE: Go on.
TWO: I will.

What can we close at a glance? Two seems determined to do something. One tries, with various tactics, to discourage Two. By the end, however, One is encouraging Two to do something, which may or may not be what Two originally set out to do. Are there any other implied closures on this scene? Let us look at two of many possible interpretations of these lines.*

---

*The two scenes are adapted and extended from two directing projects first presented under the supervision of Wandalie Henshaw, now Artistic Director for the Clarence Brown Theatre Company and Professor at the University of Tennessee, and originally published in an article entitled "The 'Open Scene' as a Directing Exercise" in *The Educational Theatre Journal.* Professor Henshaw wishes to acknowledge Kathleen George, Professor at Pitt University and author of *Rhythm in Drama,* for basic concepts and dialog.

Open Interpretations

The three elements below are the only things shared by these two scenes.

Setting: a bedroom
Characters: a young married couple
Script: listed above

Example 1   The couple lost their only child before the baby reached three. The tragic death occurred about six months ago. The wife has often been found lately, sobbing hysterically over the box of toys belonging to the child. The day has come when the husband is determined to get rid of the toys, because of the way they continue to haunt his wife and himself.

Example 2   This couple do not get along well, because their sex life is unsatisfying to both of them. The wife usually takes a book to bed, and tonight it happens to be a *Love-Without-Fear*-type manual. The husband often wakes the wife, to have a go at it, when he cannot sleep. She hates these sessions, and does her best to discourage him.

Set and Props: Both scenes require something to represent a bed, and both can share the same book if the cover is plain
Also Needed for 1: basket containing variety of toys, including a doll and a music box
Also Needed for 2: sheets and pillows, water glass, aspirin bottle, cold cream jar, any invented props for first beat

Example 1: Time to Let Go

Activity	*Intention*
1. She enters bedroom.	to find something to distract her
2. She finds and opens book.	to grab first available diversion
3. She sits on bed.	to calm herself
4. She pages through book.	to occupy her mind
5. She hears noise, starts, recovers.	to suppress her fears
6. She crosses to door.	to somehow stop what she expects

7. He enters with basket.	to make her understand his plan
8. She says, "Oh."	to get him to stop
9. He says, "Yes."	to make her understand he will not back down
10. She touches the toys.	to somehow touch her child as well
11. She asks, "Why are you doing this?"	to cause him to change his mind
12. He says, "It's the best thing."	to persuade that he is doing this because they need it
13. She takes the basket.	to stay close to the toys
14. She says, "You can't mean it."	to intimidate him
15. She kneels, puts toys on the floor.	to keep them near her
16. He moves to put a hand on her shoulder.	to comfort her
17. He says, "No, I'm serious."	to get her to comprehend he will not be dissuaded
18. She picks up doll from basket.	to cling to it
19. She says, "Please."	to get him to back off
20. He says, "What?"	to force her to at least speak of it
21. She holds the doll like a baby.	to bring back the feeling of comforting
22. She says, "What does this mean?"	to arouse his grief
23. He turns away.	to find a less devastating sight
24. He says, "Nothing."	to maintain control of his emotions
25. She picks out music box.	to find a more powerful weapon
26. She plays it.	to pull him into her perspective
27. She says, "Listen."	to remind him of better times
28. He says, "No."	to fight the music's effect
29. He crosses to other side of room.	to regain firmness and purpose
30. She rises and faces him.	to confront him combatively
31. She says, "So different."	to accuse him of insensitivity
32. He turns to face her.	to stop the charge

33. He says, "Not really."	to accept his own vulnerability
34. She goes to him.	to make peace
35. She embraces him.	to apologize and comfort
36. They hold each other.	to gain strength
37. He looks at her.	to check if she is ready
38. He holds onto her, says, "You're good."	to assure her she has the strength to give the toys up
39. She slowly returns to the toys.	to say good-bye
40. She stands up, looks away.	to end her attachment
41. She says to herself, "Forget it."	to discipline herself
42. She picks up basket.	to test herself
43. She hands it to him.	to free herself from any temptation to change her mind
44. He says, "What?"	to get a verbal commitment from her
45. She quietly says, "Go on."	to encourage him to do it quickly before she weakens
46. He says, "I will."	to accept the offer firmly and close the discussion
47. He exits with toys.	to accomplish his task
48. She listens to music box fading as it gets farther away.	to linger an instant longer in the past
49. She sits on the bed.	to support herself
50. She lies down and curls up on the bed.	to comfort herself and to help her resolve

Example 2: Try It, You'll Like It

Activity	*Intention*
1. They enter from opposite sides.	to go to bed
2. They stop to glare at each other.	to keep the other at a distance
3. They go through separate preparations (he rubs feet, stretches, she applies cold cream, takes aspirin)	
4. They get into bed.	to go to sleep
5. They fight over the sheet.	to spite each other

6. She falls immediately to sleep.	to forget she married him
7. He tosses and turns.	to find some position to get to sleep
8. He sits up.	to admit he can't sleep
9. He looks at her.	to decide whether to try or not
10. He looks away.	to find courage
11. He shrugs.	to persuade himself to go for it
12. He nudges her awake.	to warn her
13. She groans.	to avoid being awakened
14. He clears his throat.	to signal her
15. She says, "Oh."	to wither his resolve with her sarcasm
16. He says, "Yes."	to double his determination
17. He attempts passionate kiss.	to emulate screen lovers
18. She stops him.	to avoid being smothered by him
19. She asks, "Why are you doing this?"	to distract and discourage him
20. He answers, "It's the best thing."	to appear confident
21. She says, "You can't mean it."	to remind him of past times
22. He kisses her.	to encourage her participation
23. She picks up the book.	to seek mental diversion
24. She reads while he caresses.	to entertain herself
25. She pushes him away.	to free herself to concentrate
26. She says, "Please."	to keep him off while she studies passage that interests her
27. She slams book shut, stunned.	to grasp fully what she has found
28. He says, "What?"	to find out what is so interesting
29. She shows him page in book.	to share her discovery
30. She asks, "What does this mean?"	to get help comprehending
31. He takes book, reads.	to mollify her
32. He slams book shut.	to suppress shocking information

33. He says, "Nothing."   to cover his amazement
34. She says, "Listen."   to suggest book's suggestion
                                            may be worth trying
35. He says, "No!"   to free himself from
                                            experimenting
36. She reads passage again.   to memorize procedure
37. He lies down.   to protect himself
38. She looks at him.   to plan her attack
39. She grabs him and they   to act out passage in book
    disappear beneath the
    covers.

Blackout (may be accomplished by couple just flailing beneath
    sheet, out of audience view, for a while)

40. They emerge from covers.   to come up for air
41. They sit up smiling.   to glory in their success
42. She says, "So different."   to express her appreciation
43. He says, "Not really."   to persuade her he is fully
                                            capable of this and more
44. She pokes or tickles him.   to make loving contact
45. She says, "Oh."   to tease him
46. He says, "You're good."   to praise her own prowess
47. She says, "Forget it."   to acknowledge praise
48. She taps him on the   to seduce him
    shoulder.
49. He says, "What?"   to play coy, to encourage her
                                            aggression
50. She points to bed beneath   to show him the way
    them.
51. She says, "Go on."   to get him to take initiative
52. He says, "I will."   to accept the challenge
53. They disappear again   to pursue their mutual
    beneath covers.   pleasure

Exercise 4.14

Motivation Units

1. Go back over each scene and mark where you feel changes in beats
   occur. Then discuss to see if your choices matched others'.
2. If time allows, two couples should volunteer to present the scene regarding the dead child, and two other couples the sex-problem scene,

trying to follow closely the motivational units on the list. Discuss the differences between each couple doing the same scene. Which elements of subtext will vary, simply because of what any single actor will bring to a role?

Exercise 4.15

Open Scene Project

1. Stick with the sample script and format, but devise two entirely new scenarios. Working with a partner, begin brainstorming various situations that contrast as strongly as the examples.*
2. Look for opportunities to explore the power of subtext. While a comic scene and a serious one have immediate contrast, consider all the other ways contrast is possible.
3. This is one of the few times in your life when you get to cast yourself any way you want. It may be your only chance to play Abraham Lincoln, Pooh, a talking horse, Mother Teresa, Mother Nature, a hustler, God. Consider the possibilities.
4. Plan to present both of your scenes in class and to turn in a written breakdown of the scenes into beats and bits just prior to performance.

Start by looking at situations and characters instead of moods. At least one of the scenes above could be played in an entirely different mood. A couple having an unsatisfying sex life is not inherently amusing, and certainly not to those involved. While in questionable taste, "dead baby" jokes have been around for many years, obviously treating that subject satirically. Sometimes an idea that starts funny, develops sad. Or the scene switches emotional gears so that the final product has tragicomic balance, beginning in one mood and moving into another. Start with interesting people in intriguing predicaments, and then let them respond honestly. No character or encounter is too outrageous if the responses are truthful to the people and the event. Stanislavski says that acting is be-

---

*Since no scene is truly open, two ideas should be mentioned because they lend themselves so obviously to the lines. Scenes about suicide or leaving home offer little challenge. Try to stretch your imagination beyond these first obvious choices. Or if you must use them, try to explore some creative variations.

having truthfully in imaginary circumstances. This is a chance to let your imagination fly, free as a kite. The string is truth.

As you work on writing up motivational units, concentrate especially on what happens *between* each actual line of dialog. Notice there are only 20 lines, but over twice that number of bits. And in both scenes, there are more nonspeaking motivational units than there are speaking ones. Novice actors tend to rush open scene work, particularly the first beat, and to neglect the tiny stages (remember the door example?) that make up real lives. Do not ever be tempted to neglect subtext, particularly when your text is as negligible as this one. Each line in the intention column should begin with the preposition "to" followed by an active (or actable) verb.

Since you will probably be revising your score right up to the last minute, work with pencil and various rough drafts. If you prepare a document that looks too finished too early, you will be tempted to make yourself stick to it. Wait to finalize what you turn in until after your last rehearsal. Make certain that you have determined the ten basics for each character, plus the ten more advanced ingredients: given circumstances; the magic If; super objective and objective hierarchy; through-line; score; endowment; sense and emotional recall; images; external adjustments; and an open, responsive attitude towards the creative state.

As with the imitation assignments, this is a collaboration, but you may find it easier for each partner to take the primary responsibility for one scene, from conception through writing up the score. There should still be maximum input from both actors, but the process itself can be simplified if each partner focuses on the *mechanics* of one scene.

Rules   Since this is an exercise in subtext, the text, such as it is, should remain absolutely intact.

1. Actors may switch who is One and who is Two between scenes, but no other switches are possible. No single person ever gives two lines in a row and no reversals in the middle of the scene are fair.
2. Actors have complete freedom of line delivery, but are not free to change wording. By all means, put in unexpected pauses, change a declarative statement to a question, change the intent of a line right in the middle, add numerous nonverbals—those

are all actor *tools*. But do not turn "You're good" into "You are good" or "Yes" into "Yeah," and so on. Dealing with a difficult line by changing it is always a last resort. In this exercise, it is cheating.

Katharine Hepburn: *I can't understand actors who learn their lines* approximately. *If it's a good script, the writer has sweated over every part of it and a single word can throw everything. If it's a bad script, you shouldn't be doing it.*[31]

Open Scene Presentations

If time allows, scenes should be presented twice in class, with actors having the opportunity to go back and work between showings. When it is your turn to present, give the audience no more than a title or perhaps a headline ("Tycoon Weds Martian") by way of introduction. If any more background is necessary, you have not really done your homework. Every other piece of information needs to be *on the stage*. You are seeking strong, clear physical actions that reveal strong psychological states. If two characters share a long friendship and you cannot get it into the title, explore ways in which that friendship may manifest itself in their *behavior*.

It is a good idea to use props and costume pieces in an assignment of this kind. Your attention needs to be on the truth of the moment, not on the precision of miming. Keep all these things minimal, however, just what actually is used. Not set decor. In your last few rehearsals before the day you present in class, start rehearsing setting up the stage, introducing your material, getting quickly from one scene to the other, shifting props and costume pieces, and clearing the stage. I have seen actors, otherwise well prepared, simply collapse, because they forgot to work on how to get up there, how to switch from scene to scene, how to get off, on the *bookends* of their presentation. You do not work on these things because you are trying to achieve some slick level of polish. You do it to put your own mind at rest, to keep yourself from being unnecessarily distracted or scattered, and to avoid wasting the time of your classmates who must sit and wait while you fuss over your scarf. If you can avoid it, why do this to yourself?

Remember that the System is all preparation. Do not let yourself get bogged down with your homework when it comes time to perform, but give yourself permission for freedom, *earned* through your homework. As the inventor himself said: "You cannot act 'The System'; you can work on it at home, but when you step out on to the stage, cast it aside, there only nature is your guide."[32]

Stanislavski Extended

Because so much knowledge has opened up since Stanislavski worked and wrote, acting has benefited from sources as diverse as the behavioral sciences and computer research. He was in favor of anything that worked. In fact one of his admonitions was that each actor should move beyond Stanislavski to his own discoveries.

If anything would upset the great man as much as the degree to which some of his concepts have been misunderstood, it probably would be the degree to which they have been slavishly imitated. There are disciples who refuse to tolerate an exercise or a phrase not dropped from the master's lips. But his System is open-ended. At no point does it close off expansion and change. That is precisely why it emerges as the reigning school of acting in the world. Like democracy as a political system, it grows, suffers, adapts, gets battered, and survives.

The following techniques are worthy of Stanislavski and so worthy of attention.

Private Audience

Your own private audience is that group of people whose opinions are important to you. They are the people to whom you have always felt the need to prove yourself. They influence you so strongly that you cannot get them out of your head, at least not easily. Imagine that you are walking along, dragging your feet, shlumped over at the shoulders, and you hear your mother (who lives 500 miles away) telling you to "Stand up and walk right." Now, you may automatically straighten up or you may mutter "buzz off" and keep shlumping, but she is very much present in your audience in either case.

This group includes supporters and nurturers as well as major detractors, competitors, and those who have abused their authority over us. So some of the members are not friendly at all. When you have a triumph, and you think of someone and mutter to yourself, "I wish the S.O.B. could see me now," you have acknowledged a member of your private audience. Ex-husbands and wives are always private audience members. I keep waiting for the day when someone wins the Oscar or Tony and instead of thanking the world, says something like, "I won't bore you with thank-yous, but I do have a list of people who tried to stop me. I'd like to name them. First there was my terrible second grade teacher, Miss Markowitz, who didn't cast me as Cinderella. Then there was . . ." and so on. The winner would be acknowledging those truly unsung members of the private audience.

Your own vision of God has membership, whether it is abstract, such as The Force; literal, an elderly man with a beard and a scroll on a throne; or like Jerry, in *The Zoo Story,* who maintains that "God is a colored queen in a kimono."[33] A variation on this category involves those whom you idolize, but have never actually met, such as a worshiped favorite author or actor.

Exercise 4.16

Naming Members

1. Jot down at least two names in each of these categories for yourself:
   a. family
   b. nurturers
   c. detractors
   d. God
   e. idols
2. Replace your members with those of your open scene characters. Run each scene, leaving your character open for any of the members to make an appearance in her mind and influence her decisions.

The identification of the character's private audience helps you with the magic If. It also clarifies where *you* stop and the *char-*

acter begins, which influences you share, and which you, the actor, need to take on, to perceive the world as the character would.

Grouping

Grouping involves looking at others in general terms, instead of as individuals. It is a way of endowing in large numbers. Bigots are the worst groupers, branding all members of a race or creed with the same qualities, seeing cultural binding where it does not really exist. But everyone groups to some degree. Theater majors tend to view business majors as aliens. Liberals tend to view conservatives as selfish. No one is entirely guiltless of the sweeping label for clusters of others.

Grouping others (as powerful if you are cast as a *timid* soul; ignoramuses if you are playing an intellectual *snob;* thieves if you are a *miser*) helps you actively use all the other people onstage and in the character's world, in a collective magic If. It also helps you avoid playing an "attitude." You cannot play "timid," "snob," or "miser" as isolated cliches. The more eccentric or unbalanced a character is, the more essential it becomes to use this technique, so you are not tempted to play her zaniness or craziness, but instead let yourself *see people* as she does. If you place these qualities on others, quite a bit of your behavior is likely to be automatically appropriate and free of stereotyped choices.

Exercise 4.17

Group Bias

What groups do you view in the most sweeping way ? Write the name of the group and the one or two words you would use for it. Consider people who differ from your convictions in each of these areas:

1. politics
2. religion
3. pastimes or recreation
4. attractiveness
5. discipline

Imagine someone whose views are the polar opposite of your own. What terms would she use to cluster you and those who feel as you do into a single group?

Substitution

While actually inserting your own experience in the place of the character's seems thoughtless and shallow, there are certain, rare instances where you may have no choice. Something in the character's life may be outside your experience. Now, nothing should be outside the spiritual or *imaginative* experience of an actor. You certainly should not have had to rule a kingdom in order to play a king. But you may not have a frame of reference. Uta Hagen uses two of the best examples when she writes about shooting someone and being shot. Killing and being killed are experiences that are hopefully foreign to you. She suggests that stepping into the shower, expecting warmth, but being hit with ice cold water and stunned is a reasonable sensation for a bullet hitting you. And, while you may have never hounded another human with a pistol, you have probably been in pursuit, swatter in hand, of a fly or wasp that has been driving you crazy, stalking with genuine menace and malevolence.[34] Her suggestions act as "triggers" for the imagination. I think some actors would categorically deny that a character's actions are in them to perform. Substitution is a superior solution to denial.

Conditioning Forces

Many actors isolate from the given circumstances—which influence a character's general behavior *throughout* the play—factors influencing the character's behavior of the *moment*—which may change from beat to beat. *Conditioning forces* are immediate, physical, even sensual. If it is raining outside and you enter the stage wet, this force conditions at least the first moments of the scene, influencing each decision you make. Standard conditioning forces include:

1. *Temperature/Weather* (How hot/cold, wet/dry, constant/changing? May include variable conditions, as in a cold palace room with a fireplace, so that *proximity* changes feelings.)
2. *Light* (How bright or dark and what kinds of difficulties do you have as a result? Are there pools of light and shadow so that your vision and sense of security vary from space to space?)

3. *Comfort* (Any irritating little aches or pains? Any discomfort that comes and goes, depending on how you move? Any stiffness? How do your clothes fit? Do you need to go to the bathroom? Is your foot asleep? Are you hungry or thirsty?)

4. *Time* (Actual hour? Are you running late? How late? How long have you been up? How fatigued or energized? How anxious are you to get this over with? How willing to play around and sustain the encounter?)

5. *Space Familiarity* (Who owns it? How much right do you have to be here? How well do you know it? How curious are you about it? Who do you know here? Has it changed since your last visit?)

6. *Distractions* (Is there loud noise from the street outside? From the next room? Is there an unpleasant, intriguing, or tantalizing odor in the space? Are your senses diverting you from your objective? Are you terribly curious about something? Terribly aroused by someone? Is any force or activity making it hard to focus your attention?)

Actors often mistakenly play in a space that seems utterly neutral, without any discernible physical influences. They also tend to play only two physical states: vibrantly healthy or dying. Consider the effect on the scene if your character had one glass of wine too many last night and, while not truly hung over, has this tiny little irritation at the side of the temple and is just a bit sluggish. Then there is that silly cut on your little finger where the Band-Aid will not stay on. And the neon light above is a bit glaring, but you do not have the energy to turn it off and a lamp on. But there is a nice breeze coming in the window, relieving the heavy humidity in this room, and so on, and so forth.

Our state of well-being is relative, not perfect or terminal. Like endowment, a conditioning force may or may not read to an audience, but the sense of a complete human being in crisis probably will. Conditioning forces are especially important as you *enter* the scene because it is here that they often change (moving from dark movie theater into glaring sunlight, from heat wave into soothing air-conditioning, from space uncertainty to relieved familiarity as you learn this is your friend's apartment building after all) and their effect on you may then modify as you grow accustomed to the new environment.

Exercise 4.18

Adding Conditions

1. Run the first several beats of one of your open scenes, adding a strong influence from one of the six forces listed above, then with another force until you have tried all six. Now go back and layer in all six, one by one so that all are finally working at once.
2. Have volunteers improvise situations where the audience identifies a basic relationship for the actors to start with. Do the scene once in a neutral state, then select two crucial conditioning forces to add.

Rehearsed Futures

The same way actors rehearse for the opening of the play, most of us are rehearsing our futures in our heads, thinking about some moment ahead when our lives will come together, or possibly fall apart. There are three kinds of rehearsed futures: best possible; worst possible; and wildest dreams come true! Most of us feel that our present circumstances will somehow change. Sometimes rehearsing your future is a way of holding onto your sanity and surviving present misfortunes. The future can be freely fantasized in both practical/possible visions and in wild/unlikely terms requiring windfalls or even miracles.

For many actors, a best possible future would include getting a Master of Fine Arts degree from a respected program, working for some regional repertory companies, and perhaps doing some successful runs on Broadway. A worst possible might include flunking out of your present undergraduate program, never regaining the courage to leave town, and spending the rest of your days busing tables. A wildest-dream-come-true future might include being discovered tomorrow, becoming a household word overnight, winning Oscar, Tony, Emmy, Grammy all several times, having all the great writers of the world beg to create vehicles for you, and all the great lovers of the world beg to sleep with you, as you somehow manage to create peace and harmony among the peoples of the world with your art, and have a newly discovered planet named after you in honor of your accomplishments.

Taking the time to develop your character's rehearsed futures adds to the liveliness and energy of your performance, beyond the obvious additional dimension to the magic If. Knowing your character well enough to fantasize from her perspective gives great confidence. Thinking about and yearning towards her future tends to make your performance alive with anticipation.

Exercise 4.19

Open Futures

1. Identify all three rehearsed futures for both of your open scene characters.
2. Run the scenes, keeping yourself open to moments when the character might fantasize about the future.
3. Discuss any immediate impact on the scene.

Suppression

Much of our energy during time spent with others is devoted to trying *not* to reveal how we feel or at least how strongly. It is this *suppression* of emotional display that keeps us from making complete fools of ourselves, but can also stifle our freedom and spontaneity. Review the section on offstage suppression in chapter 1. Research has shown that instead of trying to cry, if you can identify, as Stanislavski has suggested, the conditions of the body that lead to crying (maybe you start to pause at odd places, your voice moves back into the throat, your fingers begin small spasmodic moves of their own) and then play directly *against* revealing those symptoms, the result will either be tears or a truthful struggle. So most actors who attempt to cry are approaching the phenomenon exactly backwards. Having planted the character's given circumstances, move specifically to planting those definite physical symptoms he wishes to avoid revealing.

Exercise 4.20

Playing Against

1. Observe yourself for the next week, whenever you are trying not to show your feelings, but are not entirely successful. Note your physical

symptoms. Begin to put these in your mental acting file to employ when needed.

2. Go back to your open scenes and identify each point where your character wishes to suppress displaying emotion. Plant the symptoms to be avoided. Rehearse the scene with the focus on playing against what the character fears to reveal.

Exercise 4.21

Observing the System

Attend a performance and identify each of these techniques for an individual performer (see Appendix E):

1. List ten of the character's most significant given circumstances.
2. Specify conditioning forces at work at the character's very first entrance and describe how and when these changed throughout the evening.
3. How would you, if cast in this role, employ the magic If to help you absorb yourself convincingly in the character's perspective?
4. How would you employ grouping if cast in this role?
5. Write three paragraphs on three different versions of the character's rehearsed futures. Write in the character's own voice.
6. Find three instances where the actor was required to use endowment in order to make use of props or set pieces effectively. Do the same for the character's view of three others in the play. Extend at least one of these endowments into detailed conjecture.

Working with a Partner

Stanislavski suggests that you must learn to infect a partner with your very soul. Never one to understate, he establishes throughout his works the need for complete respect, trust, and connection between acting partners. You share so much responsibility with and for your partner that the working relationship should be one of self-disclosure, nonpossessive caring, trust, risk taking, mutual acceptance, and open feedback. Stanislavski calls this working relationship a state of "communion," which is a step higher than simple communication towards complete sharing.

In acting, as in life, certain basic rules of courtesy should be observed, such as never standing your partner up or failing to get a message to her if there is some block to your availability to rehearse. Here are some other generally accepted guidelines:

1. Never direct your partner. This is a collaboration. Neither of you is in charge.
2. Ask for help from your partner instead. Remember the problem is always yours. If you need a response from her, state it as exactly that, something you need and she can give you.
3. Endow your partner shamelessly and allow yourself to fantasize about him, but keep this information to yourself. A lot of your ideas can be rendered ineffective by sharing them when there is no real point and only potential embarrassment.
4. Try to bring a contagious, supportive energy into the rehearsal.
5. Your relationship is like a small, short-term marriage, with all the give and take and need for mutual support which that implies.

The two of you need to know each other better than can usually be accomplished accidentally. The following exercise imposes some structure and speeds up the process. It does not force an artificial instant intimacy, however, because you always have the freedom to reveal only as much information as is comfortable. Stanislavski and his company had the extraordinary luxury of working and living together for many years, so that members of the Moscow Art Theater were much like family. This is the best exercise I know for gaining some semblance of self-disclosure, between people who have no choice but to trust each other.

Exercise 4.22

Partner Sharing

Decide who will speak first and take turns answering each question. Whenever possible, the listener should repeat in her own words what she has just heard. It is sometimes helpful to say, "What I hear you saying is . . ." and then complete the statement. If the speaker agrees that this was what he intended, then it is time to go on. Do not look ahead and do not plan or "rehearse" any answers, but respond in the moment.

In a statement such as item 2, you have the freedom to reveal as many nicknames or titles or as few as you want. This way you are not forced to share more than you want. When a statement (as in items 6 and 15) is repeated, answer it for the specific moment at which the statement is made. The exercise takes most people about an hour. If you are given some class time, but not enough to finish, why not begin your next rehearsal by completing it together?

1. My name is . . .
2. My other names are . . .
3. My romantic status is . . .
4. I come from . . .
5. The reason I'm studying acting is . . .
6. Right now, I'm feeling . . .
7. When I am in a new group, I . . .
8. When I enter a room full of people, I usually feel . . .
9. When I'm feeling anxious in a new situation, I usually . . .
10. In groups, I am most comfortable when the leader . . .
11. Social rules make me feel . . .
12. If a situation is ambiguous and unstructured I . . .
13. I am happiest when . . .
14. The thing that excites me the most is . . .
15. Right now I feel . . .
16. The thing that concerns me most about the theater is . . .
17. When I am rejected, I usually . . .
18. To me belonging means . . .
19. The thing that is most difficult for me to do in public is . . .
20. Breaking rules makes me feel . . .
21. I most like to be alone when . . .
22. The thing that turns me off the most is . . .
23. I feel affectionate when . . .
24. Towards you, my partner, I feel . . .
25. I cry most easily when . . .
26. I laugh most easily when . . .
27. When I have a day all by myself, I am most likely to . . .
28. As a performer, I feel most insecure about . . .
29. I am most likely to get really angry if . . .
30. If I believe anything strongly, it is . . .
31. The thing I am most curious to know about you is . . .

After completing the list, take a few minutes to discuss the experience generally and anything that may have come up during the rehearsal period so far that you would like to explore.

Exercise 4.23

Pulling It All Together

Review the next three paragraphs, which summarize the basic vocabulary of the Stanislavski System. Go back and review any idea still not entirely clear to you. Promise yourself not to reject any of these actor's tools until you know you have tried them, carefully and with an open, responsive attack:

You begin by determining the **given circumstances** of your character and employing the **magic If** to place yourself inside those circumstances, including **endowment** of real and imagined objects and people with physical and emotional qualities. You explore the character's **relationships** with everyone he encounters, developing his **private audience** and his **grouping** of others. You use your five senses to **recall** impressions, with **sense memory** adding detail and texture and sometimes being employed to tap **emotional memory** to connect with the character's feelings. **Release pictures** can be especially powerful in this process. You explore not only the character's past and present but his **rehearsed futures,** including his fantasies. Each time the character appears you identify those **conditioning forces** that may influence his behavior in an immediate and sensual way.

As you explore the **text** you seek **images** to bring each line to life in order to connect fully with your partner. You also work closely and in sufficient trust with your partner for mutual **communion** to occur. You discover the text's underlying **subtext,** including the character's **interior monolog** and **evaluations** where **alternatives** are explored. In each scene you find his **objective,** the **obstacle** in the way, and the general **strategy** and specific **tactics** employed to make it happen. You find many small **actions** or **bits** where any *inner* impulse has an *outer* execution. You experiment with the **method of physical actions,** balancing the psychological and physical key ingredients of each action. Instead of trying to feel the emotions for each moment, you concentrate on **planting** the physical symptoms of the emotions, including the **suppression** of emotional display. You section the role into **beats,** which change as individual transactions are completed.

You attempt to identify the character's **super objective** and to find the **through-line of actions,** connecting all of the strategies, tactics, and individual maneuvers executed by the character along the way. All this work is placed in the **score** to guide the process. While a number of changes in your own habits have occurred automatically, some **external adjustments** are likely to occur with attention to **tempo/rhythm,** especially important towards entering the character's experience. If all these ingredients have been carefully pursued, you have a good chance of entering the **creative state** and are almost certain to achieve a performance based on **truth.**

Taking the Gifts

Stanislavski created an acting system that is as flexible and misunderstood as any political system, including our own. It is based on behaving truthfully in imaginary circumstances. His contribution has been effectively summed up by the most renowned actress in the history of the Moscow Art Theater (who was also the wife of Anton Chekhov):

Olga Knipper: *Stanislavski deserves credit for posterity for "summoning us all to be scrupulous and honest in our approach and understanding of art. His name is our conscience."*[35]

The System includes a close, careful look at the world of the character and then gradually entering the character's perspective. It is composed of series of *obj*ective means for taking on the *subj*ective views of the character. It allows the actor to portray any person, however despicable at first glance, without judgment. It is based on the most humanizing trait, empathy. Any actor who chooses not to accept and employ the gifts of the System has a minimum obligation to do so *informed,* rather than ignorant. It is Stanislavski's System that is likely to provide you with the basics on which you develop your own. It is his contagious spirit that may give you the courage to change.

Constantin Stanislavski: *Create your own method. Don't depend slavishly on mine. Make up something that will work for you! But keep breaking traditions, I beg you.*[36]

5

Truth/Technique

(balancing honest, open spontaneity with steady, polished consistency)

Geraldine Page: *If you learn to be truthful first . . . it's terribly hard to learn to be heard. And if you learn to be heard first of all, it's terribly hard to speak truthfully.*[1]

Laurence Olivier: *Being bone real is not the big problem in acting in the theatre. The problem is to express what you are expressing at close distance, fifty yards away—that is the problem.*[2]

Which Way?

"Is it better for an actor to work from inside out or outside in?"
"Is it preferable for a performance to have emotion or precision?"
"Should the actor show the audience his face or mask?"
"Should the feelings be real or calculated?"
"Which is needed most? External form or internal conviction?"
"Is it more important to be honest or interesting?"

This is everyone's favorite debate topic regarding acting. It is no less interesting for being unresolvable. Like most debate topics, you can learn, without settling the issue.

Why do we not just ask the great actors and get it over with? Because they cannot agree. From Eleonora Duse (truth) and Sarah

Bernhardt (technique) in the last century, through countless others in this one, there have been celebrated advocates for both sides. Great actors, like all geniuses, skip steps, so their work process and their statements can be deceiving. And many of them simply will not speak of what they do, lest they lose the magic.

Not only do actors work differently from each other, but the same actor will work differently depending on the medium, the space, and the script. Is there a microphone? Is my partner a camera or a person? Are there 50 people out there or 5000? Is it intimate or do I need to fill a barn? Am I playing someone like *me*, or am I Mephistopheles, Hercules, the Mad Hatter, a potato chip? The same actor will even work differently from scene to scene. I was once in a musical, where I had a scene that always came straight from the heart, but minutes later was involved in a dance routine where my interior monolog never got beyond "Step-ball-change. Step-ball-change. Don't forget to smile." The same actor may even work differently moment to moment.

As True as Possible

I believe that most actors, if pressed, would say they prefer to work internally, if *possible*. It is more fun to dig inside and tap real emotion, to cry tears that are genuine, to summon laughter that is not forced. It is more of a genuine rush, to share the character's feelings. It simply is not always possible. How can you enter the character's soul if you can barely remember his dance steps? You could risk bumping into the other dancers, but there would be consequences. Nearly every actor, early in his training, experiences something like the following:

Example 1   You are in performance and it all seems to be happening for you. In your big scene, the tears come out in floods, everything is real, you are inspired, you are absolutely "in the moment." You know you are at last an actor in the fullest sense. The director comes backstage and says something like, "You know in scene seven, when you were blubbering all of a sudden, not only could I not understand a word you said, but you personally added five minutes to the running time of that Act. Are you alright?" Others come backstage and do not praise. They give you sympathetic, curious looks or they look away. A few may also inquire about your health.

You have learned firsthand, one of the classic truths of acting:

AN ACTOR'S FIRST OBLIGATION IS TO BE SEEN AND HEARD.

By "heard" here, of course, is meant "understood." Emotion, when it finally overtakes you completely, blocks communication. Especially if you are trying to speak.

Example 2   You give a performance, which seems calculated and hollow to you. You feel you were too aware of each effect and were probably stiff as a result. People come backstage. *They* are weeping. Your performance is eulogized. The director and other company members say you have never been better, that tonight you finally flew.

You have learned firsthand another classic:

THE AUDIENCE DOESN'T CARE WHETHER OR NOT YOU ARE HAVING A PERSONAL MOMENT.

They care whether or not *they* are having a personal moment. The theater is an art based on illusion, and ultimately what matters to the people out front is what *plays* out front.

Actors prefer to be as truthful as they can, while still being technically sound. If you can play from deep inside and still hit your marks, project to the back row, and give your partner support, then you have begun to marry these partners in art.

A Marriage of Necessity

Lee Strasberg, often associated with "emotional acting," still criticized actors who were all feeling, with lines like, "Blood, without flesh and bones, only spills" and "Without will, sensitivity is of no value."[3] A purely technical performance risks looking like a lifeless skeleton. A purely emotional performance risks looking like blood with no framework to flow through. Stanislavski demanded a completely trained instrument, with the *technical* repertoire to know how to respond fully to the impulses from *within*.

The actor's task is to become knowledgeable enough in technique to have at her disposal the *means* of transmitting emotion. A basic technical framework involves:

1. Being able to analyze a character
2. Examining scripts systematically for evidence to support rehearsal decisions

3. Mastering a working vocabulary of rehearsal and performance communication
4. Being able to execute a variety of physical maneuvers
5. Being capable of vocal experimentation, change, and clarity
6. Adjusting your behavior to suit the needs of the character and nature of the playing space.

At a later, more sophisticated level, it can include such diverse techniques as speaking dialects, handling rapier and dagger, scanning verse, mastering styles, and a multitude of additional specialty skills—advanced techniques called on when you are ready to tackle characters from other worlds and times. Your own world and time are enough of a challenge at first.

Exercise 5.1

Scene Project

Once the open scene work is complete, move to works by actual playwrights, which are more closed and traditional. Class demands vary, but the following restrictions are common. These limitations are freeing. They get rid of distracting hurdles and allow the actors to concentrate on the basics:

1. a scene of 5 to 10 minutes in playing time
2. from contemporary American realism (from another country if accents are unnecessary)
3. with characters rarely more than five years (and never more than ten years) outside the actual ages of the actors
4. with neither actor cast against type
5. with dialog divided fairly equally between the two (or at the most three) characters

Scene Suggestions

The following two-character scenes meet the basic guidelines and offer interesting conflicts:

All My Sons by Arthur Miller (Chris and Ann)
All the Way Home by Tad Mosel (Jay and Mary)

Am I Blue by Beth Henley (Ashbe and John)

Baby with the Bathwater by Christopher Durang (John and Helen)

Bent by Martin Sherman (Max and Rudy)

Birdbath by Leonard Melfi (Frankie and Velma)

Blue Denim by James Leo Herlihy and William Noble (Janet and Arthur)

Buried Child by Sam Shepard (Vince and Shelly)

The Death of Bessie Smith by Edward Albee (Receptionist and Intern)

The Faculty Lounge by Michael Schulman (Rhonda and Linda)

Fishing by Michael Weller (Mary Ellen and Robbie)

Fool for Love by Sam Shepard (Eddie and May)

The Four Seasons by Arnold Wesker (Adam and Beatrice)

Fugue in a Nursery from *Torch Song Trilogy* by Harvey Fierstein (Arnold and Laurel)

Gemini by Albert Innaurato (Francis and Judith)

Golden Boy by Clifford Odets (Lorna and Joe)

The Good-Bye People by Herb Gardner (Nancy and Korman)

A Good Time by Ernest Thompson (Mandy and Rick)

A Hatful of Rain by Michael V. Gazzo (Polo and Johnny)

Here We Are by Dorothy Parker (He and She)

I Am a Camera by John van Druten (Sally and Christopher)

Lemon Sky by Lanford Wilson (Alan and Ronnie)

Long Day's Journey into Night by Eugene O'Neill (Jamie and Edmund)

A Long Walk to Forever by Kurt Vonnegut (Katherine and Nute)

Look Homeward, Angel by Ketti Frings (Eugene and Laura)

Loose Ends by Michael Weller (Paul and Susan)

Love Is Where You Find It from *Where Has Tommy Flowers Gone?* by Terrence McNally (Tommy and Nedda)

Lovely Afternoon by Howard Delman (Alan and Pam)

Lovers by Brian Friel (Meg and Joe)

Lu Ann Hampton Laverty Overlander by Preston Jones (Lu Ann and Billy Bob)

Ludlow Fair by Lanford Wilson (Agnes and Rachel)

Mimosa Pudica by Curt Dempster (Diane and David)

A Modest Proposal by Selma Thompson (John and Mer)

Ordinary People by Judith Guest and Alvin Sargeant (Karen and Conrad)

Orphans by Lyle Kessler (Phillip and Treat)

Minnesota Moon by John Olive (Alan and Larry)

Mr. Roberts by Thomas Heggen and Joshua Logan (Pulver and Roberts)

The Paper Chase by Joseph Robinette and John Jay Osborn (Hart and Ford)

Postponing the Heat Death of the Universe by Steven Gregg (Nick and Randy)

Private Wars by James McClure (Gately and Silvio)

The Real Thing by Tom Stoppard (Billy and Annie)

Say Goodnight, Gracie by Ralph Pape (Jerry and Steve)

The Sea Horse by Edward J. Moore (Harry and Gertrude)

Seascape with Sharks and Dances by Don Nigro (Tracy and Ben)

Sexual Perversity in Chicago by David Mamet (Debie and Dan)

Shivaree by William Mastrosimone (Chandler and Shivaree)

A Social Event by William Inge (Carole and Randy)

The Sorrows of Stephen by Peter Parnell (Stephen and Christine)

Split by Michael Weller (Paul and Carol)

The Square Root of Love by Howard Delman (Alan and Pam)

Standing on My Knees by John Olive (Catherine and Robert)

Strange Snow by Stephen Metcalfe (Martha and Megs)

Streamers by David Rabe (Richie and Billy)

Summer and Smoke by Tennessee Williams (Alma and John)

Table Settings by James Lapine (Girlfriend and Younger Son)

Talk to Me Gentle Like the Rain and Let Me Listen by Tennessee Williams (Man and Woman)

Thieves by Herb Gardner (Martin and Sally)

The Time of Your Life by William Saroyan (Joe and Mary)

Two on an Island by Elmer Rice (John and Mary)

Uncommon Women and Others by Wendy Wasserstein (Kate and Rita)

The Wager by Mark Medoff (Leeds and Ward)

When You Comin' Back, Red Ryder? by Mark Medoff (Angel and Stephen)

The Woolgatherer by William Mastrosimone (Rose and Cliff)

Character Analysis

Regardless of where your performance ends, it starts with the script. Actors are recreative artists, not pure creative ones. Actors start with the playwright's vision and attempt to realize or *complete* that vision. The actor does not start with a blank sheet. The work begins with the text.

Peggy Ashcroft: *One begins with the text because it's the text that leads you to the character.*[4]

Some playwrights, like Shaw and O'Neill, give microscopic character details, down to the titles of books you keep on your shelves. Others simply give your role a name like The Boy, minimal dialog, and leave a lot for you to discover. To make certain all evidence is examined, go through the following stages:

The Three *I*'s: Investigation, Inference, Invention

1. Investigation This is just facts. No hearsay. You find everything in the script and playwright's notes about your character. If the character is well known, it is crucial to make sure you are looking at the person the playwright *wrote* and are not too influenced by some famous actor's performance, by an acting tradition for this part, or by the public image of this character. There will still be gaps, so you move to inference.

2. Inference From the facts, you draw conclusions. If everyone keeps calling you "child" you assume you are younger than they are. If your stage directions are filled with indirect movements and pauses, you infer you are hesitant and nonassertive. This is a fascinating process. And easy to confuse with investigation but inference must be *based* on facts. Blanks still remaining can be filled with invention.

Harrison Ford: *Acting is interpretive by nature. An architect may have an overall vision, but it takes the attention of craftsmen like plumbers, carpenters, sheet-metal men and roofers to bring it to life. I'm quite happy being a craftsman. I don't feel lessened by that at all. It's the facts, Jack.*[5]

3. Invention Some actors are tempted to skip to this stage, without earning their way through the first two. Others neglect it, contented with unactable generalizations like "she's in her teens" or "she's in high school." Remember, no real person thinks of herself as *in* her teens, but is concerned precisely where. Remember Stanislavski's admonition that "in general" is the *actor's greatest enemy.* After inferring an approximate age, this is where you decide you are 16 and you were born March 4, at 7:00 P.M., on a still, moonless night, by Caesarean, the whole picture.

Following this progression (investigation to inference to invention) ensures the actor that the writer's will has been served, and leaves him free to discover. The list that emerges is filled with *technical details* to rehearse and master, plus *emotional conditions* to plant and let develop.

The document you prepare is often kept with the score and strongly connected to it. Fortunately, you have already done a character analysis on yourself in chapter 2, so you are not only familiar with the standard questions, but you can compare and contrast yourself with your character. This time each category is phrased with acting vocabulary developed in the last few chapters (see appendix F).

Exercise 5.2

Character Past

Complete the statements from the character's perspective (with a strong need to tell the truth), except for those instances where questions are specifically addressed to the actors.

I come from . . .
My childhood was . . .
Family conditions were . . .
Major influences on me include . . .
Experiences making the most lasting impression on me were . . .
Strongest cultural binding involves . . .
Ten most important given circumstances are . . .
Five most powerful members of my private audience would be. . .
Crucial actions prior to play/scene were . . .
The moment before my entrance in complete detail involves . . .
Outlook on life was primarily determined by . . .

Exercise 5.3

Character Present

Complete the statements from the character's perspective (with a strong need to tell the truth), except for those instances where questions are specifically addressed to the actors.

Immediate conditioning forces are . . .
Others in script (and/or playwright) describe me as . . .
I characterize others as . . .
In groups I . . .
I am basically . . .
My physical appearance is . . .
My physical life involves . . .
My usual style of clothing and type of accessories include . . .
My vocal life can be outlined as . . .
My most distinguishing characteristics are . . .
My favorites would have to include . . .
My temperament could be described as . . .
My lifestyle involves . . .
I am most and least interested in . . .
I am different from the other characters in this play in that I . . .
I most need to use the magic If for this role in . . .
Three examples of endowment would include . . .
The location of this scene can be described . . .
My silent script during one page of script is . . .
Two crucial moments of evaluation (including all alternatives considered and rejected) are . . .
My scene breaks down into the following beats . . .
The moment-to-moment victories within the first two beats of the scene are . . .
I make the following discoveries in the scene . . .
What is most important to me is . . .

Exercise 5.4

Character Future

Complete the statements from the character's perspective (with a strong need to tell the truth), except for those instances where questions are specifically addressed to the actors.

My super objective is . . .
My intentional hierarchy would include . . .
My immediate scene objective is to . . .
Obstacles I face are . . .
My strategy in the play and in the scene could be described as . . .
Specific tactics I enploy in two pages of text are . . .
Clues I will look for from my partner to gauge success . . .
My best possible future would be . . .
My worst possible future would be . . .
My wildest dreams come true would be . . .

Abstracting

Since much analysis work is systematic and logical, a useful balance can be achieved by also working in an abstract and fanciful mode. The following questions should be answered, not thinking of what the character would *choose* to wear, drink, or drive, but which qualities sum up the character's essence.

John Gielgud: *Barker (the director) said to me, "Lear should be an oak, you're an ash; now we've got to do something about that."*[6]

A person may choose the finest champagne to consume, and still be warm draft beer to those who know him. Someone may drive a truck, but clearly be thought of as a Rolls, by everyone she meets.

Exercise 5.5

Character Abstracts

This exercise is based on a party game, sometimes called "Abstracts" or "Essences." The class may wish to play. In the first version, one person picks one other in the room and then everyone poses a question, until someone guesses who is being abstracted. In another, a guesser leaves the room, while everyone agrees on a subject in their midst. When the guesser returns, she questions each person there until she guesses correctly or gives up. It is always surprising how often people agree on these indirect ways of describing others, and how clearly the final image emerges. Ask yourself, If the character were actually one of the following, which would he be?

1. fabric	11. type of day
2. animal	12. decade or era
3. beverage	13. film or TV series
4. mode of transportation	14. landmark or building
5. city	15. snack
6. tree	16. mythological or fantasy figure
7. color	17. spice
8. play	18. musical instrument
9. scent	19. painting or photo
10. song	20. toy

Abstracting helps you discover some images (all you need are four or five) to snap you into character, to help drop the day's distractions, especially if you are not in the mood. You walk into rehearsal feeling like "milk" and a "bus shelter" but you think of "dry sherry" and the "Taj Mahal," and you shift your *sense* of yourself. It is whimsical but it works. Abstracting also provides a way of communicating when traditional terms are inadequate. Gielgud the actor really *is* an ash, and the character King Lear *is* truly an oak. There is no clearer, kinder way to make that distinction than in abstract images.

Exercise 5.6

Character's Autobiography

1. Take all the information you have accumulated and write an autobiography, no longer than two pages, in the voice of the character.
2. There is way too much available material to include, so pick what the *character* would consider important.
3. Take the character only up to his first entrance in the play (or in the scene) and end the essay by completing the statement: "What I want most out of life is . . ."
4. Give yourself a strong motive for speaking the character's truth as he sees it. Maybe the essay is being written for a psychiatrist who can only help if the answers are genuine. Maybe to a priest, with the complete conviction that deception will be seen through by the man of

God. Maybe to a child, who deserves to know the truth about her parent and you are determined to finally tell it. If the only way the character would ever prepare a manuscript of this kind is to write a letter to someone, then use that format. Try to find a condition that suits who this person is.

5. Use the character's language, spelling, and sentence structure. Experiment with altering your handwriting (if the character would not type this document) to suit the writer. Pick the texture and color of paper and pen this person would choose. The difference between using lavender stationery, purple felt-tip pen, all small letters, and *i*'s dotted with circles, maybe even some *smiles* in those circles (which would be the right way to express some characters) and a legal size document in triplicate, and using a word processor (which would be right for another) is a vivid way to express differing personal approaches. Enjoy the process of finding just the right mode of presentation.

Exercise 5.7

Analysis into System

1. Score the scene based on Stanislavski's concepts.
2. Armed with new information about your scripted character, go back and execute each of the exercises in chapter 4 from the perspective of the person you are playing: Other's Givens, Planting, Hierarchies, Tiny Triumphs, Adding Consequences, Bringing It Back, Release Album, Imagining, Naming Members, Group Bias, Adding Conditions, Open Futures, and Playing Against.

Work with your scene partner when appropriate. Work alone when you need time and space and no pressure to react quickly. Make a promise to yourself to let none of your analysis and research remain theoretical, but to actively apply the results in rehearsal.

Exercise 5.8

Warming In

Pick the most evocative images from your character analysis, those that seem to thrust you most vividly into the character's experience and feelings. While warming up to present the scene, let these particular images drift over you so that as your body and voice prepare, your mind releases your own biases and accepts those of your character.

The World of the Play

It is important to know, not just who your character is, but how she fits into the world of the play. It is a lot more significant, if your character is gregarious, bubbly, and personable, if all the other characters do *not* share those traits and if being outgoing is not rewarded behavior in this play. The *style* of a play is often described as what all of the characters have in common (truths assumed to be self-evident, standards, knowledge of what is appropriate, plus the ways each of these manifest themselves in behavior) while *characterization* is what makes your role unique within the style. You may have heard a performance described as striking, but not in the same play as everyone else. Here are some questions to use to find out what play everyone else is in:

Exercise 5.9

The Playwright's World

What choices are made in the following areas by the majority in the play? Scan the list to discover the degree to which you understand the world of the play, and how much your character fits into that world. Again, there are many more categories than you can explore in depth. But look for those which leap out at you as worth considering. Ask yourself how close or far away you are from the mainstream:

1. Time

How rapidly does it move for most people?
How conscious are they of time passing?
What is the dominant tempo/rhythm?
Do people focus mainly on the moment, on whole lifetimes, the future, the past?
What lengths of attention spans do these people have?
Is age revered or feared? What is the relationship between youth and maturity?

2. Space

How large a bubble do most people carry around?
In what ways do personal spaces alter? How flexible?
To what degree are privacy and open space respected?

What are attitudes towards invasion and physical force?

Is space simply literal or do people think in terms of spiritual or philosophical space?

3. Place

Is the setting rural, metro, urban, remote?

Does it have a specific or generic character?

Do people feel great connection with where they live or indifference
to it?

How aware are they of *other* places?

Are they citizens only of this specific spot or are they citizens of the
world?

4. Recreation

What is most people's idea of fun?

What would be an ideal social occasion in this world?

Are they doers or watchers?

Thinkers or mindless hedonists?

What are common hobbies, pastimes, concepts of having a good time?

Most people's vision of an enjoyable evening, party, vacation, day?

Differences between the sexes?

Favored food, drink, drugs, snacks?

Relative importance of recreation in life?

5. Beauty

What is the look most aspired to in this group?

Who are the contemporary ideals of male and female perfection?

Most coveted skin, hair, coloring, proportions?

Which colors, shapes, textures, silhouettes are favored in clothes, furnish-
ings, props?

How important is fashion? How fast does it change?

To what degree is nature accepted or altered in order to create a thing
of beauty?

How is taste defined?

6. Sex

How significant a part of the collective consciousness is sex?

What is considered a turn-on and turn-off by most people?

How is seduction defined?

How is sexuality acceptably communicated? What are sexual stereotypes?

Is the emphasis on the act or the chase? On pleasure or procreation?

How much tolerance for deviation?
Accepted attitudes towards infidelity, towards promiscuity?
What degree of suppression or expression of sexuality occurs?

7. Values

What are the beliefs most widely shared? What ideals?
What are the traditions and how large is the commitment to them?
How are friendship, family, trust, and community defined and how are
    these bonds broken?
What is the predominant mood?
How do people define sin, consequences, forgiveness, ethics?
What gets attention? What holds it?
Value placed on money? Uses for it?
What kind of humor dominates? What role has laughter in society?
How is fear defined? Sources of it and ways of coping with it?
How and to what degree is emotion expressed? How suppressed?

8. Structure

Who rules and who follows?
How easy is it to bring about change?
How absolute is authority and what is the voice of the individual?
What governmental system?
How is justice brought about?
How is the pattern of daily life ordered and followed?
How are family and marriage defined? How much sanctity do they have?
How are manners, etiquette, rules set?
Degree, type, and emphasis of education? For both sexes?
How are groups created and identified?
What professions dominate and how is work viewed?
How is information gathered and spread?
Most widely held view of God, power of church, and role of religion in
    life?

9. Sight

How do all the above manifest themselves in the way the world of the
    play looks? In shapes and angles, light and shadow? In dominant
    patterns of movement and gesture?

10. Sound

How does it all come out in common speech, nonverbals, the degree to
    which listening and speaking are prized?

How close is your character to the average member of the group? How likely would he be to defend his right to be different if pressured to conform? Analyzing the world of the play becomes more and more crucial the farther that world is from the one you live in offstage.

Exercise 5.10

Fitting into the World

Create a situation in each of the ten categories above where your character is confronted with a group that conforms to the expected behavior in the world. React as your character would and either give in completely, make an adjustment, or defy the standards altogether. Complete, in some other way for each category, your sense of how your character will or will not blend with all the others.

Body Maneuvers

We have dealt with the body in a number of contexts. Now it is time to identify what it needs to do onstage. If you are new to the stage, think of this as a crash course in the jargon used there. If this is review for you, skim the lists quickly to brushup and see if there are any new terms. Try to tour the theater itself, associating each item with something concrete.

The Acting Space

The following items represent theater geography. They are the landmarks on the map, helping you explore this world. Knowing where each is helps communication in rehearsal. If a director asks you to move to the third stage right leg and face the teaser, you do not want to be looking at the audience's legs and looking God-knows-where to find the teaser.

Above: area away from the audience, upstage
Apron: part of the stage that projects into the auditorium, close to the audience, downstage of the proscenium arch

Arch: short for proscenium arch, the frame that defines the stage, the opening through which the audience sees the stage

Arena: form of staging where the audience surrounds the stage on all sides; sometimes called theater-in-the-round

Backing: flats or drops used to mask the backstage area by limiting the audience view through doors, windows, or archways on the set

Batten: long pipe or strip of wood on which scenery or drops are hung

Below: toward the audience, downstage

Border: short curtain hung above the stage, used to mask the flies

Box Set: standard set for contemporary, realistic theater, showing a back wall and two side walls, with the fourth wall understood to be the transparent one, through which the audience views the play

Callboard: bulletin board backstage, where notes for a show are posted

Cyclorama: curtain or canvas hung at the back of the stage, usually to represent the sky; also called the cyc

Downstage: the part of the stage nearest the audience

Drop: curtain or flat hung above the stage and dropped or lowered when needed

Flat: single piece of scenery usually made of muslin, canvas, or linen stretched over a wooden frame, used with other similar units to create a set

Flies: area of the stage where scenery may be stored and "flown" in or out

Forestage: part of the stage nearest the audience (see *apron*)

Fourth wall: imaginary partition through which the audience watches

Green Room: actor's lounge backstage

Grid: framework of wood or steel above the stage; also called gridiron

Ground Plan: scaled floor plan that shows the ceiling view of the set, including entrances, windows, doors, and furniture

House: all areas of the theater not onstage or backstage: auditorium, lobby, box office, lounges

Legs: flats or curtains at extreme right and left of stage used to mask wings (see *tormenters*)

Mask: to conceal from view of the audience

Props: any articles handled or carried by the actor

Proscenium: opening through which audience views the stage (see *arch*)

Rake: to place the floor of any area of the set on a slant, like a ramp

Scrim: net curtain, stretched taut, that can become transparent or opaque depending on how it is lit, so that the audience may or may not be able to see through it

Sight Lines: areas of the stage visible to the audience

Spill: light leaks around the edges of a lighting area

Stage Left: left side of the stage from the actor's point of view, facing the house

Stage Right: right side of the stage from the actor's point of view, facing the house

Teaser: border curtain just upstage and in back of the front curtain

Thrust: form of staging with the audience on three sides of the stage, which is thrust from the fourth side into the house

Tormenters: flats or curtains at the extreme right and left of stage (see *legs*)

Upstage: the part of the stage farthest from the audience

Wings: left and right offstage areas

Acting Areas

The terrain of the stage is mapped out with the following major areas. Some directors elect to break up the acting area into more or less separate areas, but these are where you move on major crosses during the process of staging a play.

Which of the areas in figure 5–1 are stronger and which are weaker? The centerstage areas are relative, but the most commonly accepted hierarchy for the others, from most powerful to least, is shown in figure 5–2.

Figure 5-1 Acting Areas

Up Right	Up Center	Up Left
Right Center	Center	Left Center
Down Right	Down Center	Down Left

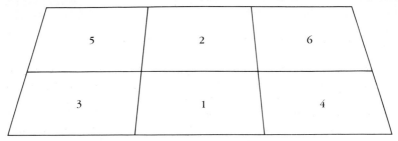

Figure 5-2 Area Power

Can you see why? Areas 1 and 2 are center and framed by the arch. As a culture, we are trained to look left first, because we read that way. Any of these factors may be changed by adding a platform (which will put a character on a much higher, more compelling level) or any number of other manipulations of the space. The relative power of areas also alters with nonproscenium staging.

Exercise 5.11

Using the Map

Execute the following basic moves:

1. Walk from the cyc to the apron, then to the downleft leg.
2. Stand downstage of the downleft tormenter and look at the grid.
3. Start at the border and move in a triangle with the other points being a tormenter on either side of the stage.
4. Move from the right arch to the cyc, then to beneath the batten.
5. Make up additional problems for individual class members to practice.
6. Have each person write down a three-part problem, draw each other's slips of paper, and do the map maneuver written there.

Stage Movement

As anyone who has ever been lost will tell you, reading a map and using it are not the same thing. Once you have locations down, there is another vocabulary for *using* the space:

Bit: a particularly striking or theatrical piece of business, not to be confused with a single motivational unit

Blocking: those movements of the actor that are set by the director at some point in the rehearsal process

Breaking*: dropping character suddenly, often by laughing or in some way "breaking up"

Bridge: transition from one unit to another

Business: pantomimed action with or without props, the smaller movements not involving full crosses

Cheat: to turn toward the audience while appearing to focus on another player onstage in order for her to be seen better

Closed Turn: turn executed so that the actor turns his back to the audience

Composition: stage pictures created by placing actors and properties in various arrangements

Counter: small move in the opposite direction from a move made by another actor in order to balance stage composition

Cross: to move from one area of the stage to another

Cue: final word, move, or tech change (lights, sound, scenery) that signals you to proceed to your next line or movement

Cue to Cue: skipping lengthy passages and running only those moments where change in responsibility occurs, moving from one cue directly to the next

Focus: directing attention towards a focal point so that the audience's attention will follow

Freeze: to suddenly stand completely still to form a tableau

Front Curtain: curtain hanging in the proscenium arch, concealing the stage from audience view

Give Stage: assuming a less dominant position in relation to another actor

Hold: any deliberate pause in the play's action

Indicating*: showing the audience, rather than letting them see, playing actions without intentions

Mugging*: exaggerating facial expressions and reactions to the point of caricature

Open Turn: turning so that you are always facing the audience during the movement

---

*These three terms represent degrees of failure in physical reaction. The actor moves himself farther and farther from the character's perspective and truth as he "progresses" from indicating to mugging to finally breaking, where complete control is lost.

Places: instruction to take positions for the beginning of the play or scene

Presentational: acknowledging the audience, the theatricality of the event, and playing generally towards the house

Read: to register with the audience, often used to describe the difference between the way an action feels onstage and the way it actually looks from the house; also called play

Representational: creating the impression that the audience is not present, that a real-life situation is being represented onstage so that the audience seems to be eavesdropping

Run-through: an uninterrupted rehearsal of the play, an act, or a scene

Schtick: silly or cheap piece of business, usually designed for laughter

Share Stage: assuming a position of equal importance in relation to another actor

Stretch: to take longer to execute something than would normally occur, often done to allow time for a difficult costume or set change

Strike: to remove an object from the stage

Take: a reaction of surprise, usually involving looking again at the source or the audience; takes may be single, double, or triple depending on how many times the look is repeated

Take Stage: to draw audience attention, to assume a stronger stage position

Exercise 5.12

Maneuvering

Execute the following maneuvers. Two actors together onstage.

1. A cross downright, B counter, both cheat.
2. A and B face each other. A do a closed turn to face the wings. B start an open turn a beat later and A stretch your turn so they finish at the same time.
3. A and B stand downcenter. A take stage from B through movement. B regain focus by a piece of schtick.
4. A and B move freely, conversing about the stage in a presentational manner, finding as many opportunities for takes as possible.
5. Add other problems from the class for pairs of classmates onstage either with the audience calling out directions or drawing tasks.

Movement as Technique

Once you understand stage vocabulary and maneuvers, you are ready to use the space to achieve *effects*. The more you know about how stage pictures are continually created and dissolved, the more comfortable you will be in the space. It will feel more and more like home, and you will look, to the audience, as if you really live there.

Exercise 5.13

Living Pictures

If you and your partner are onstage, before you ever physically move to another spot, there is the feeling of an active *relationship* between the two of you and between each of you and the audience. Try each of the following pictures. Ask yourself what the impression is if:

1. The two of you stand quite close, facing each other, in profile to the audience?
2. Same as above but with considerable distance between the two of you?
3. Same as above, but with pieces of furniture actually separating you?
4. You are standing close, but your partner's back is turned to you?
5. You are standing close, but your back is turned to your partner?
6. You are close, but both of you are facing opposite directions?
7. If the distance of 2 (above) and the separations of 3 are added to the relationships of 4, 5, and 6, what results?
8. You are standing close, but both of you are facing full front?
9. Both of you are full back?
10. Both of you are 1/4 left or right? 3/4 left or right?
11. One of you is 1/4 left, the other 1/4 right? You switch?
12. The same combinations of 3/4 left and right?
13. One of you full front and the other full back?
14. Any other combination, including profile?
15. Take any of the close-to-each-other combinations and put it up-center?
16. Move it downcenter?
17. Move it to any of the other four major acting areas?
18. Take situation 4, but you are in the upright area and your partner is downcenter? The two of you reverse?
19. Any other situation with the two of you in different acting areas?
20. Same as 19, but with varying proximities to pieces of furniture?

21. Back to situation 1, but you are both sitting?
22. You are both kneeling?
23. Both of you are on a staircase or ramp? Both up on a platform?
24. Any situation above, with both of you reclining? Both lying down?
25. Any situation listed so far, with each of you in one of the following positions, but always different from each other:

Figure 5-3 Implied Relationships
What seems to be changing besides the picture in each of these situations?

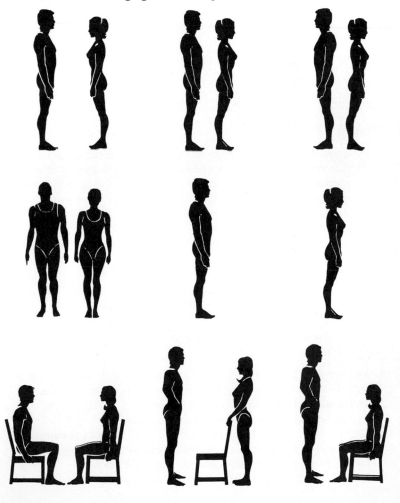

on platform
on staircase or ramp
standing
sitting
kneeling
reclining
lying down

Before even adding business or overt movement, strong messages would have been sent, about how open the two characters were to each other and to the audience, about how equal they were, or about who was dominant and who subservient, about degrees of dominance, barriers to contact, and about the relative involvement or indifference of each participant.

Exercise 5.14

Offstage Pictures

1. If you are not already aware from the imitation exercises, try to note whether you have a tendency to face people at 1/4 instead of straight on, whether you tend to stand when others are sitting, which of the above combinations are most and least characteristic for you in life.
2. When you see two people from a distance, note the immediate judgment you make regarding exactly what might be going on between them.

Exercise 5.15

Adding Motion

If the two of you are standing in profile as in the very first picture above, what is the impression if:

1. You are both gesturing with full large bubble, extending arms all the way out and even involving legs in the conversation?
2. You gesture in a normal, everyday range?
3. You gesture in a tight, close to the torso manner?
4. There is any contrast between the two of you in gestural patterns?
5. You both use hand props to emphasize everything you wish to say?
6. One of you uses hand props, but the other does not?
7. You both make long crosses every time you speak?

8. You both make short crosses of just a few feet?
9. One of you moves a great distance and the other a short distance?
10. One of you moves and the other is always still?
11. One of you moves a lot but does not really gesture, while the other stands in place but gestures fully?
12. The movements are relatively constant throughout the scene?
13. Large moves come after at least a minute of no movement at all?
14. One of you moves in an erratic, varying pattern while the other is quite predictable?
15. You both tend to move directly and then stop, or instead both move to an intermediate location, then change directions before you finally stop? If there is a contrast of directness between you?
16. Recalling your basic body positions when static, what if your movements tend to be largely pointed straight upstage or downstage?
17. There is constant countering with moves seeming to go back and forth before the proscenium arch?
18. There is a greater use of the diagonal by both or one of you?
19. There is a tendency to circle each other and to move in curves, S shapes, or figure eights? If one person uses these circular moves while the other is always heading straight for a target?
20. The movements themselves are rapid and darting?
21. All movements are slow, steady, almost lugubrious?
22. There is a contrast in tempo/rhythms between characters or at various moments in the scene?
23. A movement comes just prior to a line?
24. The line comes first, then the cross?
25. The line is broken, with a movement occurring somewhere in the middle? If one character falls into a pattern while the other is quite surprising?

These tools, combined with the prior list, give the actor an almost unlimited combination of ways to communicate a relationship. The more you practice and observe these maneuvers as pure technique, the more responsive the body becomes to discovering appropriate moves in a more spontaneous way. Once you have been exposed consciously to all the modulations, it is amazing how many simply *come* to you, when you are exploring, within a scene.

Exercise 5.16

Exchanges

Use the following brief exchanges of dialog to explore the staging relationships covered so far. Which changes in basic stage picture, business,

stage movement, and timing alter the impact of the lines most signifi-
cantly?

"Your place or mine?"
"Neither."

"I'm so excited. I'm just going to hold my breath 'til we get the news!"
"You do that."

"How cold, crude, and rude."
"Yes, those are my lawyers. You'll be hearing from us."

"How do you like my outfit?"
"You know, a lot of people couldn't get away with a look like that."

When you get larger groups of actors in the space, many var-
iables are added. The most important principle is contrast. Whenever an actor does something different from all the others, it will
take focus. So you may be sitting in a weak area of the stage with
your back to the audience, but if it is full of actors in stronger areas,
all standing and facing forward, *you* will be what we watch. Also,
no matter what kinds of pictures exist, the minute someone moves,
all eyes will go in the direction of the moving target.

Exercise 5.17

Contrast

Go back over the lists in the preceding exercises, and find situations in
which an actor might position himself in such a way that it would normally be considered a weak choice, but could be quite powerful, simply
because of contrast.

Onstage/Offstage Comparisons

Some things that have been learned, as simple good manners offstage, need to be modified, for purposes of audience attention.
Most of us have learned to be less assertive in life than is necessary
in the theater, just to be seen and heard.

1. You usually cross in front of another character, unless that character is seated, and you can be seen the whole time.

2. You do generally look at people who are entering or exiting to help direct attention.
3. Entering characters move well onto the stage and do not linger at the entrance. They also leave completely. Half-moves distract out front.
4. Actors do not often move at the same time unless momentary chaos is intentional. The audience gets confused about where to look.
5. You move on your own lines and usually need to remain absolutely still on those of other actors.
6. You remain as open to the audience as possible when speaking, with particular awareness of keeping your face, especially your eyes, visible much of the time.
7. All other factors being equal, if you are standing and the other person is sitting, you will dominate. Even though possessing the chair may seem the more powerful position, as it would be offstage, the audience, looking through the picture frame, sees one person looming powerfully over another. The possession does not read nearly as strong as the height. All such assessments of dominance need to be considered as seen through a picture frame.
8. Minimize eye contact. Inexperienced actors look at each other either not at all or too much. Michael Shurtleff, the famous casting director, estimates real people look at each other only 10 percent of the time.[7] He may be right. Connecting with your partner does not mean staring at her relentlessly. In fact if there is only one other person in the scene, eye contact tends to lower, because there is no need to signal to whom your remarks are being directed.

    Offstage, even when you are in a position that forces you to face each other (like a restaurant booth) note how often your eyes dart away or settle on other targets. When you are in the vast outdoors with a companion, note how seldom the two of you lock eyes and how much of the time you focus on surroundings.

Patterns

Worried about having to figure out a floor plan for your scene? Don't be. Though the possibilities are infinite, when you sit in the audience, a majority of the time, you see some variation of the set in figure 5–4.

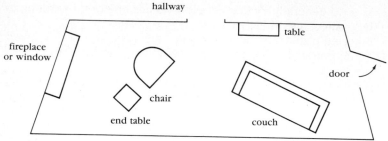

Figure 5-4 The Generic Floor Plan
This stage arrangement is used constantly in the theater. Why?

Why? Because it is simple, and provides most of the opportunities to explore relationships, while keeping everyone easy to see. It has:

A strong upcenter entrance

Two "islands" that can become territories so that any actor may assume one space as his and the other as his partner's

Opportunities for actors to play space invasion or space sharing games

Easy movement around the furniture so they can protect themselves at one instant, then step forth the next

A couch and an armchair, which offer the widest possible range of leaning, sitting, reclining, lying possibilities

The smooth and effortless use of figure eights around the two main sections as well as employing other curving patterns

Two isolated areas upright and left for retreat and reflection, as well as an alternative, if weaker, entrance/exit

This is not a bad space to start exploring with your partner as you begin work on a scene, especially if you know little about scene design. Alter it, as the scene requires, but try to keep the same opportunities for variety and visibility. What it lacks in originality, it offers in reliability. Ultimately, the space is made compelling by what people do there.

Voice Maneuvers

While word choice is determined by the writer, the actor is responsible for adjusting the control knob on each of the other categories (quality, tempo, rhythm, articulation, pronunciation, pitch, volume, and nonverbals) which we have covered. Each of these is worth working on separately offstage. You might pick a day when rhythm is what you are listening for, in others, and experimenting with, on yourself. Try working your way through each category, on a different day, aiming to expand your range in that particular aspect of vocal life before the day is over.

The most frequent request from directors and coaches is for variety, for the actor to simply use *more* of everything, to break out of a very narrow vocal life. Most actors need to expand their expressive mode by letting the pitch slide into the upper registers and down into the lower; the quality move into different textures as they describe a range of feelings; to speed up, slow down, and hit a middle stride with less *predictability*. We are not talking about changing your own vocal tendencies, so much as *broadening* them. Most of us tend to trap the voice in a tiny expressive mode. Actors learn to use more voice, period.

Vocal Directions

The following are terms used for standard requests, made at rehearsals, during notes, and in class critiques:

Anticipate: to respond earlier than your cue, revealing that the actor knows what is coming, even though the character would not

Build: to increase any combination of vocal techniques for a speech to reach a climax

Curtain Line: last line in scene or any other line requiring pointing up; also called tag line

Diphthong: two consecutive vowel sounds

Drop: to omit or to say inaudibly

Dynamics: energy, color, and variety of speech

Elongate: to stretch out or take longer to say

Emphasis: pointing out, by stress or any other technique, particular words or sounds

Inflection: a change in pitch

Intonation: a series of inflections or pitch changes

Melody Pattern: a predictable use of pitch, which can be graphed like notes on a musical scale

Onomatopoeia: characteristic of a word that sounds, in speech, like what it identifies (saying "slap" sounds similar to the act of slapping)

Overlap: to begin speaking during another actor's speech, not to be confused with anticipating since overlapping may be both deliberate and natural

Paraphrase: to say words that convey the meaning of the line but are not those of the playwright

Phoneme: any single sound of the English language

Phrasing: sectioning speech into units for emphasis and breathing

Resonate: to use as sounding area

Set-up: first of three parts to comic line in which subject is introduced, followed by a pause, then the punch line

Speed-through: running lines as rapidly as possible while still maintaining sense, mood, and relationships

Stress: placing greater weight on a particular portion of a word or phrase; see *emphasis*

Stretch: to take longer with a speech, often by elongating individual vowels

Substitute: inserting one sound in place of another

Support: sustaining sound, projected from within, without allowing waste of breath

Swallow: to fail to project or resonate certain sounds

Tap: to hit a consonant lightly, firmly, and briefly

Throw-away: to give a line only the slightest emphasis, usually for comic effect, because the words themselves register so strongly

Top: to register more strongly than a preceding line, usually by speaking louder and faster

Trithong: three consecutive vowels, employed in few standard sounds, but often true of regional speech or dialects

Undercut: to deliver a line with much less intensity than the preceding one, usually to deflate, the opposite of topping

Voice/Unvoice: to vibrate the vocal folds so that a sound reverberates or not, as in "p" (unvoiced) and "b" (voiced)

Exercise 5.18

Vocal Changes

1. Pick a line of dialog. Face one wall of the room. Begin the line in your head voice. When you get to the corner, switch to your sinus voice. When you get to the next corner, switch to your throat or pharyngeal voice. At the last corner, employ your chest voice. Change lines and expand to other resonators until you feel aware of the differences.

2. Play catch with sound. Throw a "one" to your partner, with one of you onstage and the other out in the house. Give the "one" definite weight and shape so he knows what kind of ball to catch. Partner repeat "one" as you catch it. Then throw a "two" back. Vary the distance between you, the weight and mass of the sound, and the degree to which the receiver needs to move quickly or some distance to catch the sound where it has been thrown. Work backwards when you hit twenty.

Vocal Technique

Even though mastery of your own voice starts later and happens slower than mastery of your body, it is worth the daily grind when your sound is finally really yours. The first step is to expand your own speech repertoire so that you have more choices, whenever you start to speak a line. Every time you hear another version of the basic voice elements (review Vocal Awareness in chapter 3) or of the directions above, play with it and try to capture it. The following exercises, if pursued regularly, will offer you a wider range of possibilities.

Exercise 5.19

Adding Repertoire

1. Go back over the two-line scenes employed for movement exercises and use each of the vocal directions above to add yet another dimension to the relationships. Even if the direction appears to imply a negative speech characteristic, explore what it may achieve.
2. In groups of two, draw slips of paper with each of the items on the list above. Quickly improvise dialog to demonstrate the concept. Class guess which vocal maneuver was being employed.

Exercise 5.20

T-shirt Philosophy

These lines appear on T-shirts I have seen. Their humor works without taxing the delivery of the line. Relax and experiment, knowing that variation can only enhance each line's impact:

"Better to remain silent and be thought a fool than to speak and remove all doubt."

"The future isn't what it used to be."

"Having sex is like playing bridge. If you don't have a good partner, you'd better have a good hand."

"Life is a bed of roses, but watch out for the pricks."

"Conform. Go crazy. Or become an artist."

"The difference between genius and stupidity is that genius has its limits."

"I refuse to have a battle of wits with an unarmed person."

"You're twisted, perverted and sick. I like that in a person."

"Obviously, the only rational solution to your problem is suicide."

"A woman without a man is like a fish without a bicycle."

"Don't tell me what kind of day to have."

"Reality is for people who lack imagination."

"You're the reason my children are so ugly."

"Men should come with instructions."

"Keep America beautiful—stay home."

"Sex is like snow. You never know how many inches you'll get or how long it's going to last."

"Stupid people shouldn't breed."

"Experience is what you get when you didn't get what you wanted."

"Onward through the fog."

Word choice is, of course, set but:

1. Which voice quality best brings out the line's impact? (Review Resonators and Classic Voices exercises in chapter 3.)
2. Which lines should be rapidly or slowly delivered? Should some alter tempo as the line progresses?
3. Where should pauses be used and where should a word or syllable be punched for effect? Where should emphasis be placed and how strong should it be? What rhythmic variations are possible?
4. Are there specific sounds that can be crisply emphasized as spoken? Any that might be slurred or thrown away? How might articulation alter?
5. Would any line be enhanced by a dialect or accent, by a pronunciation other than standard?
6. Do any lines seem to cry out for a high or low pitch or for a change mid-thought? Where does a change in pitch prove most effective?
7. Does the line work well almost whispered? Bellowed? With the volume knob adjusted as it progresses?
8. Are there any nonverbal additions that might be amusing or enlightening? Any places for a slight stammer, a growl, a deep sigh, any other sound beyond the words themselves?

Improvisation and Freedom

In the search for the healthy blending of truth and technique, no activity can be as liberating as improvisation. Once the basic language and maneuvers of the body and voice are comfortable, and the actor begins to feel playful again, improvisation can channel that playfulness and help renew a sense of spontaneity. Without some playfulness, how can you do plays?

Improv (which is how it is always abbreviated) gets a bad name when the games do not lead anywhere. Some theater groups spend a lot of time improvising and none of it shows up in the final product. Original works, created exclusively through improv, tend to be amusing, even satiric, but rarely memorable. Some people *only* want to improvise, nothing else, so they drive everyone else crazy with their refusal to set anything. Ever. It is easy to abuse it, but when properly focused, few activities can be as invigorating.

Improv is aimed at tapping your intuition, your knowledge that does not rely on reason or rational processes. It can help sharpen insight, the capacity for guessing accurately. And it can help you dare to decide quickly, and dive in, without wasting time speculating or reflecting unnecessarily. All of us would like to make better decisions, faster, without mentally debating an issue to death. On the other hand, no one wants to turn into a reckless fool. Improv can help you avoid the extremes of careful and careless, in favor of *carefree*.

Improv Ground Rules

Any game needs rules or there is no structure to the freedom. The more wild and freewheeling the game, the more important are those rules that keep it from chaos. In improv, actors agree to:

1. Participate without evaluating—this is an exploration without a judgment.
2. Stay involved until the teacher/coach calls the session over. Accept side coaching, without breaking concentration.
3. Play to solve the problem, not search out the clever line or cute ending, which may be untrue to the character.
4. Remove any preconceptions or plans and respond only in the moment.
5. Accept whatever another actor brings into the scene as true.

Regarding number 5, if an actor enters an improv scene, looks at you, and shouts "Brother!" with open arms, you do not answer, "I've never seen you before in my life." All new information is accepted. You are his brother. Hug him. If a new actor comes on while you are holding a broom and asks you whether your baby is a boy or a girl, your broom is indeed your baby. You get to decide the sex.

Basic Awareness Improvs

Earlier chapters in this text have improvs designed to illustrate acting concepts and terms. The following improvs have two specific and separate purposes: basic awareness (for your general growth) and script awareness (for effective character development).

Exposure

This exercise is almost universal in an introductory improv session because its lessons are fundamental to performance situations of all kinds.

Exercise 5.21

Being and Doing

1. Stand in groups of five or more onstage and look at the rest of the class and have them look back at you for at least three full minutes. Everyone should get a turn up there.
2. Repeat the process with these tasks: Count the number of book bags in the room, the number of women versus men, the number of people with each hair color, the number of people wearing running shoes. Take suggestions from the audience of what to count. Try to beat the other members of your group and shout out the answer when you have it.
3. Discuss the differences between numbers 1 and 2.

Exercise 5.22

Changing

In the same groups follow these directions, remaining up there in a line:

1. Be interesting.
2. Be sexy.
3. Try to appear indifferent.
4. Look intelligent.
5. Be mischievous.

Now replace each of these instructions with:

1. Think of a secret that no one here knows.
2. Quietly scan the room and note those people who turn you on and whose qualities especially appeal to you.
3. Count the number of separate items of clothing you have on.
4. Decide which controversial topic intrigues you most at the moment? What is the best argument for each side?
5. Find someone in the room you know you can play a favorite trick on.

Discuss the differences in relative relaxation and the reasons. This is a lesson every actor needs to learn deep in his bones.

Reactions

The capacity to respond with all the senses to an imaginary event calls on the full range of your ability to remember deep inside the mind and body. It also requires a complete return to a state of Let's Pretend. Perform in groups of five to ten:

Exercise 5.23

Spectator Sport

Agree as a group on the sport that is going on at a great distance from you. Watch without interacting with each other, but feel free to speak and move around. Accept whatever changes the teacher adds.

Exercise 5.24

Sounds of Music

Same situation as above only at a concert where you are enthralled by what you see and hear.

Exercise 5.25

Senses Alive

Pick an agreed-on eating or drinking task and concentrate fully on the act, with as many senses involved as are needed.

Exercise 5.26

Weather Watch

Add to the above a change in weather that breaks, to some extent, your dwelling on the task, dividing your focus between consuming and climate.

Exercise 5.27

Five Alive

Agree on a spectator situation that will allow you to combine all of the reactions above. Several groups layer them in one by one. Later groups try to begin with all reactions working, never allowing any single influence to disappear for long from consciousness. (Example: group watching square dance at county fair; add sound of fiddler, midway noises, bright glaring sunlight, mix of cooking smells, odors from animal exhibits, eating corn dogs, drinking lemonade, and so on.)

Joining

Working as a unit, balancing and supporting each other, and using each individual's contribution are what make acting the ultimate collaboration. Groups of five to seven:

Exercise 5.28

Where Are We?

Focus is on establishing an environment. First actor enters an open space and starts a task. Second actor does not enter until he is absolutely sure where scene takes place and how he might fit into the space. Public places (supermarkets, student unions, libraries) should be selected so that the actor can choose any characterization he wishes and still fit it into the location. All interact with the environment and use all the senses.

Exercise 5.29

Helping Out

First person goes onstage and begins an activity, such as yard work or house painting, which can be done alone, but can also benefit from help. The task should be physically involving and apparent even to someone who speaks a foreign language. Others join, one by one, concentrating on completing the task with free-flowing group interaction. Every person's objective is to effectively accomplish the basic shared task at hand.

Exercise 5.30

Building

First person enters, assumes an identity, and starts an activity, but he is the only one who knows both of these. Others join as they are called on and *given* an identity by the person preceding them, until the group is complete and functioning on the task. (Example: detective calls in assistant who calls in eyewitness who spots and calls in a suspect who calls her lawyer . . .) Everyone is concerned with accomplishing the shared objective, unless the person calling you on gives you an identity that justifies your working against the others.

Exercise 5.31

Changing

Variation on above, with each new person arriving and deciding both who she is and her relationship to others onstage. They do not know until the entering actor reveals her connection to them and the task at hand. Character entering is free to decide whether to help or hinder the task at hand.

Concentration

The double task of pursuing two activities at the same time or doing one thing while thinking about another always faces the actor, who is constantly juggling or splitting his focus.

Exercise 5.32

Who Am I?

Done with two actors. First is onstage seated on a bench and second (who is the only one who knows their relationship) enters. The first actor needs to find out who she is and what her connection to the second is, by studying the other's behavior towards her, without revealing her ignorance. If time allows, actors should switch, once relationship is clear, so each gets a chance to initiate.

Exercise 5.33

Eat, Drink, and Be Merry

Two to four actors. Same as Senses Alive, above, but this time, actors agree on a topic of conversation, which engages them actively. Consume a large meal at the same time. Keep all the areas of concentration balanced. Once secure, add sounds, sights, and weather conditions to the scene.

Exercise 5.34

Preoccupation

Two actors. A shared physical task is undertaken that necessitates that the two people interact. But each is totally preoccupied with his own subject and neither listens to the other at all, except for matter related to the mutual task. Alternate which person is chattering and which is silently thinking of something else, with moments where both are talking or momentarily drifting away. Keep the *task* active.

Exercise 5.35

I've Got a Secret

Five actors. Two actors decide on a topic that they must discuss in the presence of the other three without *revealing* the topic. They are trying to mislead the others, without saying anything that is actually untrue. Others join, one by one, when they think they know, but never ask if they are right. Two talkers may challenge any participant to a huddle and if the joiner is wrong, she has to leave. Everyone gets two chances to join before being permanently on the outs.

Selectivity

It is important to know what *not* to think about, so that distractions do not get in the way of objectives, onstage or off. Since the mind can only hold so much at once, only the essentials can stay.

Exercise 5.36

Drawing and Drawing

Entire class in two teams. Each team has a pile of scrap paper and pencils. Each team sends forward its champion to be shown the name of an item, written on a slip of paper which the scorekeeper has drawn from a hat. Each champion runs back and tries to draw a sketch of the item fast enough but clearly enough so that his team guesses it first. Get only the essentials on the paper. Keep score between teams until everyone has had a turn.

Exercise 5.37

Slow Motion Tag

Entire class. Begin by simply forcing all movement to slow down, even though someone is chasing and others are escaping. Once this becomes comfortable, each person who is "it" sets a particular movement, which everyone imitates, while still trying to keep from being caught. Each new "it" changes the mode of movement.

Exercise 5.38

Passing Sounds and Moves

Entire class. First everyone stands in a circle and one person starts a peculiar sound, accompanied by a movement. He carries these across the circle, to someone else who catches both, until they are perfectly imitated. When the new person reaches the middle of the circle, both sound and motion evolve into others, which the new initiator carries to another actor. Neither sound nor move should just jerk into a new mode, but *selectively* move out of the former set, into the new one. Once the group is responding fully, transfer into tag, this time with both sound and movement involved and everyone required to imitate the person who is "it" both vocally and physically, while avoiding being caught.

Exercise 5.39

Coming and Going

Entire class, but one actor at a time. Each person picks a place she just was, and another she is headed towards, and all we see is the moment between. The actor tries to be selective enough that both are clear. (For example: a man zipping up his fly and then pressing an imaginary button on the wall has come from the men's room to the elevator.) Once procedure is clear, actors should draw slips of paper that assign one of the two places, then finally draw both places. Variation: actors work in pairs.

Nonsense

The use of gibberish, or nonsense syllables, forces you, just as when traveling in a foreign country where you do not know the language, to call out the full range of *body* language and vocal expressiveness. In each particular exercise below, even your partner is simply making an informed *guess* as to the precise meaning of what you have just said. Remember to use sounds with no recognizable meaning at all (not even letters and numbers) so all information is nonverbal.

Exercise 5.40

Help Me

Work privately, in pairs. Alternate asking favors of your partner, warming up your sense of freedom from words. Ask for specific physical tasks so that your partner is able to literally help you out.

Exercise 5.41

Translating

One of you is demonstrating some product in nonsense, while the other "translates" to the audience at large what he believes his partner has just said. Not even the identity of the object is decided on beforehand. The object should have little relationship to its usual function (so a pail may be the latest in hats or an open notebook may be a bathing suit top) but the speaker should try to be as clear as possible about intentions and new function.

Exercise 5.42

Selling

Working in pairs to *persuade* the audience to buy some product, the two of you alternate physical demonstration with the sales pitch, helping each other out, until the end of the commercial.

Exercise 5.43

Interplay

Working in pairs, select any of the above conditions: a request for assistance, a demonstration, or a sales pitch. This time the audience is free to ask questions (in English), which you comprehend, but always answer in your own language.

Calls

As you have probably already figured out, a "call" is a signal that is given to you by some other source: drawing a slip of paper, side coaching, or the audience itself. Calls usually involve the given circumstances of the scene.

Exercise 5.44

Three *P*'s

Groups of two to five. Each group draws three slips of paper from three containers marked People, Places, and Projects. People will be members of the same profession (doctors? hairdressers?) or background (Martians? Elizabethans?). The Place (a stadium? a sauna?) may or may not have anything to do with what they share. The Project (spring cleaning? playing poker? having a quilting bee?) may also be unrelated to their background. It is all in the luck of the draw. Audience shouts out guesses. Stick with the task until it is finished or well under way.

Exercise 5.45

Audience Coaches

Groups of two to five. Those not in the group decide on the setting, an identity for each participant, the occasion, and the basic conflict, as we have done in earlier chapters. Audience is free to side coach the scene as it progresses.

Exercise 5.46

Audience Handicaps

Same group sizes. Actors decide on everything except the conflict, which comes from the audience. At various points in the scene, the audience layers in no more than a total of five handicaps (someone cannot speak, a dark secret, a case of amnesia) which are incorporated. Keep within the character's perspective and do not succumb to parody.

Tranformations

The ultimate effortless skill of childhood, which every actor needs to recapture, is changing whatever you look at by just believing it is now something else.

Exercise 5.47

Play Ball

Entire class in partners. Begin tossing an imaginary ball back and forth between you. Teacher will call out changes as it turns into football, medicine ball, Ping-Pong ball, and others as you let size, weight, and attitude influence you. Later, the ball may become other objects of varying shapes, values, and complexity, which are still sent through the air.

Exercise 5.48

Passing Objects

Entire class in a circle, sitting on the floor. First chosen actor creates an object out of air so that her fellow actors can see it, then passes it to the person next to her, who handles it until it transforms into something else, and is passed again.

Exercise 5.49

Passing Masks

Groups of five to seven. Sit in a tight circle. First person picks up an imaginary mask from the floor in front of him, puts it on and lets it change him, takes it off, returning to himself, passes it on to the person next to him. Each person gets to try on this particular mask and each person gets to initiate a mask of his own.

Exercise 5.50

Magic Clothes

Entire class. Everyone wanders around room ignoring others until discovering before you a magic pair of shoes. You decide what they look like and what their power is but once you put them on, they control you and change how you move and relate to the world. After a time you spot a magic sash, belt, or girdle which again takes you over and dominates not only that area of the body, but your entire relationship to the space around you. Finally you encounter a headdress, hat, helmet, or crown which you put on and it sends your energy up while transforming how you move and what you feel about the area around you. After allowing the headgear to dominate who you are, for a while, the three garments begin to fight each other and your sense of self is pulled in different directions. You remove the influence you like the least, then the second choice, and finally allow the one discovery that seems to have freed you most to transform you completely.

Exercise 5.51

On and Off

Groups of five to seven. First actor begins a task and establishes an identity which, once clear, makes a second actor enter and change, by virtue of his first line. Once the two of them fall into the new pattern, actor three enters and again *changes* everything. Allow each new relationship to function before the next change. Once the entire group is on and involved, first actor finds a reason to leave which transforms the group again, and each actor departs, leaving a change behind. The last actor *transforms himself* before leaving.

Script Awareness Improvs

Anything that appears in your character analysis could become the basis for an improv, in order to help get the information fully assimilated, especially if you wrote it down but you are not yet using it in the scene. Here are some possibilities:

Exercise 5.52

First Meeting of the Characters

Set up all the circumstances of the first time the two of you laid eyes on each other. Then enter the scene from a point of innocence and discover

your partner. Leave the encounter when you have some idea when you
will see this person again.

Exercise 5.53

Crucial Offstage Event

Select the single most influential experience, either before the play begins
or away from the script, on your actions. This may or may not involve
your partner. Set yourself up to simply respond without scripting the
experience. Solo examples: a character anticipating an abortion goes to
an actual clinic for counseling, an alcoholic attends an AA meeting, an
expectant mother goes to a birthing class. It matters far less how many
demands you place on yourself than the range of *feelings* the experience
allows you to share with the character.

Exercise 5.54

Character Wake-up

On the morning of the beginning of the play, move from sleep to the
character's anticipation of the day ahead. Get a strong sense of the bed
(if it *is* a bed), the space, your feelings about where you sleep, the time
you wake up, your expectations about the coming day, and all the circumstances that launch you into this event. Go through each detail of
bathing, choosing what to wear and eat, what to take with you. Arm yourself with everything the character carries onto the stage.

Exercise 5.55

Stop Partner from Leaving

Imagine that one of you simply wants to leave and not deal with the
encounter at all. Using the actual dialog, one actor should employ any
tactic available to keep the partner from going. Partner should actually
walk out of the space, if not stopped by some riveting sense of urgency,
need, or power. Reverse positions and run the scene the other way
around. Then alternate every four lines whose turn it is to feel the need
to get away.

Exercise 5.56

Unrelated Activity

As you run lines with your partner, pick a variety of ways to involve yourselves physically at the same time. You might set the table for dinner or do laundry or clean the rehearsal hall or any task that will involve the two of you equally. Let the lines and the activity influence each other so that neither is independent of the other.

Exercise 5.57

Scoreboard

Place a blackboard (or some other prominent means of visibly displaying who scored the last point) somewhere on your set. Play the scene with particular attention to one-upping your partner. When you know you have scored, walk up to the board and give yourself the point. Take time out if the point is contested. Relish each point you score. At the end, tally who wins and by what margin.

Exercise 5.58

Talking Beats

Walk through the scene, negotiating, in character, about where each beat begins and ends, and what it should be called ("This is the beat where I show what a fool you've been and it should be called 'Sheila's Revenge.'"). Disagree as your character might ("What is really shown here is your mindless cruelty and it should be called 'Sheila the Bitch.'"). Negotiate until you find a mutually acceptable spot, for the beat's beginning and end, and a title that both parties can deal with. Try it with larger clusters of beats (measures or subscenes), giving titles to them as well.

Exercise 5.59

Typical Time

Spend an evening or an afternoon as the two characters, doing something they would likely do together. Agree on the exact point at which you leave yourselves behind and take on the characters. Try to view each event and line heard from the character's perspective and to relish the change. Pick up a sense of how the two of them deal with each other and others outside the script itself.

Exercise 5.60

Character Interview

If possible this exercise should be performed in class, but it can be done with your partner or a friend playing the interviewer. You decide the circumstances. Are you interviewing for a job, a deposition, a biography, an article, a grant, a TV show? The group is free to ask you any questions and you must answer at all times from the character's point of view.

Exercise 5.61

Character Encounters

In character, go through the list used for Partner Sharing at the end of chapter 4. Imagine the circumstances under which these two would do this together (to save their marriage, to satisfy the urging of one of them, to help them get over a misunderstanding). Answer fully as the character would, and later note where you and the character intersect and where you divide.

The activities above can be accomplished fairly early in the rehearsal process, once you have completed a character analysis draft and are just off book, with lines barely memorized. For more intensive improvs done at a later point in rehearsal, see chapter 6, Shaking Up the Scene.

Keys

Actors are always searching for the key to a character. They often discover what they are looking for in a costume prop (a hat, a handkerchief, a pair of shoes or glasses) or some physical characteristic (set of the jaw, hands deep into pockets, feet turned in slightly when walking) or vocal quality (a slightly nasal sound, a nonverbal hum, a startling laugh) characteristic. The actor will talk of searching and searching "until I put on this scarf and that was the key" and suddenly the door to the whole characterization opened.

This search and discovery represent vividly the way in which a single technical element can unlock an emotional awareness. They also show how much technique the actor needs, to experiment with all those physical and vocal traits, to know what to *do* when he picks up the hat or the cane, to even recognize the *value* in picking it up. Stanislavski refers constantly to "unconscious creativeness through conscious technique" where the actor earns the *right* to discover by carefully opening himself up to possibility. When a simple physical object or tiny change can suddenly make him feel like another human being, with detail after detail rushing in to complete the character, the actor often feels as if he is experiencing a miracle. A well-earned miracle.

Exercise 5.62

Key Searching

1. Select a character and spend a half hour wandering around your own room (or, if available, a prop room) trying things on, picking up and handling props, examining small objects, letting each work on the character's sense of self. Keep the best of what you find, but keep your personal antennae out everywhere you go for objects that might open character doors.
2. Do the same thing with isolated physical and vocal characteristics and techniques. Try them on like glasses or scarves, seeing if they fit (or even release) the character.

Blending and Balancing

This particular marriage of truth and technique, like most marriages, requires time and adjustment, but is worth it. Many actors search for, yet do not find, a key that allows them shortcuts, but every conscientious actor experiences moments that in themselves are tiny miracles. There are few things more wonderful than finding yourself in rehearsal, with an impulse you know you can support. Let us say your heart wants to cry out with a desperation to your partner that suddenly seems absolutely right for the character.

You know how to extend an "s" sound masterfully, how to support a plaintive vowel sound so it is mournful but not weak. You know how to land on a consonant like "p" so that it seems to explode. You have learned to focus almost all your energy momentarily in your eyes. So when you call out "Stop!" to your partner, the other actor is frozen, feels a chill, and turns, mesmerized, looks up, and is locked into your eyes. Your sense of truth launched you and your technique carried that truth to capture your partner. Now you feel a chill. Of power. And then delight.

Geraldine Page: *If you want to be able to express the maximum variety of things, then the more technical mastery you can achieve, the more* fun *you're going to have!* [8]

6
Performance Process

(recognizing standard procedure
and appropriate behavior from
first audition through closing
night)

Dustin Hoffman: *The director's job should be to open the
actor up and, for God's sake, leave him* alone![1]

Helen Hayes: *Childbirth is easy compared to giving birth
to a role in a play.*[2]

We in the theater like to believe we have no rules. We are more
tolerant of personal eccentricity and more encouraging of emotional display than most groups. We hardly require our members
to all be the same. We are unusually loving and supportive of each
other. Actors, who are forced to compete against each other for
parts, nurture each other in every other way. But the process of
putting together the performance of a play has definite rules of
procedure and personal behavior, most of them unspoken.

There *have* to be rules for any large group or the group
will not work as a unit. Look for the silent standards of *any*
world you wish to join. Every rule in the theater is made to be
broken. But a rule needs to be learned before it can be broken.
Only if you master it do you earn the right to break it, when the
time is right.

200

Acting Etiquette

Every year talented newcomers enter the acting brotherhood. Full of potential, some get well cast, and then offend so many people that they are immediate history. Or it takes a long time for anyone to risk working with them again. Often the offending newcomer is no more than a victim of ignorance, unaware of what is happening next, much less how to handle it. I once heard a veteran actor refer to this phenomenon, while watching a recently fired young actor depart, as "choking the baby on meat."

Some things you are better off not having too early. You do not play Lear when you are seventeen and you do not want to play *anything,* until you understand basic behavior in the theater. This chapter will deal more than any other with what makes onstage different from off.

Taking Time

The biggest surprise for most newcomers is, inevitably, the enormous time commitment. While the process of putting together a production varies wildly, this list will do as a model of traditional rehearsal patterns:

1. *Audition Notices:* Posters and ads describing when, where, and how try-outs are to be conducted.
2. *Auditions:* Basic try-outs, often spread over more than one day, usually held in the evenings.
3. *Callbacks:* Smaller group narrowed down by director for another look, possibly a different set of audition activities (often no one is actually "called" on the phone, but rather a list is posted).
4. *Cast List Posted:* Notice of casting may involve initialing next to your name by way of acceptance.
5. *First Company Meeting:* Introductions of participants to each other, and sharing of director's production concept with the company.
6. *Show and Tell:* Costume and set designers (plus other possible specialty designers) demonstrate their renderings and explain visual concepts.
7. *Read-throughs:* Exploratory sessions, often sitting in a circle, just reading aloud, focusing on script, possibly stopping to cut some passages and discuss relationships.

8. *Blocking:* Physical staging, slow and laborious, may range all the way from director meticulously preplanning and simply instructing actors to director planning none of it and weeks of exploration.

9. *Fittings:* Costume pieces tried on you and adjusted at various points in construction process.

10. *Character/Ensemble Development:* Rehearsals geared towards getting individuals into character and feeling like a group.

11. *Coaching:* Sessions devoted to individual acting problems, seldom involving more than director and one or two actors at a time.

12. *Intensives:* An "anything goes" period, usually working very small portions of script, over and over, in great detail out of sequence.

13. *Polish:* Work on flow and builds for whole show, more and more running through an entire act or whole script, without stopping.

14. *Promotion:* Taping media ads and interviews, taking scenes to special events, posing for publicity photos, selling the show.

15. *Tech-ins:* Adding lights, props, sound, set pieces, all technical elements, lengthy sessions requiring infinite patience from everyone.

16. *Dresses:* Rehearsals just before opening, done as close as possible to actual performances, with all ingredients present; seldom more than three rehearsals, one of which is sometimes a preview.

17. *Opening:* Official first night, after months of prior work.

18. *Run:* Scheduled performances, usually with adjusted calls or times you are expected to arrive at the theater.

19. *Brush-ups:* Rehearsals called, when considerable time exists between performances, to review lines and get it back in shape, often done without technical elements, unless cues are tricky and also need review.

20. *Closing and Strike:* Final performance followed by taking down set, storing props and costumes, cleaning makeup and dressing rooms, taking down lights, and so on—process involves both actors and technicians.

Audition notices tend to go out two to three weeks before tryouts, the audition process takes usually under a week, the show itself most often rehearses at least four weeks, and an educational or community theater production rarely runs longer than three weeks. (Commercial productions may close after a single performance or run for years. In fact all time frames vary wildly in commercial theater.) So the entire process takes, on the *average,* two months, but this time can be greatly expanded if the show is large and complex. Big musicals and Shakespeares often rehearse a good twelve weeks, because of all the extra dance, singing, fighting training, and special skills needed to develop the styles of performance. Most shows rehearse at least five evenings a week for three to four hours, and in the final stretch may rehearse daily, with tech and dress rehearsals going into the wee hours.

A popular statistic for minimum play rehearsals is one hour for every minute of running time. So a small cast, single set, contemporary, realistic play which runs two hours (120 minutes) plus intermission, would rehearse a bare minimum of 120 hours. This figure could easily quadruple, with large casts and difficult scripts. Obviously, you need to determine if you have the *time* to do all this, before you ever attend auditions.

Rehearsing Outside of Rehearsal

A common error made by new actors is to schedule yourself so tightly that you can fit in rehearsal, but very little *else* during each day. This is what you are generally expected to do outside of rehearsal:

Character analysis
Memorizing lines
Researching the role
Applying the director's notes from last night
Experimenting with character approaches
Developing the vocal and physical lives of the character
Brushing up material that has not been worked in a week
Attending costume fittings
Participating in publicity photo sessions and interviews

This list could also expand if you need to work with a coach on a particular skill or if you and one of your acting partners need to explore some aspect of your characters' relationship together.

To keep your bases covered, it is a good idea to plan on an hour of offstage rehearsal, usually by yourself, for every hour spent onstage, with the rest of the company. You may not need this much every day, but you may sometimes need more. And few things are worse than having a director say to you, "Your work was sluggish tonight. You've got to get more rest." Then, after she walks away, you turn to your crammed schedule, and ask yourself, "When?"

What follows are some basic questions to consider at each stage of the performance process.

Audition Preparation

— Are **scripts** available to check out and read beforehand? Find out where and for how long. Why go in blank?

— Is there a definite production **concept** that might affect how you could be used? Is there something about yourself that you can punch up? Ask around.

— Are any roles **pre-cast** and not worth your shooting for? Ask only people who *know*. There are always false rumors on this one.

— Will there be **cold readings** or are you to prepare material? If you need to present something **memorized**, need it be from the script? Even if it is cold readings, there is nothing stopping you from practicing and making *your* reading at least lukewarm.

— Can someone who knows your work and the play advise you on where your best **casting potential** is, in this show?

— Does this director regularly use certain audition methods, ask certain questions, show definite preferences? What kinds of actors does this director seem to admire? What kinds of procedures are known to be standard when this person is in charge? You can **research the director**, not just the script.

— Can you get into the **space** beforehand to get comfortable and maybe have a friend help you check your projection?

— What to **wear**? Something that will not get between the director's imagination and visualizing you in the final production. Full costume and makeup are too much, but try not to look all **wrong** for the play. If it is an elegant drawing room comedy, your sweats and your sneakers are a bad choice. Pick the closest thing, in your closet, to the *spirit* of the play.

— Have you thought of all your potential **time conflicts** over the next few months, so that you can list them? Have you thought of your **responses** to questions that might be on the forms?

Audition Behavior

— **Which night(s)** are you going to attend? Most people suggest going the first night, especially if you are new. Directors go home with actors in their minds, after the first night, no matter how hard they try to wait to cast.

— How **early** should you get there? Right at the beginning, when a series of instructions are often given and questions answered.

— Is there someone in charge here besides the director? A stage manager or assistant or some **trouble shooter**? This is the person to ask things.

— Is the director the only one who can help you? Leave him alone until there is a **break**. Never, ever talk to him while another actor is up there reading.

— Are there **instructions** written down? Read anything handed out carefully so you do not need to request info that has already been given to you.

— What if you are asked (on a form or in person) if you will accept any part? If you will work on a crew? If you can miss work for some rehearsals? If you will change your hair color? Lose some weight? Grow a beard? *Gain* some weight?! These are fairly standard requests and no one can tell you how to answer. But give yourself some time to **think about it,** so you are not so staggered by the question that you can no longer concentrate. It is always O.K. to say you will think it over, and let them know by the end of the evening or the next day.

— Are you **tensing** up? It is always alright to warm up. Are you getting too loud and chatty because you are nervous? Remind yourself to support every person who reads. Do not ever get so thrilled that a hot-shot actor you admire is talking with you that you distract from someone else, struggling onstage.

— Are you studying the other actors? This session can turn into a master class if you observe closely. Watch not only those who do well, but those who do not. You probably have tons of **examples** of what to do and what not to do right before your eyes.

— Do you need to leave? Make sure it is alright. If you cannot do that, tell at least one person who plans to stay that you have gone and where you will be. Do you know when you might hear something? Where the list will be posted? Are you absolutely clear on all **details** for callback time, place, procedure?

Audition Activities

— Are you asked to do something weird? Think of it as a game and give yourself **permission to have fun.** Often your poise, imagination, and sense of adventure are being tested. It does not all have to make sense.

— Do you get a chance to **choose** a partner to read with? Check out everyone, for those you think will look right with you, people who make you comfortable. This is a real chance to use your insight, instead of just grabbing someone.

— Are you being asked to **change** your reading? This is always a good sign. Respond positively. Directors rarely direct people at auditions who do not interest them.

— Are you puzzled by the **range** of activity? Remember, anything that could happen in acting class can happen here, in a highly condensed form. You study improv to release your spontaneity. If improv is used here it is probably to *test* your spontaneity.

— Do you sometimes just have to stand there while the director studies you and others? She is looking at combinations: families, lovers, ages (review chapter 5 improvs on exposure). Let yourself relax and try not to look like a hunted animal. You are being **considered**.

— Is there a chance to **volunteer**? Take it. You have just been up there. Fine. They will see you again. Within reason, actors are aggressive, and enthusiasm to be onstage now says you will carry this enthusiasm through rehearsal.

— Are you rushing and not **connecting** when you read? Stop and ask yourself what you want, what is in the way, what your plan is, how much the person opposite means to you, the quick basics. Do not let yourself forget the way you always act most effectively. Take time to feel the words and to see the person reading opposite you.

Callbacks

— Is there something you need to **prepare**, check out, a person you are to work with in advance, information you still need to provide? Read the notice with incredible care, so your joy over making the list does not cloud your sense of detail.

— Are you not on the list? You still need to **check** the cast list, because some directors only call back people they are undecided about, and do cast some roles based on the initial reading.

— Is there something the director would like to **see from you** that you have not yet shown? Ask. If you make callbacks, you are a contender. A mannerism she would like you to modify, a quality to punch up, some alteration in your appearance? You have a golden opportunity to show the kind of actor you will be if cast.

— Any last-minute **reservations**? This is the time to get out. If you drop out *after* the cast list is posted, you seriously damage your reputation. You inconvenience many. And no matter how thrilled the person is who replaces you, he and everyone else will always know he was *not* first choice. All because of you.

Preparation for First Rehearsal

— Are you supposed to check out a **script** beforehand? Probably. This is a good time to mark your lines with highlighter or in some way that helps you focus.
— Is there a **callboard** for this production? Start checking it daily. This is where they tell you they need to take your measurements for costumes and each time you are needed for a fitting. This is where you may get a deadline for a form that needs to be filled out, so something can be sent to your hometown newspaper. This is where last minute messages of all kinds are posted.
— Do you have your rehearsal **supplies**? Several pencils (not pens, you may need to do a lot of erasing), a notebook or journal, basic supplies (mouthwash, mints, whatever you need to "feel good about being close"), script, special clothing or shoes that may be needed? It helps to keep all this stuff together and ready.

Rehearsal Behavior

— What is the scheduled **starting time**? Whatever it is, it means that you have already arrived, unpacked, gone to the john, warmed up as necessary, and taken care of chitchat. It is not the time you breeze in the door out of breath. It is not a bad idea to aim to arrive a half hour before the scheduled time and take care of business.
— How long ahead will you know when you are called? There is no guarantee. Some directors post each day what will be on that night and some never post ahead. That is an extreme, but even if you have what looks like a detailed **schedule**, check the callboard daily for last minute changes. Someone may be sick, and your scene is going to be worked instead of hers.
— Some of your favorite lines are **cut**? Try not to gasp, moan, or collapse on the floor. Strive for grace. Should you try to get these words put back in? Only if you are completely convinced

they are essential to your character. Not just because you like them. Think about this for a while.

— Feeling inhibited by some big guns in the cast? Get to know them as soon as possible. Work past the image to the real people. Feeling cautious generally? Do not let yourself start bottling up. No one expects a performance yet. Rehearsal is where you need to feel free to **experiment** before finalizing, where you dare to be foolish and vulnerable.

— **Conflicts** with class demands and show demands? Can you expect theater teachers to let you out of assignments or delay them because you are in a play? No. You can ask, but realize it is a big favor you are asking, and it is due to your own failure to structure your time.

— Missed a fitting? Beg the designer's forgiveness. Go volunteer to work in the shop. Costumers can put pins in places you would rather not feel them. Need help in feeling like your character? Wear the closest you can come up with to the right **rehearsal clothes**, either checked out from the costume shop or from your own closet. If the character wears heels and fitted skirts, do not wait. Get into these the first week. The character is a cowboy? Your running shoes have got to be replaced by boots. Even throwing your coat over your shoulder, in place of the cape that will eventually be there, is better than nothing. Do not underestimate the power of clothes to transform you. Do not be embarrassed by adding these things. Some in the company may tease you, and secretly recognize you as a serious actor.

— Blocking coming at you fast and furious? Write it in **shorthand**. There is standard code for common stage movements. In addition to using only the initials (DR for downright, UC for upcenter) the codes in figure 6–1 are often employed. Or make up your own. Confident you will remember the movements without writing them down? Do not be. There may be lots of time before this scene is called again, and you may be struggling with lines by that time, so your concentration will be scattered. Write it down. And **check** it again before you sleep tonight to make sure you have got it.

— Being asked to do things you do not understand? Unclear about the objectives of some rehearsals? Ask, right away. Unlike an audition, there should be no hidden agenda here. You have a **right to know** why and wherefore. Never assume that you should understand, unless you already know you do not listen well.

cross ✕	table ⊤
sit ⌐↓	chair ⌀
enter E	door ⊓
exit ∈⤡	couch ▭
pivot right ↙	pivot left ↘
kneel ↵	fall or lie down ↧
face direction ↘	rise ↗

Figure 6-1 Stage Shorthand
Here are some common codes, but if you don't like them, invent your own.

— **Tech staff or crew members** attending rehearsals? Contact with box office and front of house staff? Treat every person on this show with maximum respect. Do not succumb, for an instant, to acting like these people are your servants. They are fellow artists. And they do not get curtain calls.

— Feel like a haircut? Lightening your hair color? Going on a crash diet? Clear any potential **change in your appearance** with the director beforehand. Do you have any idea how many actors have foolishly altered the very thing the director liked best about their looks?

— What to eat and drink **before rehearsal?** Keep it light, so you do not get sluggish. Most actors choose long-term energy food, instead of stuff that gives you a surge but dies long before the end of rehearsal. No, do not even consider arriving even mildly drunk or stoned (or stunk and droned, a combination). Any experimenting (like rehearsing a character who drinks heavily by drinking) is on **your own time,** or by mutual agreement with the director and anyone else involved.

Shirley Maclaine: *I had a lot of trouble working with my co-star, who was from "the Cocaine School of Acting."*[3]

— Getting **bored or tired** waiting for your scene to come up or to be called in to work? Bring other work that can be done while waiting. Write in your acting journal! See if the costume shop needs someone to sew on buttons. Or work on your character in these stretches. Keep yourself energized and occupied.

Likely Deadlines

— For your analysis work? Usually about two weeks into the rehearsal period. Handed in? No, not usually, but shared with the group or just integrated into the rehearsal process by this time. Be **prepared** to answer all the questions noted earlier.
— **Outside** research? Varies. Anything you do not know about the historical period, country, art, music, styles of the people in the play is worth a few trips to the library. Will others feel disdain for you as an eager beaver? Only the motivationally impaired. And the jealous.
— Lines? Some directors want them as soon as possible, most expect them the second time a scene is called after it is blocked. Rarely are there less than two full weeks with everyone off book before opening. If you are a slow study, start scheduling daily **line workouts** from the first day. Realize you tend to lose a lot of solid memorization once in front of the other actors, so consider checking memorization with the other people in your scenes before the actual deadline.
— Running lines? Usually an assistant director will help you. Other actors will usually be glad to. **Calling** for lines? Stay in the scene. Try not to look at the prompter. Give yourself a beat for the line to come. Try not to break character or concentration. Lines will come much faster if you stay in the moment itself, even when the words are rough.

After Opening

— **Adjusting** performance? Only in consultation with the director and anyone else influenced by being onstage with you.
— Reviews? Look for trends, if reviewed by a number of publications. If by one not-very-respected-local critic, ignore altogether. Never take a copy to the theater or quote it or grumble about it or in any way inflict the review on others, who may wish to rise above it.
— Let down? Inevitable after the rush of opening night. Do not succumb to second night blahs. Consider yourself a source of energy and fresh air for everyone you work with. It is always opening night for the audience. Always. **Renew** that night every night.

— **Brush-ups?** May be called if show has been dark for a while. Lots of plays just perform on weekends, so may go Sunday through Thursday dark, and need at least a run-through before going up for an audience again. Give yourself the same charge as above.

— Some performances better than others? Inevitably. But these things happen for a reason. Try to make sure *you* are not the reason. Which performance is best? Ideally, closing night. You **grow a little bit** every time you go out. And on closing, you look forward to the next time you will get to work with this script or develop further this kind of character.

— Strike? In most theater settings, actors become crew members until everything is put away. A **tradition** and not to be violated. This is not the moment to suddenly decide to have a fling with being irresponsible. See the experience through to the end.

Adaptations

Adapting Show Process to Class Process

What happens in a production can simply be scaled down for a course in acting. How? You just look at the time frames, responsibilities, and deadlines, then modify them. The number of actors who function brilliantly, when someone *else* imposes the schedule, and then collapse, when they have to do some scheduling themselves, is alarming.

It is a ten-minute scene? That means the bare minimum rehearsal period prior to the first time it is done in class is ten hours. Remember? The operative phrase here is "bare minimum." Full productions develop a cumulative effect. Scenes late in the play sometimes require less rehearsal, because so much groundwork and layering has preceded them. Once you really know these characters and have experienced them in previous situations, you somehow earn the right to discover quickly in the final stretches. Obviously, a scene never has this advantage. So you only add. Also your entire rehearsal period is more likely to be a few weeks, so you are condensing the performance process.

Shortcuts? You and your partner have discovered you are soulmates and probably are really brother and sister separated at birth? You are so well cast that each line of dialog sounds as if it rolled off your very own tongue? A shining light descended on a rehearsal and every word uttered for the next five minutes was magic? There *are* no shortcuts. You can always rehearse a few more times, and discover some more values.

Look at each stage of the traditional preparation of a play and make sure that, to some extent, that period exists for your scene. Any chance to develop and share your work with an audience is a very big deal. Your scene is an important production, in miniature.

Schedules and Objectives

As soon as you get a partner, sit down together and map out a rehearsal period. Reserve generous time frames between now and the due date. You can always cancel an unnecessary rehearsal easier than you can squeeze in an unanticipated one at the last minute. In class, you often have a partner before you have a scene, so selecting one may be your first objective, with a definite deadline. If you have an actual copy of a rehearsal schedule for a full production, you may find it helpful to literally work with this model, crossing off irrelevant items (like photo calls) but keeping some version of everything else.

Many actors just sit and read through the script for lots of sessions without any progression. Then one day it becomes obvious that they have got to stand up and do some blocking so they do that, and from then on in they just run through again and again, without progression. A certain amount of progress takes place in spite of this vapid approach. But not nearly as much as if you establish an objective for each time you get together. One meeting might be for no purpose but to get to know each other better, another to work on vocal technique and line delivery, another to clarify only subtext, another to develop the characters' shared history. There are so many tasks to be accomplished that the main problem is just which one today.

Stated objectives will also make you feel, when you leave, that you know why you were there. A great deal of acting is magical and mysterious. There is always plenty of *that,* no matter what. Some organization will actually free you to unlock the magic.

Cutting the Scene

Time limits on acting class scenes have to be enforced, simply because there are so many people in class and so little time for vital individual attention. If you present a scene that goes way over the assigned limit, you have wasted time in a number of ways. First, you are eating into your own period of getting critiqued or having your scene worked. You are probably eating into *other* people's time, which is worse. Also, you have spent all these valuable rehearsal hours working on a giant, unwieldy rock of a scene, when what was wanted was a little jewel glistening in the sun. You have probably heard the standard theatrical adage "Leave them wanting more." As advice, it has no peer. It stands to reason that the shorter your excerpt, the more times you can run it, work it, try something else, polish it, right? No epics allowed.

Time the scene regularly as you work. You will probably add time as you get more layers, find inspired pauses, consider incredible alternatives during your evaluations, and so on. So if your scene timed near the limit at first reading, you will inevitably have to cut. It is very common for a scene to run 15 minutes and for actors to say, "But it was only ten last week." Last week? That was before you found all that glorious subtext.

What can be cut? Every line is perfect? Here are some standard edits:

1. Anything connecting with other parts of the play, but not directly connected with the scene. The scene can have a life of its own.
2. Start closer to the climax than you originally intended, or consider ending with more of a cliff-hanger than full closure. Find the portion of the scene that gives you the best *acting work out.*
3. Any passages where you have found you can imply, or communicate physically, without stating specifically. Some speeches may be overwritten, others you simply find can be edited, once your subtext is clarified.
4. Cut for balance, if one character has been given lengthy monologs, so that the scene becomes more of a duet. This experience should serve both partners.
5. Lines you have trouble with: trouble pronouncing, motivating, clarifying. *Not* until you have tried to make them work, but eventually to relieve yourself from unnecessary pressure. There is no

point approaching a word or phrase with dread because you have rarely been able to say it right.

6. Dated or obscure references that the audience is unlikely to grasp.
7. Bleed the scene, instead of looking for giant amputations. Sometimes you do need the entire body of the scene, but can ease out a word here, a phrase there, so you have a cleaner script but a complete one.

Cutting is a valuable skill for actors. Too many leave it all up to directors. You are much closer to each line, more intimately aware of potential nuances within each speech. In play rehearsals, if you are able to offer suggestions for cuts, you are also far more likely to be able to keep your favorites. Respecting a text is not synonymous with needing to present it all. Some magnificent texts can be enhanced with surgery.

Memorizing

Some actors are quick studies and others are painfully slow. There is a definite trend to ask for lines earlier and earlier in rehearsal. It used to be thought that if actors memorized too early, they would lock the actual *delivery* of the line as well. So many exercises are now designed to liberate and vary delivery that the problem of locking is rare. If you have trouble getting lines down, here are some suggestions:

1. Work from your cues, not from the first word of each of *your* lines. Memorize at least the *last half* of your partners' speeches. Many actors are sent into paralysis because they were not expecting their partners to stop talking.
2. Cue yourself off of motivating (action cues) words within your partner's speeches, the words that stimulate response, not off of the last word (line cue) of his speech. Responders always start gearing up on a certain word or phrase while the other person's talking.
3. Work on lines for short periods, ideally a single beat mastered at each session. Marathon sessions are rarely retained.
4. After you get about half a page go back over and drill, then drill again. Never assume you have got it without backtracking.

5. Place a card over your lines and reveal only as much to yourself as absolutely necessary as you cue yourself and master each speech.

6. Try taping your partner's lines with spaces or, if your partner is feeling helpful, have her tape her lines, so you can run yours when she is not around, but still hear the right voice, giving you cues.

7. Some actors find using flash cards helpful, with the other actor's lines on one side and yours on the other. Putting the cards together is time-consuming, but frequently the mere act of doing it gets you off book.

8. Always memorize according to what the character *wants,* rather than doing words by rote. Memorize thought clusters and intention clusters rather than word clusters. At worst, you should be able to paraphrase in a pinch. Actors who forget, or go up on, lines are invariably those who have just placed the words in their heads, with narrow computer logic, so that when the word is gone, so are they.

9. Remember Stanislavski's images and use them to get a firm film and/or still shot to associate with each group of words. The visual image as it pops back into your mind will tend to bring the lines with it.

10. Every time you memorize, review everything *else* you have memorized in the last few days too. Go back to the beginning for a brush-up, which serves as a warm-up to get you in the "memorization mode."

Working with a Director, Coach, or Teacher

All three of these guides attempt to help you, but in different ways. It is important to separate their functions, so you know what to expect. There are many exceptions to the following distinctions, but they hold true most of the time.

An acting *teacher* creates an environment (physical and emotional) and provides exercises, to help you explore and discover your own potential. The teacher rarely inflicts his will or forces change. He is aiming to make you self-sufficient and, particularly in beginning acting classes, is usually more concerned with your overall awareness and growth as a person than with technical precision.

An acting *coach* functions much like a coach in sports, working with you on specific problems, having you try a number of solutions, fine tuning the same moment, over and over, driving you a little farther than you thought possible. You go into a coaching session with definite problems to be solved. If it is a good session, you leave with some solved, and more to work on, because the coach has stimulated you to move ahead in specific areas. A coach's attention is in many ways the most direct or personal, and the efforts the most precise.

A *director* is the most likely of the three to impose his will on yours. He is the most likely to tell you (at some point, sooner or later in the rehearsal process) exactly what he wants and (very late in the process) to lock much of what you do. This is because he has an opening night and a huge group of other company members to think about. In a show, you are part of a much larger package, a package that will ultimately be, in some way, marketed. One of my favorite directors said regularly to casts, "You are all like hands on a clock, very important, but I'm standing out here, and I'm the only one who can tell what time it is." The director is ultimately concerned, to a larger degree than the coach, and much larger than the teacher, with a finished *product*. The teacher is the most concerned with *process*.

These distinctions are arbitrary and are often contradicted. Sometimes a director is mounting an experimental work that is highly process-centered, for example, with no interest in slick surfaces. Some teachers act as gurus, and instead of making their actors self-sufficient, they make the actors highly emotionally dependent on *them*. A director mounting shows involving styles or skills unfamiliar to his cast may move through *all three* roles. He may start by teaching, then evolve into coaching each performer, and only towards the end become a traditional director. The distinctions between the three are useful, however, in terms of your own anticipation. Actors are sometimes naively disappointed because their work is not "polished" in a class, failing to realize that surface is not the purpose. Others will go for a coaching session, expecting everything to be "fixed," and be upset when they leave, aware of even more work that needs to be done. All of these people, if they are conscientious artists, are trying to help make you strong. Even the director will only "fix" things for you because he has an audience to think about. Work with all three guides, with realistic expectations, for long-term growth.

Working Without a Director

For years I went around saying, "What I really like is a strong director who knows exactly what he wants and will tell me." It took me
quite a while to realize that what I was really saying was, "I don't
know what I'm doing so I want to be told." The ideal relationship
with a director is collaborative, full of mutual strength and support.
No one has summed up the *ideal* more vividly than Stanislavski,
who said, "A talented director may come along and drop just a
word, the actor will catch fire and his role will glow with all the
colors of his soul's prism."[4] How's *that* for a good working relationship?

A director who tells and shows you everything, with no exploratory encouragement, is hardly treating you like a collaborator.
Such directors are probably eagerly awaiting the time when robots
get polished enough to use them instead of you.

At the other extreme, any actor should be prepared to survive
the absence of a director's help. There are many productions where
someone is listed in that capacity, but that person did precious little
to provide vision and coordination. And remember, the director
can leave the theater, the town, the country. You are the one who
has to go out in front of the audience.

So, if you are lucky enough to have help, grab it and relish it.
But if you are on your own, you *can* do it. You can survive. The
primary switch you need to make is in attitude. Every time you have
to block yourself, or go to a friend for feedback on a speech, or
make *up* a rehearsal objective, without being told by the resident
authority figure, think of it as one more chance to grow self-sufficient. "I need a director" is too easy to say and impossible to survive.

Working with a Nondirector

Sometimes you simply get no feedback whatsoever from the person
in charge. It does not usually work to go up to her and say, "Give
me some feedback." You tend to get an answer like, "You're doing
fine." It does not usually work to stop her after rehearsal and ask,
"Got any notes for me?" You'll probably be told, "No, I'll let you
know."

Now, it is important to remember that if everything is going smoothly, NO NOTES ARE GOOD NOTES. There are many directors who *only* address what is wrong, and you may indeed be doing well. But if you feel insecure and awkward, you have to devise a strategy. Your best bet is to ask questions that *must* be answered like, "Why do you think my character does this?" or "Which of the ways I tried that sequence have been working best?" or "Tonight, I'm going to try this character element. Tell me if you think it adds, or if we should go back to the other approach." Always, of course, keep it friendly and respectful. You need to be, not only aggressive, but a bit clever. If you are getting no help, you can take the initiative. But you must provide the framework for a reticent director to respond to you.

Working with Untrained Observers

Almost anyone who lives, observes human behavior. And most people are quite good at detecting when that behavior is dishonest, phony, stiff, or distracting. So you do not need to go to a supposed theater expert to get feedback while working on a scene or monolog. Sometimes friends and family, who are completely unconnected with the theater, can give you some of the best information, and a fresh perspective on your work.

Obviously, you are not going to drown them in actor lingo, or in any way make them feel less than experts. Just show them what you are working on and have them respond, human to human. Here are some questions that you can ask absolutely anyone about your scene:

Exercise 6.1

What You See

Show your work to a friend with no specific theater background and use the following questions as the basis for soliciting feedback:

1. What kind of a person do I seem to be?
2. How old am I? What kind of background? Beliefs?
3. Where am I when this speech takes place?
4. What had happened to me just before the scene? Where did I come from? What had I been doing there?
5. What do my movements and gestures say about me? When do my moves look unnatural?

6. How would you imagine me dressed and looking if the show were fully produced?
7. To whom am I talking? What is my relationship to her? Her reaction to me? Does my listener ever move or respond? When? How?
8. Which moments do you find hardest to understand? Most difficult to believe?
9. What do I seem to want in this scene? What does this person seem to want out of life?
10. What do you notice going on between my words? What am I deciding *not* to do or say?
11. What, if any, changes do I seem to go through? How do I modify my behavior?
12. Is there anything getting in the way between me and what I want? What is it?
13. What about this character is just like me? What different?
14. Do I remind you of anyone else when I do the speech?
15. When do you find the whole thing least interesting?
16. How would you feel about being friends with this kind of character?
17. What effect did my imaginary surroundings have on me? Any you could see?
18. Does this scene take place right now in the present time? If not, when? How can you tell?
19. What kinds of feelings did listening and watching me create in you?
20. At what points did you think my concentration seemed to be more on myself the actor than on the needs and desires of the character?

Notice that all these questions are open-ended, the same kinds of questions needed with nondirectors. Nothing can be answered yes, no, or maybe. The person you are talking to has *got* to give you information. There are also almost no value judgments or implied requests for compliments. Why? Most people want to tell you what you want to hear. So if you just do your speech and say, "What do you think?" your friend is likely to say, "Great."

"Any suggestions?"
"No. Boy, I could never do that."

"Was I believable?"
"I guess so. Sure."

"The character is younger than I am. Was I young enough?"
"Oh, absolutely."

"Could you see the wind blowing?"
"Wind? . . . Uh . . . Yeah, wind."

You can see that this goes nowhere. You are implying a desired answer. If you just ask how old the character is, you get exactly what the other person really thinks. If your friend says 53, and you are doing Juliet, you know you have some youthening work ahead of you in rehearsal.

Clearly, you will not want to ask everything, on the list above, of everyone you know. Expand or contract the list according to the needs of the scene and your personal respect for the opinions of your auditor on life in general. Substitute other questions, based on your character analysis. An added benefit to sharing your work regularly with friends and family is that the unveiling in class is less tense, because you have already unveiled in bits and pieces. Do not neglect this source. You may get a lot of the help you need, right at home.

Criticism: Give and Take

Criticism in acting class is a free gift that actors give to each other. It is especially important in assignments that will be repeated to give your classmates all the reactions you have, in order to help them go back into rehearsal, armed. If you are worried about sounding like an expert, but the terms are not coming as quickly as you want them to, just revert to the kind of vocabulary and categories above. If you say to a fellow actor, "I wasn't always sure what you wanted from him," that is a valid expression, which may mean the actor's objectives were not clear. It could also mean that you were not looking very carefully, but at least you have *shared* it. What the actors do with these free gifts is up to them.

Many beginning actors simply will not take part in critiquing a classmate's work, leaving it all up to others. It is one thing if you are simply drawing blanks, but if you are still worried about others thinking you are cruel, opinionated, or out of line, you are sabotaging yourself and them. It is selfish to keep to yourself and not to dare to risk disapproval. Remember you are invested in these people and they in you.

How to take criticism that seems harsh? Remind yourself that nobody criticizes unless he cares; it takes too much energy. It beats not being noticed at all. And it goes with the territory. Drama critics have the right to print comments on actors that would get other writers sued for libel. The healthiest actor I know carries the following review with him in his makeup kit and puts it up on the mirror in each new dressing room he occupies:

> "Mr. _____ spends the entire evening onstage making a pitiful attempt to prove his masculinity. The attempt is not just pathetic; it's boring and he completely fails."

The actor manages to find humor and solace in this old review. He's home free. No one will ever write anything worse about him.

Shaking Up the Scene

Not all improvisation work has to be done in early stages, as groups begin to form or as the scene is just taking shape. Some rehearsal experiments should come later in the process, when the scene is relatively solid and ready for some new life. The following exercises work best when lines and blocking are quite secure. In class, these fit best when the work has been shown once, critiqued, and gone back into rehearsal.

Your teacher and classmates may suggest some specific ones, based on the first showing, but all are worth trying. Sometimes the very aspect of the scene about which you feel most complacent turns out to benefit from a jolt of a different kind of energy. If this experimenting is not done in class, it helps to have some observers, at your rehearsal, to help you identify your discoveries. It is possible to get so caught up in doing an exercise that you fail to register the benefits. After each exercise below is an indication of what often happens when it is accomplished. Do not *force* that result, because in your case it may be something altogether different. Or like any improv it may fizzle out. Not all mining trips lead to treasure. Not all lead to the *same* treasure. Leave yourself open.

Character Explorations

Exercise 6.2

Spoken Silent Script

Actually speak your continuous interior monolog in addition to the lines themselves, so you are speaking both text and subtext. Take all the time you need to recognize inner thoughts and get them into words. Go ahead and overlap with your partner, as your tapes run simultaneously. Remember, a lot of your silent script will not make sense to others, and that is as it should be. Speak the "silent" parts in a slightly less projected voice than the actual lines, which are punched up for clarity. This exercise starts rough, but once you get it, it rolls. Stanislavski suggests trying it in four stages: speaking the silent script 1) as above, in a lower tone of voice; 2) merely a whisper; 3) soundlessly; 4) expressing it only with the eyes.[5]

What happens   You find out where your thinking is muddy and some gets cleaned up. Some awkwardness drops away because you are so *busy*. You discover business and movement as your body takes over.

Exercise 6.3

Shadowing

Hand two other actors your scripts, and have them go through the scene. You and your partner shadow them, telling them where to move, asking to have some words punched, to repeat some lines or moves, with greater emphasis, encouraging prior to an important moment and after a maneuver is accomplished successfully, acting as alter ego and coach. When you are ready for your "stand-in" to read the line, press her lightly on the back.

What happens   You get a new perspective. Countless little insights come out of just peering over another's shoulder and seeing the scene from another place altogether. You are able to put this alter ego onstage with you in places where encouragement would help.

Exercise 6.4

Isolating

Pick any two tactics and use them exclusively in the scene. Do not let your partner know which ones you choose. (This may also be done by simply drawing slips of paper so the decision is made for you.) Make sure every inch of mileage is gained from each tactic.

Variations:

1. Both of you employ the same tactic on each other.
2. Both select tactics you are relatively sure your character does *not* employ in the scene.

What happens   Focus shifts from lines to maneuvers. Evaluations have more excitement. You see tactics as possibilities that you failed to consider before. The scene becomes more like a game and partners are studied more carefully.

Exercise 6.5

Role Reversal

1. Switch parts with your partner and run the scene.
2. Keep the major shape of the scene the same, but feel free to use your own line readings and character business whenever you wish to do something differently.
3. Listen closely to your partner when he gives a new and interesting twist to a speech, when it sounds the same as the way you usually do it, when your sense of timing is altered.
4. Most important, enjoy playing the other role and doing all the things you might wish the other actor would do, but would never "direct" him to do.

What happens   You learn immediately how well you know the whole scene and how often you have simply been biding time and not really listening when your partner speaks.

There is a theraputic release in getting to say the words and do the other part the way you want. Whether or not your partner hears, notices, or decides to use anything of yours, at least you have had the chance. You tend to feel somehow freer.

You find places you may have been making the other guy wait forever, or where you may have been jumping on his cues, or a cross you have been making more difficult than necessary. You get all the benefits of the magic If for your partner.

If you are alert, your partner will show you some better alternatives and will give you permission to try things.

William Hurt *(on role reversal in rehearsal for* The Kiss of the Spider Woman*): So I said, "Okay, let's just switch roles." It's tricky; you have to trust the other person, because when he plays your role, he's gonna be telling you how you should play it. Well, we just* flew. *Raul was the one who took off first. I was dazzled by his flamboyance. So I took up the gauntlet and made that revolutionary one tough son of a bitch. We were giving each other what we* needed *from each other.*[6]

Exercise 6.6

Passing

Start with a simple object, such as a rubber ball, a bean bag, a tennis ball, and run the scene, passing it to the other person at the very end of each speech. Use the object to punctuate your lines while you have it, and really pass it to your partner the way the *cue* is passed (violent, sly, flirtatious, outraged, and so on). Let the relationship between the characters centralize in the object. Remember, you do not have to just hand it to the other person, you can put in his pocket, on his head, down his pants. You can nudge it over to him with your foot or your little pinkie. You also can do more than hold it, while you speak. You can crush it, roll it, bounce it, or put it down your own pants.

Variation:

Move to a game that is most appropriate to the conflict in the scene (Ping-Pong or croquet if it is witty repartee, boxing if it is all frontal assault, wrestling if it is basic, noncerebral, and gutsy, chess if it is sly) and explore in the same way.

What happens Line readings tend to have more color. As the energy goes into the object, it also goes into the words, so variety and clarity both rise. Individual consonants and vowels, within words, get more liveliness and variety of attack. Both partners are more alert hearing and receiving cues.

Exercise 6.7

Animal Abstractions

Assume the animal images you have chosen for your characters and perform the scene with all the animal's physical characteristics you can summon, with an animal voice (animal *sounding,* but with real words, punctuated by a generous dose of nonverbals). Your animal can be a combination of animals, instead of one that exists in real life. Let the blocking of the scene alter in any way that seems right, and go ahead and scratch where it itches. Open the scene up to all the nonintellectual, sensory, sensual, sexual, purely physical realms. Repeat the scene immediately without any effort to animalize.

What happens   A greater playfulness often emerges as well as some carryover of pure animalism. An effective counterbalance for actors who tend to talk a scene to death or to act too much with the head.

Exercise 6.8

Contact

Touch your partner at some point, within each of your lines in the scene. Take your time and find some way to physically connect with her, every time you speak. Touches may be anything from traditional moves (slapping on the shoulder, nudging, pointing into someone's upper chest) to those that are simply discovered (touching elbows, pulling someone's shirt untucked, even pressing your nose to someone's knee). Some combination of the conventional and the new will probably emerge. Do not try to be clever, but let your body tell you some way to connect at the same time your words do.

What happens   A surprising number of these moves end up being serious possibilities to put into the actual scene. Others provide an emotional memory for the body to suppress interestingly later. The emotional contact is inevitably punched up by the physical contact. And some unexpectedly pointed line readings are discovered.

Exercise 6.9

Gibbalog

Select agreed upon nonsense syllables and run the scene, using these limited lines, instead of the actual dialog. Make sure you have communicated as fully, through the gibberish, as you would through the words. To accomplish this you will need to intensify your physical and nonverbal responses. The face will need to get involved and the range of vocal life will need to be more vivid. Do not go on to the next line until your partner has made your cue perfectly clear.

What happens   Much as when struggling with a foreign language, the body gets engaged. As in the Nonsense section of chapter 5, the communication suddenly has higher stakes on the part of both participants. Often you decide to keep some of these vivid choices at moments of high intensity.

Exercise 6.10

Handicaps

1. Play the scene sitting back to back, with your partner's arms and yours locked, and neither of you having any possibility of seeing the other. Communicate everything through your voice and whatever pressure you can manage on the other person's back and your arms, where looped.
2. Sit against the wall, facing each other at opposite ends of a large classroom or rehearsal hall. Communicate over the vast space, keeping the scene intimate and complex, not allowing it to become loud and flat.
3. Invent a handicap for the scene, based on removing anything you agree either of you has grown to rely on heavily. If that is different for each of you, try it both ways.

What happens   Just as those who are sight or hearing impaired tend to gain, by necessity, a heightening of other senses, adding some limitation to the scene can sharpen the intensity of communication in other areas and get both actors thinking again.

Exercise 6.11

Counterpoint

Decide what your character is *not,* and play the scene as if she is just that. Deliberately interpret each line so that it conveys a meaning opposite to that which seems intended by the text. Create a character who would be the polar opposite of yours and relish the difference. You may need to repeat this once, for the obvious amusement you will experience, then for listening very carefully, to determine once and for all what you know is absent from the scene. And also to find the occasional contrast within people, which makes them interesting, the touch of villain in the saint and vice versa.

What happens   Initially, there is a relief of laughter as in seeing a parody of something taken as deadly serious before. Then a security comes from eliminating some options completely from the scene. Finally, some spice and unexpected twists may be discovered.

Exercise 6.12

Layering

Add gradually into the first beat of the scene extreme conditioning forces. Make the space arctic cold or swelteringly hot and humid, blindingly light or all dark shadows. Make the characters dreadfully late or having had to wait forever. Give yourself an extreme physical condition (dreadful cold, worst hangover of your life, a devastating injury). Manipulate various combinations, then back off to more subtle, nuanced circumstances, but ones with constant influence.

What happens   If you tend to play in a bland, neutral state, this will shake you out of that quite firmly. It opens up the senses. Even though the exercise choices will largely be too extreme to retain, an intense physical awareness tends to linger later. Also, with the concentration so strongly on the body, some surprisingly natural lines readings emerge.

Exercise 6.13

Rally Squad

1. Select four class members to serve as a cheering section for each actor (eight altogether). Each squad stands at a separate end of the room.
2. Perform the scene, returning continuously to your squad for encouragement and advice before returning to give your next line. Squads should react to the other side much as you did to opposing teams in high school. They should cheer their hero or heroine on to victory. They should speak out encouragement and comfort to their player.

Variations:

Split the class down the middle and have the actors play, each to his own half of the house. If the actors are a man and a woman, let each sex root for its own. Or divide class between those over and under age 20. Some group identification that gets the adrenaline flowing.

What happens   All the competitive elements of the scene are suddenly quite clear. The scoring of points is sharper. The rally squad can carry over into the private audience, so that each character feels supported in his part of the conflict. Most important, there is an infusion of relish, each actor savors his chance to play, and the resulting scene tends to have a greater feeling of playfulness, once the shouting dies down.

Exercise 6.14

Speed-through

Run the scene as rapidly as the words and moves will come, keeping all the values present and playing it in the same emotional key as always.

Save this one for the very final stages of rehearsal close to the last time the scene will be presented in class. Try to go through all your normal evaluations and interior monologs as well as the script and blocking itself so that all ingredients are included, only faster.

What happens   An antidote to potential indulgent pauses or subtext work that has gotten labored. You find places where the lines *do* work that fast because of the urgency of the moment. You may even find some places to overlap each other's lines in a believable and realistic way. You discover where you can evaluate *during* lines, when you thought you had to isolate your alternatives between speeches. Conversely you find out which pauses and extended evaluations are absolutely essential to accomplish transitions.

Character Confidence

These next two exercises, in which each actor faces the audience as the character, but without the script, can make you feel you *own* the role. If your preparation has been inadequate, they can also make you aware of how much more you need to dig in. But most actors, however, develop confidence the more they get to take the *character* before an audience, without the absolute necessity of the playwright's *words*. When the security of the words is then returned, a new surge of authority may enter them.

Exercise 6.15

Character Hot Seat

A variation on the Character Interview but with somewhat greater intensity, more like a grilling by a district attorney. Audience gets to ask any questions they want of the character, but all should focus on forcing her to justify her behavior, much like a prosecutor might approach the defendant. A class member may be chosen to play head prosecutor. Any ethically questionable act by the character should receive particular attention.

What happens   By this time, actors are secure enough to enjoy the confrontational challenge and take on all comers. The magic If gets a genuine workout, since it is essential to become the character from a totally nonjudgmental perspective. You retain the character's own sense of conviction regarding the appropriateness of her acts.

Exercise 6.16

Comparisons

The character appears before the class and speaks about the actor.

1. What does the character think of this person presuming to play him?
2. What does the character feel the actor still needs to accomplish?
3. What does the character feel the two of them have most and least in common?
4. Would the character like to know the actor or would they probably not get along?

The character presents this basic information, then the audience is free to ask questions about this actor who is being described.

What happens   The perspective is pleasurable and illuminating since the actor is being discussed as if he is not here. The actor tends to feel he has finally got the character down if he can actually discuss himself *as* the character. It is as if the immersion is finally complete.

Exercise 6.17

Character Encounter, Part II: The Sequel

Unlike most sequels, this one can be as good as the original. Now that the actors have been together as the characters for some time, a more challenging encounter is possible and productive. With the same format as the Partner and Character encounters from chapters 4 and 5, complete the following questions as the person you are playing:

1. You tend to hurt me most often when you . . .
2. The single time you hurt me most was when . . .

3. What I love most about our relationship is . . .
4. The part of my life I prefer not to discuss with you is . . .
5. I cannot stand the way you . . .
6. I was proudest and most moved to know you (be your friend, related to you, married to you, and so on) when . . .
7. You and I are most similar in . . .
8. You and I are completely different in . . .
9. I envy the way you . . .
10. If I could wish and make something happen for you, it would be . . .

(If you are feeling adventurous, you might try doing this with your partner as *yourselves.*)

What happens   The relationship is explored with greater depth and emotion than in the past, than indeed would have been appropriate before. The shared histories of the two people solidify and their relationship often emerges with more layers.

Exercise 6.18

Meet Another Character

1. Either the teacher or groups of classmates should pick characters from different scenes and set up circumstances in which they might encounter each other.
2. A public place, where these two could conceivably run into each other, works best.
3. Keep your character's point of ignorance regarding the other person and respond without your audience knowledge of the scene, which you watched your classmates perform earlier.

What happens   In addition to absolutely requiring character perspective and concentration, this lets different scenes benefit from each *other* more than in the simple act of observation. These characters you have seen in other contexts now provide enjoyable challenge to yours. Actors inevitably begin to think about how their characters would respond to all the others.

Process versus Product

Process does not stop one day, in rehearsal, as suddenly product replaces it. If the distinctions between these two are too sharp, the work changes radically, rarely for the better. People who do lousy, lazy shows will announce that they are concerned with process, as a rationale for a complete lack of discernible quality and polish on opening night. Others will refuse to tolerate experimentation and exploration because "we have a product we need to get out here." So everyone involved in such a production is forced to *set* work at the earliest possible moment, without any real chance to grow or discover.

In the rehearsal of a play or a scene, as opening or class due date draws near, a shift in energy often occurs among actors. A sort of panic that undoes a great deal of earlier work, as if now is the time to get serious and lose all the delight and spontaneity of our past weeks together. Then there is the procrastinator-actor, who does absolutely nothing until a performance date looms on the horizon, then suddenly crams—a very bad idea. A performance is not like a term paper, where you can write all night, then drop the product off and collapse. Remember *you* are it. Not only can you not do work worth watching if exhausted and stressed, but your performance will have had no chance to grow. You need to start working seriously early, then give yourself periods where you let things work on your imagination, where you allow the character to visit you. The famous actress Laurette Taylor (the original Amanda in *The Glass Menagerie*) used to compare it to bread dough rising. The whole process of making bread from scratch is an apt comparison for a performance, because there are interludes where you have to stop forcing the product and just let the process take its course for a while.

If you expose your evolving performance in bits and pieces, as suggested earlier, to your loved ones and some of your classmates, it will enhance the *gradual* nature of the performance process. Doing things at least twice in class helps. Being asked to preview scenes and speeches from a production and being allowed to have an invited audience or a preview performance also help. Process is a way of thinking. Opening night is like a rehearsal, where the new problem is adjusting to the change in acoustics and to playing the house. Each night of the run is a chance to set a personal objective the way the director may have set objectives during rehearsal. Closing night as your best work is an ideal to shoot for. Looking *beyond* closing is an even better idea, so that you keep yourself in the future, looking ahead to the chance to repeat this role or play another of this type again sometime. There should be no moment in the process where growth stops, and fear or sentiment replaces it.

Kiss the Line Good-bye

There is a great temptation at the close of a play to get maudlin. You love these people, and this project has engaged you for a long time. A constant in your life is being eliminated. Actors sometimes go out onstage and relish each moment (usually a good idea), to the point where the performance is much like a memorial service. "Good-bye little line. Good-bye little prop. I'll never use you again. Good-bye little upstage turn."

Do not misunderstand. We all tend to do this. I have been one of the worst offenders in the world. If you have loved it, how can you let it go? At least without saying good-bye?

The answer is the audience. They deserve nothing less than your opening night best. What have they done to deserve attending a wake? The other answer is your memory. You want to remember this last performance as crisp, strong, full of control, a work of art. Backstage, afterwards, during strike, that is where you have earned the right to get messy and mushy.

Offstage Process

You decide to join a club, a co-op, or a corporation. You seek membership in a fraternal order, team, party, family, secret society, navy, monastery, or the Daughters of the American Revolution. What do you do? The exact process outlined in the preceding pages, since each group has particular quirks, but universal questions to be answered. Those who do not do well, socially and professionally, do not research. So they do not know how to (pardon the expression) act. Because theater has so many restrictions, so many freedoms, and so many peculiarities, if you can case it out, you can case anything. These are topics covered in this chapter:

handling interviews	adapting procedures
taking initiative	working well with others
mastering etiquette	editing
managing time	handling criticism
working unsupervised	maintaining perspective
setting goals	finding innovative ideas
meeting deadlines	gaining confidence

One of the largest employment agencies in the country has reported continuous success placing students, who have studied acting, in other fields, because they have such highly developed skills in each of the areas above. The theater teaches these topics by necessity. If you get involved in a play production, it can do more than take up a lot of time and be lots of fun. It can teach you fundamental survival skills.

Exercise 6.19

Processing

1. Go back over the 14 categories in the list above and adapt them to a job or group, familiar to you, but outside the theater.
2. Pick a new area you know nothing about. Use the list above and material in the beginning of this chapter to help you investigate.

Circular Experience

The theater is a circle. Impulses generate from the stage, out into the house and back, as laughter, gasps, or utter silence feed the actors to throw something out again. It goes on all evening. It is the reason the theater (often called "the fabulous invalid") will never die. Nothing like this interplay exists elsewhere. (Rock concerts are actually far more predictable, and a smaller emotional range is asked of the listeners.) This wild circle keeps whirling invisibly for the whole evening. The audience has power to change the actors and vice versa.

For the actor, her life in the theater is circular: audition through rehearsal through performance through closing and back to audition as the pattern begins again. If the actor auditions and is not called back or cast, the circle is simply smaller. Whatever happens, the actor is perhaps the ultimate optimist. She anticipates the future, and keeps, sometimes only by sheer force of will, the circle flowing round and round.

Glenda Jackson: *Acting provides the fulfillment of never being fulfilled. You're never as good as you'd like to be. So there's always something to hope for.*[7]

7
Acting Anticipated

(setting goals for the future that allow both artistic growth and personal satisfaction)

Interviewer: *What do you want to be doing a few years from now?*
Ben Kingsley: *I'd like to become a slightly older actor.*[1]

Looking to the Future

Everyone who takes a beginning acting class wants two things:

1. An increased level of self-awareness and confidence: the capacity to take an actor's poise, command, and concentration into your own life, even if you never go near a theater again.
2. An increased understanding of what is needed if you *do* decide to enter the theater again, part or full time, casually or seriously: a sense of how you might be able to make onstage acting a part of your life.

Most onstage awareness can be taken offstage and used. And the theater does wait patiently, ready to have you back when you are ready to return.

Is the Art for You? Are You for It?

A primary question about acting right now is whether or not you want to stick around. Expressing yourself artistically *somehow* is essential to living fully. Those who do not see the performing arts as basic, like the 3 R's, fail to realize it is fundamental to feed the spirit. There are many deceased creatures walking around, still breathing, but with dead, starved spirits. You probably realize this, or you would not have chosen to study acting, even briefly. But is this the right place for you to feed regularly?

Ask yourself if acting has *rewarded* you, and ask yourself if you can *collaborate*. This art form has pressure, deadlines, and constant candid criticism. It is a communal art form, where the group has got to be put above the individual. It is uneven. It is always starting and ending, as another play goes into production or closes. There is no slow, steady flame, but rather bursts and explosions of light and heat.

Are the bursts, the explosions, and the group interaction what you love? Or do you find yourself frustrated and stressed by them? The god of the theater is Dionysus, who embodies the irrational, the powerfully emotional, who gave the world wine. The actor who puts on the mask may take on the power of the god himself, but he risks the mask overcoming him. Unable to take it off, he flirts with madness. Do you need something less frantic and more constant? When you think back on your time so far, were you unsettled during quite a bit of it? Lots of performers could be called acting addicts. They are so desperately unhappy that acting seems more like a needle in their arm than a source of strength. They are wrapped up in acting, but without joy.

Do you find the brotherhood a source of strength? Or do you have trouble being on time, not letting partners down, not flirting with irresponsibility? Was it a strain meeting obligations and deadlines involving all those partners? If you are a flake, get out of the theater. You can always go write verses on the beach, strum a guitar, get out the easel and oils—none of these objects can be hurt by your irresponsibility.

There are lots of reasons to stay with acting. The two big reasons for leaving it are the recognition of how easy it is to hurt yourself and to hurt others.

Training Objectives

If you decide to stay, take the self-awareness you have recently developed and translate it into goals, including the following possible training routes:

1. Pursue a theater degree where you are now, assuming each course in the sequence will address areas of concern.
2. Transfer to a school that is larger, smaller, more or less professionally focused, closer to an academy or to a scholarly university, in order to match your needs.
3. Take courses in dance, movement, singing, and voice to release and express your physical and vocal instruments.
4. Study privately, with a coach, on areas where you particularly want to move quickly ahead.
5. Set up sessions with a specialist, counselor, or therapist trained to address tension or inhibition which is standing in the way of your exploration.
6. Pursue a tangential therapy which addresses your own special concern and also appeals to you: bionenergetics, functional integration, Feldenkrais or Gestalt therapy, yoga, zen sports, shiatsu, reflexology, Rolfing, relaxation response, biofeedback, meditation, aikido, t'ai chi ch'uan, hakami, Alexander technique, psychodrama, or visualization are all possibilities.
7. Turn acting into an avocation or serious hobby, with no more formal training but some involvement in your theater community.
8. Spend some time as a newly aware audience member, studying the work of actors from a distance, determining how much you miss the activity itself.
9. Postpone any decision until you have had a chance to take another course or two and determine whether your infatuation survives a test of time and familiarity.
10. Learn everything you can about auditions, because they are the next hurdle if you stay involved. In fact they are always the next hurdle to leap over (and over) throughout an actor's life.

Before you pack your bags, take a good look at where you are. If you are learning here, chances are you should stay. When you stop learning is the time to go. The most pathetic actors are those who keep transferring to smaller and less reputable departments so that their casting chances improve. Is it really worth it to be surrounded by mediocrity, when your chances for growth may be much higher where you are?

Many actors never stop taking classes, even repeating the local version of Acting One, in different locations, just to stay in touch. Each acting class is a separate event because the people are so different. And acting is not like the measles, where you have it and then it is over. A veteran once explained to me his penchant for always taking class as "just like going to the gym to stay in shape. No one would ask why someone *still* does sit-ups." Acting class is where your emotional muscles and imagination muscles can always get a good workout.

Production-proof Actors

Aspire, as you train, to become a *production-proof actor.* As an audience member, you have surely identified a few performers who always seem to do good work, no matter what vehicle they take part in. The film or play can seem like chicken poop, but the actor always transcends and illuminates the material. This is a good goal for any novice performer. Way too many actors go down with the ship in an ill-conceived vehicle that bombs in a big way. Way too many go down with the dinghy, in smaller, inept projects.

This means not only managing to work with or without any kind of director, but enough security in *all* areas of production to survive everything that touches your performance. The more production tasks you learn, the better able you will be to save yourself. You do not study props or costuming just to fulfill course requirements; you need to be able to communicate effectively with every member of the design team to get the best work possible from them. It is insulting to their artistry for you to fail to understand how they work. Keeping yourself ignorant increases the chances of your ending up in a dumpy frock, lit like a cadaver, holding the world's most pathetic prop, while sound effects drown out what you are saying. And finding it very difficult being transcendent.

Post-Audition Mortem

Why deal with auditions at the end of the book? Because the audition is always the next step. In chapter 6, the process of performance went directly from auditions to beginning rehearsals. For many, there is a stop between these steps, because they were not cast. On a professional level, acting has the largest unemployment rate in the entire world. And even on an amateur level, there are many more people than parts. So there is a lot of auditioning going on that *does not* lead directly to the rehearsal hall. What then?

You audition for a show and give it your best shot. You are not called back. Or you are called back, but not cast. What to do next? (For the moment, we will omit giving up because you cannot stand the rejection. That is always an option.) In educational theater, in order to learn from the experience and train for next time, the actor may naturally seek out the director for feedback. Asking is appropriate, because these people are there to educate you. You do not need to feel that discussing your audition with a teacher/director is a terrible imposition. That is their job. Review the following guidelines, which should help the process:

1. Never talk to the director until after the show is cast. Her efforts are entirely focused on that task. She probably does not have time right now.
2. Wait a good two or three days until after the final cast list is posted, in order to give yourself time to put the entire experience in perspective. Only *time* will give you some objectivity. Only time will help you minimize responses that are purely emotional.
3. Use this waiting period to put together your own list of reasons why you may not have been used. Move beyond "no talent" as an explanation to real, concrete events that occurred during tryouts and to the specific needs of the production. Review your own participation in the audition process, step by step, and try to determine when you were functioning most and least effectively. When you consider all the decisions you made, which were most and least appropriate?
4. Use this checklist against your own castability:
   Culturally Bound (conspicuously contemporary, regional, ethnic, or any other characteristic that makes it hard to imagine you outside your own culture and *inside* that of the play)
   Wrong Appearance for this show (shape, size, bone structure, capacity to look right in the costumes, to seem like a member of that family, to fit into the visual world of the play)
   Company Balance (Sometimes an actor is very good, but would throw off a sense of focus, would be distracting, or would alter the dynamics of the ensemble.)
   Movement Limitations (There are demands, like mastery of intricate dance routines, handling period costume pieces, or radically altering your physical bearing, that are outside your range right now.)
   Voice Limitations (There are specific skills, like handling verse rhythms, singing in a certain range, or speaking in a different register, that you have not yet mastered.)

Inexperienced (You simply lack essential experience, both in training and in living, to possess the technical and *spiritual* capacity for certain roles.)

5. Extend the list above with your knowledge of this particular show. Separate those things you cannot do anything about from those you can. Use the "can" list to set some of your training objectives.

6. You may find that you do not need to see the director after all, because you have answered your own questions. If you still need feedback, go in with your own list of conjectures regarding your audition and needs for growth. Ask the director to verify, clarify, or help alter your own perceptions, *not* to do all your thinking for you.

7. Focus your conversation on the future. Consider the difference between these requests:

> "Why didn't you use me? What did I do wrong? What is it about me you don't like? Why did you pick her instead of me? What did I do to blow it?"

and:

> "I'd like to work with you as a director sometime and I'd like to work in this play sometime. Can you offer me suggestions for how I need to train? What would you like to see from me in future auditions that you didn't see in this one? Where do you see me needing the most growth?"

The same information is being asked for, but the spirit and the focus are entirely different. The show is cast and auditions are history. You want to move on to the rest of your life, with a sense of obtainable objectives. You want to leave this office with some idea what to *do* next.

8. Do not expect the kind of detailed response you would get in an acting class or a coaching session, where work is centered on how to improve a performance. Remember, a director has been doing *eliminations,* not pondering how to *fix* things. She has not been asking herself why various readings did *not* work; she has been looking at those that did. There are only so many categories possible to focus on at any moment. The director is not thinking about critiquing work presented.

9. As you prepare for next time, do not let the cloud of an unsuccessful audition hover over your efforts. There is no such thing as an unsuccessful audition if you learn from it. Far from going into the next round negatively predisposed towards you, those

who might direct you will be thrilled if you show any progress or development from last time. The most common reaction to weak auditions, however, is that, with the exception of the actor himself, nobody remembers them!

I have been visited by actors apologizing for lousy auditions they gave a year or two ago. I draw blanks. I ask others who were present, and they do not remember either. While casting, one is so clearly an editor that inept work simply fades away. You almost need to walk out, knock over a few pieces of scenery, mistakenly assume that Juliet is the boy's role (Julio?), and interrupt your reading with painful personal anecdotes, explaining why you think these lines are poorly written (especially if they are Shakespeare's), in order to register in a powerfully negative way. Take comfort in this.

Constant Reminders

For future auditions, you should develop a strategy based on your own responses to pressure. If we need reminders of the lessons born from experience regarding auditions, I would like to offer some contenders as "suitable for framing" (see figure 7–1).

If your experience has not led you to believe that maxim 1 is true, it will. Regarding maxim 2, look at the number of times that superb writers, directors, and actors collaborate for months of their lives and still come up with a bomb. Look at the number of unquestionably superb, critically lauded works that are ignored by the public and die. Look at the virtual crap that can rake in $40 million at your local cinemas.

You can set out to be a theater designer, stage manager, box office manager, shop supervisor, technician, or historian, and find a reasonable path to follow for career development, as well as actual employment potential. Superb actors run into career snags and unemployment for interminable stretches. Terrible actors who are good at marketing themselves work all the time. There is maxim 3.

And maxim 4? When you go out on opening night, at least you know you were chosen for the part. Even if you bomb, you were designated by someone as better than someone else. You own

1. *Life Is Unfair.*
2. *Theater Is Less Fair Than Life.*
3. *Acting Is The Least Fair Part of Theater.*
4. *Humans Submit Themselves to Nothing Less Fair Than the Audition.*

Figure 7-1 Life

the role, even if it may shortly be repossessed. At an audition, you are as vulnerable as at any moment in your life. You lay out your skills and sensitivity with no guarantee of anything beyond a curt "thank you" and the memory itself. You may prepare for weeks for an exposure that may not last minutes. Yes, Auschwitz and Hiroshima were worse than auditions, but the participants did not willingly *submit* themselves. Yet auditions are the best way anyone has found so far to cast and, while technology surges ahead so rapidly as to take your breath away, auditions have remained virtually unchanged for the last two hundred years. Figure 7–2 is also a contender for framing and hanging.

Selling yourself without feeling crass or immoral is tough. It takes a firm belief in who you are and a capacity to separate essential marketing strategy from the artist within. The water of the art of acting and the oil of the business of acting do not mix painlessly. Consider this testimony from one of the more respected actors in the world:

> **Katharine Hepburn:** *Being an actor is such a humiliating experience, because you are selling yourself to the public, your face, your personality, and that is humiliating. As you get older, it becomes more humiliating because you've got less to sell.*[2]

So what is your strategy? The audition is a separate entity from the performance. The world is full of brilliant actors who cannot audition and brilliant auditioners who cannot act. Theater shares this irony with politics, business, and many public service professions. Many actors give in to their own worst tendencies in an audition. Things they got over long ago and blocks they surmounted early in Acting One loom again like giants, as they go to try out for a show or interview for a summer job. The same self-sabotaging occurs in offstage application/interview encounters.

What do you do? You find warm-ups, ways to focus your energy, philosophical positions that get you back to the creative state you have achieved onstage. You personalize and adapt warm-ups to

Figure 7-2 Rounds

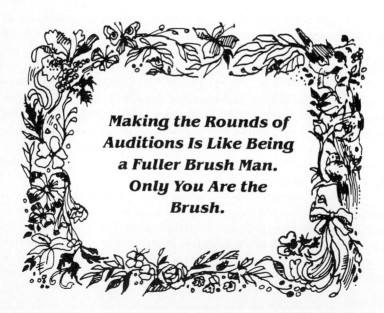

Making the Rounds of Auditions Is Like Being a Fuller Brush Man. Only You Are the Brush.

serve you in multiple circumstances. You develop a playful attitude towards the audition experience itself that allows you pleasure. You put this into perspective. You step out of the center of the universe. You decide to enjoy being there. Eventually you either get used to it or you get out. Or you become an inevitability:

Katharine Hepburn: *But if you survive, you become a legend. I'm a legend. I'm revered, rather like an old building.*[3]

General Casting

Early in your training, almost every audition you go to is *specific;* you know the play being cast and often the parts for which you are being considered. If you decide to pursue acting further, the *general* audition is inevitable. The format and objectives are different because a much broader look is being taken. The preparation level on your part is expected to be quite a bit higher. The general audition is often used for:

1. moving on in an acting program where there are large numbers of applicants
2. transferring to another school
3. gaining admission to an academy or professional school
4. studying with a private instructor
5. getting into a restricted seminar or master class
6. being accepted for a Master of Fine Arts program
7. gaining representation by an agency
8. winning a scholarship or some other acting competition
9. employment in summer stock
10. seasonal contracts in regional repertory

You need to learn this format, even if you are not yet sure how big a *place* acting will have in your life. Even if you are just a serious shopper, this audition is needed to get into most of the sales.

In general casting, instead of saying that you fit into one play or part perfectly, you are saying that you are interesting, versatile, disciplined, and gifted enough to be taken on by the auditor for some long-term venture. If the season has a variety of plays, you will fit in them all. If the program takes a series of approaches to acting, you will adapt well to each of them. If the agency deals with various media, you fit them all. In offstage terms, it is similar to being hired by a company to function in a wide range of tasks (troubleshooter, Person Friday, fund-raiser, spokesperson) instead of a narrowly defined desk job. When you looked for your very first job, the requirements for delivering papers, pumping gas, or frying burgers seemed quite specific. Becoming a public relations representative or cultural ambassador is general. You are demonstrating a wider scope.

Fortunately the format is almost identical for all of these auditions, so that once your basic presentation is in hand, you can use it repeatedly. Usually the conditions are:

1. You are given under five minutes to present two memorized monologs and time limits are enforced.
2. Strong contrast between the two pieces is encouraged so that your range can be examined.
3. One monolog should be quite close to you and your evident type, while the other has some surprise. Fairly often, one of them is requested to be classical and/or verse, to show technical mastery and a sense of style.
4. All choices should involve material for which you are well cast now. The versatility should not come by playing radically out of your age or from shock value.
5. Introductory and transitional material is to be kept at an absolute clean mimimum.

Why should this concern you if you are still in Acting One? Because the search for the right material is endless. It is almost impossible to start the search too early.

There are two main exceptions to the format above:

1. Auditions for teachers and coaches will sometimes involve only one monolog. You may be worried about demonstrating your range, but trust the perceptions of the observer. Do the monolog that is closest to you. The feeling, shared by many teachers, is that if the person comes across as interesting, truthful, and focused, versatility and virtuosity can come later.
2. The Irene Ryan competition of the American College Theater Festival requires that one of your two pieces be done with a partner. This is a rare opportunity and one to be relished. You normally spend so much of your effort trying to play to your *imaginary* partner in an audition that having a real partner there to support you can be wonderful.

Exercise 7.1

Audition Observation

The best way to quickly assimilate the general audition is to watch one. Ask around for local versions. Then take note of the following categories, which tend to be employed to evaluate actors. Ask yourself which decisions you would make in the actor's place. A glance will show you that these exact same categories can be used to evaluate any presentation in almost any line of work. This exercise is worthy of consideration for any presentation of self, offstage or on.

1. appearance/attire (care, attractiveness, appropriateness)
2. selection of material (suitability, originality, scope)
3. control of material (understanding, analysis, credibility)
4. use of voice/speech (quality, clarity, variety)
5. use of body/space (movement, staging, focus)
6. dynamics (stage presence, energy, imagination, poise, attitude)
7. flow (set-up, introduction, transitions, ending)

1. Appearance/Attire

Does it look like the actor gave some thought and preparation to how he looks today?
Does this look suit this person? Does it seem to fit who he is?
Is it the human being we are looking at or are we watching clothes and hair? Is hair out of eyes and the actor fully visible?
Is the outfit in any way fighting with the actor for attention?
On the other hand, is the look so bland that it is impossible to remember?
Is there a balance between stiffly dressed up and so casual that the performer does not seem to respect the occasion?
Is the look versatile enough that it works for both characters and the actor herself?
Does the actor accomplish any changes in appearance during the audition?
Were these changes creative or merely distracting?

2. Selection of Material

Has the actor picked pieces that seem to reflect herself?
Do either of the choices indicate a lack of self-awareness?
Are either of these characters too familiar or done too often?
Are the roles too strongly associated with famous actors to view without being too reminded of the great original performances?
Is there a feeling of having searched and uncovered new material?
Do the lines have a sense of the unexpected and the fresh?

Do the pieces provide the opportunity to share two entirely separate human beings?

Do the monologs satisfy? Do they seem complete, clear, and fully realized?

3. Control of Material

Do you feel the actor fully comprehends his characters and that each word is under his control?

Is it evident that homework and research have taken place?

Do you ever question the thoroughness or accuracy of the analysis behind the presentation?

Are either of these characters outside the actor's range at this point in his growth?

Is the actor believable as these people?

Are you watching real human beings in crisis or are you always aware that this is a performance?

4. Use of Voice/Speech

Does the voice seem comfortable and pleasant to listen to?

Do you ever have any trouble understanding?

If so, is it because of volume, articulation, or any other cause you can identify?

Does the voice change enough between roles for you to hear a new person?

Is there any tendency to make predictable or regular choices that are tiresome?

Is the sound varied enough within the body of each speech?

What is your response to the actor's sense of timing?

Are any vocal effects labored or forced?

Does this actor possess a rich, expressive instrument? Does it serve him fully?

5. Use of Body/Space

Does the actor move with assurance and authority?

Does the actor appear agile and coordinated?

Is there enough of a use of the space so that you can tell if the actor knows how to move?

Is the action so busy that you cannot tell whether she can be still?

Does action ever make you tense or uneasy?

Can you see the imaginary listener(s)?

Is the focus consistent or do you ever lose track of listener relationships?

Can you always see the actor's facial expressions? Does she focus down-
or offstage too frequently? Does she ever upstage herself or throw
attention elsewhere?
Does the actor have any trouble staying in the light?
Does the actor appear at home in the acting space?
Did you ever feel the need for more or less physical activity?

6. Dynamics

Does this person compel you? Does he command your attention?
Do you want to watch him? Are you curious to know more about him?
Is the actor the primary source of energy in the room?
Is that energy contagious or pushed?
Do you feel you are in the presence of a lively, creative spirit?
Does the actor seem to like being here, being an actor?
Does the actor appear gracious and friendly to the observers?
Do you ever get a sense of defensiveness or tightness?
Is there any feeling of apology or self-deprecation?
Does the actor put you at ease with his effortless assurance?

7. Flow

Does the audition proceed with a smooth efficiency?
Are there awkward adjustments of furniture, clothing, or lines? Any un-
filled pauses?
Is the introduction brief, pointed, but conversational?
Does each person go through realizable changes?
Do you get to watch a metamorphosis between characters?
Are you ever confused in a way that is clearly not intentional?
Do vocal and physical changes appear in sync with each other?
Does the actor bring it to a definite clear end, so that the curtains can
close in your own imagination?
Does the actor return to herself after the last character so that you get to
see the real person again?
Does the actor leave the stage with a sense of completion and pride?
Does the audition last all the way offstage?

Exercise 7.2

Choices

1. Note at least two instances in each category where you feel an actor
made vividly appropriate and inappropriate choices. (See appendix F.)

Debate with friends. Justify your reactions through the explanations above. Avoid simple rating words in favor of concrete information. Which auditions linger in your mind now and which rapidly fade away? Why? What separates outstanding from adequate work?

2. If you know any of the actors, ask if the person you know really appeared in the audition? Were there any essential qualities that you find appealing in the *human being* that were missing in the *presentation*? How can these be integrated?

Post-Application Mortem

Everything in the past section would have a direct parallel in those offstage situations where you have put yourself on the line for the scholarship, the grant, the job, the admission to a certain school or program, the fellowship, the contract, or the commission, and it does not come through. Do not retreat from a defeat. Force it to teach you.

Whether or not the person making crucial decisions is available to counsel you, a systematic review of your participation, objectivity gained from some passage of time, and careful development of positive objectives are still the secrets to recovery and growth and the way for setbacks to set-forward. Auditioning is what you are doing whenever you are in a situation that is now tentative/temporary, but may or may not become definite/permanent. Learning to audition is learning to open up the full range of your offstage life.

Exercise 7.3

Offstage Auditions

Pick one of the following events and observe choices made in exactly the same categories employed for the last two exercises. After observing others, make decisions regarding your own habitual choices that will help you the next time this kind of event comes your way.

1. an important social occasion
2. a public hearing on a controversial issue
3. a committee meeting where varying proposals are considered
4. an instance where competing bids or designs are dependent on rehearsed presentations

5. an informal or private encounter where the stakes are high enough to involve careful preparation

---

Interviews

Being questioned is standard procedure when you are applying to move ahead. Here are some of the most commonly asked questions for actors, which you should be able to quickly adjust for situations outside the theater:

The Dreaded Thirteen
1. Tell me something about yourself.
2. Why do you want to be an actor?
3. What have you done?
4. Why should we use you?
5. What's special about you?
6. What can you do for us?
7. Can you be . . . (funny, sad, sexy, commanding, and so on)?
8. Why do you think you're right for this . . . (part, company, agency, and so on)?
9. How do you feel about . . . (subject which follows may be anything impossible—vague, controversial, or private)?
10. Would you be willing to . . . (change something about yourself, play a role that is demeaning to your heritage, sex, and so on)?
11. By next week, can you . . . (relocate, leave your family, learn to do some tricky skill, and so on)?
12. What are your real strengths as an actor? As a person? What do you like best about yourself?
13. If you could change one thing about yourself, what would it be?

Oddly enough, the ones with the widest choice of answers (like items 1 and 2) seem to unhinge people the most. The good news is that almost any interview comes down to the list above or some variation. Think about *all* the ways you might answer, and feel no need to always answer the same. Realize that what you say matters far less than *how* you respond to the question. Interviews, from politicians stepping in to press conferences to beauty contestants stepping out of soundproof booths, come down to *attitude*. No one expects the senator or Miss Ohio to have a startling, illuminating, pungent response (and they usually do not). What is expected is that neither recipient will be rendered comatose by the question, that both will keep a sense of poise, humor, perspective, and a willingness to give it a go. Almost any answer is better than drawing blanks. Just give yourself permission to respond like a reasonable human being.

What if you *want* to be startling, illuminating, and pungent? Remember l'Esprit de l'Escalier? The beauty of interviews is that they are so relentlessly predictable that you can start reading, borrowing, quoting, shaping, practicing *now* for an answer you may not be called on to give for years. I attended an audition once where the director (who had a reputation for unsettling actors) stopped the woman who was reading and asked her what she had done. She answered that, and then he asked, "And what is your favorite sexual position?" There was an audible hush and a sudden tension in the room. The rest of us were in a state of shock. She paused, smiled, and said, "Number twenty-three." Everyone laughed and the audition went on in a normal way.

Was the director really trying to get personal information from her? Maybe, but I doubt it. He was testing her poise, humor, and reaction. She managed to say to him (subtextually), "You can't unhinge me. My humor is in good shape. And I'm not telling you a thing." The question is only a variation on item 9 from the list above.

The spirit of adventure essential in an audition can be carried into countless moments of your life. If you approach a job interview with a sense of the person on the other side of the desk functioning like a casting director (can you comfortably co-star at IBM?), a great deal of this process can be fun. You are constantly auditioning in life for further chances. A first date is, in many ways, an audition for a second. And when you go home to visit the family of your current companion, you are, without doubt, auditioning for the role of son/daughter-in-law. Even if you are not sure if you *want* the part, you are auditioning. If what you have *now* is temporary/tentative, but it *could* become permanent/definite, you are auditioning, even if you are nowhere near a theater.

Personal Objectives

If you never again darken the door of the theater, you should now have a sense of the kind of figure you cut in space, the sort of sounds you generate, the impressions (accurate or not) you leave on those you encounter. You may also recognize circumstances where you are easy/exploratory contrasted with those where you are inhibited/stiff. A basic knowledge of self and of what constitutes a character should clarify certain life choices.

Choosing Partners and Playmates

Most of us search for a life partner with whom we need to do a minimum of acting, someone who makes it easier to deal with what the world wants or who helps us not care. Feeling comfortable in a relationship because everything is so *predictable,* however, is hardly the same as feeling comfortable because unqualified love and acceptance are present, so whatever comes will be all right. The ideal companion for the full journey of life is one with whom we do not *need* to act at all but who will also, when we get the impulse, be there as an enthusiastic audience or as a dynamic scene partner, who will join the fun. So why do so many people pick the wrong mates, friends, even the wrong one-night stands? Many fail to recognize the difference between having a relationship and playing scenes. Many cast companions based on surface impressions and misread signals. Sure, some "professional actors" are the worst cases of multiple failed marriages and destructive relationships. But these victims are rarely *students* of acting, who should be better armed and need not be anyone's victim.

Your understanding of acting principles can help you choose better who you want to play with, to make informed selections regarding friends and lovers. You should be better able to recognize playful performance versus destructive self-deception, and to distinguish between nurturing comfort and mere predictability. The more you know about acting, the more you know how much you *want* it in your relationships.

Theater in Your Life

There is plenty of opportunity for theater in your offstage interactions.

Michael J. Fox: *The oldest form of theater is the dinner table. The same people every night with a new script.*[4]

You can always continue to train yourself to perform your life better:

1. Take what you have learned about your body, voice, and personality and set up goals to clean up what is misleading in your behavior.

2. Identify the suggestible conditions present when you have given your most memorable life performances so far. Aim to set up those conditions deliberately more often.

3. Seriously scrutinize any role models you have been using and ages you have been lingering in too long. Make edits and replacements. Start shooting to become someone's role model yourself.

4. Either accept and acknowledge your own dominant influences (of your private audience and cultural binding) or free yourself from them. Make peace with them in any case. Take the long-run dueling performances of your life and make a judgment in each, deciding which will win and freeing yourself from the tiresome pressure.

5. Examine those strategies and tactics that you overuse in your life and those you neglect. Freshen your strategic choices. Expand your own working repertoire. Stop playing tired worn-out tapes that nobody listens to.

6. Warm up for potentially difficult encounters, rather than just thinking about it.

7. Observe all the performances being given around you more intensely, both for enrichment and pleasure, and to avoid being taken for a ride.

8. Conquer space! Not necessarily in a space ship seeking unbridled intergalactic ambition. Start with just keeping cool in any medium-sized room. Any space you enter may or may not become yours. You now understand what personal bubbles are and the various means people use to break or invade them. You know how movement, composition, and business all make an impression. You understand the varying powers of sustained, intense, indirect, and darting eye contact. You can, if you will, stage yourself.

9. Conquer sound! Dare to use your voice to *influence* others' behavior. Let your voice be known to you, useful to you, no longer a stranger. Devote at least as much time to "working out" your voice as you do your body.

10. Confront the way life has typed you so far and the various parts that you have been cast in whether you wanted them or not. Cast yourself more assertively. Vow not to *accept* some roles.

Casting Yourself

Probably most actors would like to be viewed by the world as a romantic leading man or a leading lady. Those types, on the other hand, lament the fact that interesting, offbeat character roles are not open to them. Why are they forced, role after role, to be commanding, attractive, romantic? Why will the public not allow them to scratch and itch? It is obvious that no one is completely delighted with what he or she has got. You can waste an enormous amount of time lamenting. Or you can separate "can change" from "can't" from "don't want to anyway," and get on with your life. And you can begin to savor what is extraordinary about you.

There are roles that life has undeniably and sometimes cruelly cast you in. If you look and sound more like Woody Allen than Robert Redford (or vice versa), the world expects certain behavior from you. In case you have not noticed, there are a number of people who look more like one of those two, but *feel* more like the other. Their lives are often chaotic. Certain genetic, cultural limitations are placed on each living creature. Motivational and spiritual limitations are more often placed on the creature by the creature. While genetics is undeniable, your capacity to transform yourself is considerable. I do not mean plastic surgery or psychotherapy (sure, those are alternatives) but rather the simple way you think about yourself and elect to present yourself to the world.

Marlon Brando: *Acting is something that most people think they're incapable of but they do it from morning to night.*[5]

Transsexuals are vivid examples of people whom the genetic game has dealt a tough set of cards. Most people are lucky enough to be able to discover their true selves with less radical measures than surgery. Surely you have discovered something as simple (and, at first glance, superficial) as a hat, a pair of shoes, a hairstyle, a way of moving, a song, a new color that suddenly made you feel you had found a way of expressing who you actually are. These items can be far more than trite indulgences. Like the keys to a character, they help you find *you,* and help you feel much more as if you live inside your own body. With an actor's awareness, you can be far more alert, not just to finding keys to unlock other characters, but also keys to your own.

Here is one extraordinary story of an actor's transformation for the stage. Similar offstage metamorphoses are accomplished all the time.

> PAUL NEWMAN's Broadway debut was in *Picnic.* He did not play the commanding hunk leading man, Hal, who mesmerizes every woman in town. He played the well-meaning, ineffectual rich boy who loses the leading lady to a man of physical magnetism. The director (Joshua Logan, one of the most respected and successful in Broadway's history) would not even let him read for Hal. He said Newman had no sexual charisma or danger. "At that point I probably didn't. That sort of thing has a lot to do with *conviction.*"
>
> The director also told him to get in shape. "The way I translated that was six hours in the gym every day." He eventually won the role on the show's national tour after working diligently on both pectorals and presence. How? He studied acting and women. "You can measure a woman and find ways of being gallant, of listening, of crowding and pursuing."[6]

If Paul Newman could lose a role because he was insufficiently sexual and commanding and still become Paul Newman, what might others do? What might you do?

We are all looking to cast ourselves in the world. But much casting is just thrust upon us. The groups you deal with daily may force you into Earth Mother, Trusted Confidant, Charming if Bubbly Airhead, Somber Companion, Brick, or Jaded Sophisticate, depending on the needs of those around you. Now is the time to identify those roles that you have had long runs in and are ready to close. Now is a good time to promise yourself some overdue performances that you have wanted to give for a long time. Now may be the time to decide to star in your own life, instead of doing only featured roles and cameos in the lives of others. Or if you have been phenomenally self-centered, now may be the time to do just the reverse. Now may even be the time to create an altogether new type: The *(fill in your own name)* Type.

Living Fully: Onstage and Off

Ted Danson: *You can become a better actor by becoming a more complete human being and you can become a more complete human being by becoming a better actor.*[7]

Acting can liberate you as easily as it can imprison you. It can give you a wide range of choices and the means of cleaning up the distractions that are cluttering your communication. You can enjoy watching tactics being employed that you might not have recognized before, taking pleasure that you are seeing and hearing more around you. You can look across a room and savor the compositions, enjoy the body language, which may now make more sense, catch bits and pieces of conversation and idly analyze how a point might have had a different effect with a drop in pitch or by twisting the final consonant. The small details accumulate into a wealth of perception and pleasure. Acting can not only help you play your own life better, it can help you more playfully observe others living theirs.

The tools are now at your disposal. There is no doubt that you will continue to act, offstage at least. How well you act, or how long each performance lingers in the memory of those who observe it, is largely up to you. How much you discover and how much you enjoy yourself is also up to you. If you are open and alert, acting will offer you the potential for profound insight and a phenomenally good time—not a bad combination.

Meryl Streep: *Acting is simply my way of investigating human nature and having fun at the same time.*[8]

Tom Robbins: *It's never too late to have a happy childhood.*[9]

Name _____

APPENDIX A   My Acting History

Ages Experienced, Ages Observed

infant _____

schoolboy _____

lover _____

soldier _____

justice _____

pantaloon _____

second childhood _____

Quasi-theatrical Events

pageants _____

disguises _____

alter egos _____

role models _____

understudying _____

suppression _____

deception _____

Media* _____

film _____

TV/video _____

radio/voiceovers _____

Theater _____

productions _____

showcases _____

scene study _____

Dueling Performances _____

*If you have performed in plays or scenes or in front of the camera already, write out separate chronological lists in these categories: Theater (productions, showcases, scene study) and Media (film, TV, radio). These last three subcategories are probably clear, but under Theater, if in doubt, any full-mounted, publicly performed play (either full length or one act) should go under productions. Workshop presentations, with minimized or no technical support, involving excerpts from longer works or a collection of scenes and speeches (but still publicly presented to an audience), should go under showcases. Almost anything else, done as part of a class, seminar, or private lessons (but still worked on and performed with some degree of polish at the end of the session), should be listed under scene study. If you have done none of these things and are getting chills reading about them, don't worry about it. This is beginning acting and there is no reason to expect that you would have. Be calm. The rest of you, use your list to compare to the other "performances" on the list.

APPENDIX B   Acting Observed

Setting _____

Other Character(s) _____

Situation or Title _____

Character's Objective _____

Strategy _____

Tactics _____

_____

_____

Text and Subtext (four lines of dialog, TEXT IN CAPS and subtext lowercase)

1. speaker _____ : _____

2. speaker _____ : _____

3. speaker _____ : _____

4. speaker _____ : _____

Evaluation

cue _____

rejected alternative 1. _____

rejected alternative 2. _____

rejected alternative 3. _____

rejected alternative 4. _____

choice _____

Beats

1. _____
2. _____
3. _____
4. _____
5. _____
6. _____
7. _____
8. _____
9. _____
10. _____

261

Observee _____

Observers _____

APPENDIX C   Physical Life Observation

Habits (Still)

Standing _____

Sitting _____

Expression _____

Habits (Active)

Tempo/Rhythm _____

Motion _____

Gestures _____

Adaptations

Groups _____

Contact _____

Mood _____

Cultural Binding

Geography _____

Family _____

Conditioning _____

Interests _____

Age _____

Sex _____

Isolations

Head _____

Torso _____

Hands/Arms/Feet _____

Observee _____

Observers _____

APPENDIX D   Vocal Life Observation

Habits

Quality _____

_____

Tempo _____

_____

Rhythm _____

_____

Articulation _____

_____

Pronunciation _____

_____

Pitch _____

_____

Volume

Word Choice

Nonverbals

Adaptations

Cultural Binding

Isolations

Observer _____

Character _____

Event _____

APPENDIX E   Observing Stanislavski's System

Given Circumstances

1. _____
2. _____
3. _____
4. _____
5. _____
6. _____
7. _____
8. _____
9. _____
10. _____

Conditioning Forces on First Entrance _____

_____

Changes in Conditioning Forces _____

_____

How You Would Use the Magic If to Play This Role _____

_____

How You Would Employ Grouping _____

Character's Super Objective _____
Primary Obstacle(s) _____
Character's Rehearsed Futures _____
Best Possible _____

Worst Possible _____

Wildest Dreams Come True _____

Endowment
other people
1. _____
2. _____
3. _____
props or set pieces
1. _____
2. _____
3. _____
detailed conjecture (complete on separate page) _____

267

Actor _____

Character _____

Play _____

APPENDIX F   Character Analysis

Character Past

I come from _____

My childhood was _____

_____

_____

Family conditions were _____

_____

Experiences making the most lasting impression on me were _____

_____

_____

_____

Strongest cultural binding involves _____

_____

Ten most important given circumstances are _____

1. _____

2. _____

3. _____

4. _____

5. _____

6. _____

7. _____

8. _____

9. _____

10. _____

Five most powerful, influential members of my private audience would be

1. _____ because _____

2. _____ because _____

3. _____ because _____

4. _____ because _____

5. _____ because _____

Crucial actions prior to the play were _____

In the play, but prior to this scene, were _____

Details on the moment before my entrance include _____

_____

_____

_____

(continued)

Character Analysis (continued)

Character Present

Immediate conditioning forces are _____

_____

_____

Other characters and/or the playwright describe me as _____

_____

_____

_____

_____

I characterize others as _____

_____

_____

In groups I _____

I am basically _____

My physical life involves _____

_____

_____

My usual style of clothing and type of accessories include _____

My vocal life can be outlined as _____

_____

_____

_____

_____

My most distinguishing characteristics are _____

_____

My favorites would have to include _____

My temperament could be described as _____ For example _____

My lifestyle involves _____
I am most interested in _____

(continued)

271

Character Analysis (continued)

I am least interested in _____

I am different from the others in this play in that I _____

_____

The actor playing me most needs to use the magic If in _____

_____

Three examples of endowment are

1. _____

2. _____

3. _____

My silent script for one page of script is (finish on separate page or write on script)

_____

Two crucial moments of evaluation, including rejected alternatives, include

1. _____

first reject _____

second reject _____

third reject _____

fourth reject _____

choice _____

2.

first reject _____

second reject _____

third reject _____

fourth reject _____

choice _____

My scene breaks down into the following beats:

_____

_____

_____

_____

_____

I make the following discoveries in the scene _____

_____

_____

What is most important to me is _____

(continued)

Character Analysis (continued)

Character Future

My super objective is to _____

My intentional hierarchy includes _____

_____

_____

The obstacles I face are _____

_____

My strategy in the play and in the scene could be described as _____

_____

Specific tactics I employ in two pages of text are (mark script copy if you prefer) _____

_____

_____

_____

Clues I will look for, from my partner, to gauge success, will be _____

_____

_____

My three rehearsed futures are

best possible _____

_____

_____

worst possible _____

_____

_____

wildest dreams come true _____

_____

_____

Character Abstracts

helpful images _____

_____

_____

World of the Play (crucial information about how my character fits into the total world created by the playwright)

_____

_____

_____

(complete on separate page)

275

Observer _____

Event _____

Actor(s) Observed _____

APPENDIX G   Audition Observation

Identify *why* you felt a choice worked or did not, through the impact it had on you as you watched. Use suggestions in chapter 7. Someone who was not present at the audition should be able to picture it based on your remarks.

APPROPRIATE CHOICES	INAPPROPRIATE CHOICES

Appearance/Attire

_____   _____

_____   _____

_____   _____

_____   _____

Selection of Material

_____   _____

_____   _____

_____   _____

_____   _____

Control of Material

_____   _____

_____   _____

_____   _____

_____   _____

Use of Speech/Voice

Use of Body/Space

Dynamics

Flow

277

APPENDIX H   Sample Scene: The Rehearsal

[Two actors enter the room tentatively]

FRED: I can't believe there's no one in here.

ETHEL: It's freezing in here.

FRED: You know what Katharine Hepburn insists on whenever she rehearses?

ETHEL: No. What?

FRED: She insists that the temperature is always 60 degrees.

ETHEL: Really?

FRED: Yeah.

ETHEL: Why didn't you ever tell me that before?

FRED: I just read it. She says it keeps actors from getting sluggish. She also brings sweaters for those who need them. A box full of sweaters.

ETHEL: Well, Fred, you're a good actor, but you're no Katharine Hepburn. At least not yet. And you haven't brought me any sweater. It's still freezing.

FRED: Maybe we need to warm each other up.

ETHEL: *[Pause]* What do you mean?

FRED: I mean that we both need to read this scene so well, so brilliantly that we get the blood rushing. You know.

ETHEL: Oh. Right. Well, let's read it and see.

[They begin reading Beatrice and Benedick from Much Ado About Nothing, *Act II, scene iii]*

FRED: "When I said I would die a bachelor, I did not think I should live till I were married—Here comes Beatrice: By this day, she's a fair lady: I do spy some marks of love in her."

ETHEL: "Against my will, I am sent to bid you come in to dinner."

FRED: "You take pleasure in the message?"

ETHEL: "Yea, just so much as you may take upon a knife's point, and choke a daw withal: You have no stomach, signior: fare you well."

[Exits]

FRED: "Ha! Against my will, I am sent to bid you come to dinner—there's double meaning in that." [to Ethel] Do you think I should give those first and last lines to the audience? Like I'm confiding in them?

ETHEL: *[Reentering]* Sure. I would. Do you think she knows she loves him yet?

FRED: I think she loves him, but I don't think she knows it. She thinks she hates him.

ETHEL: Yeah. That's what I think too. Let's just take it from my entrance. Okay?

FRED: Right. I'll cue you in. "**I do spy some marks of love on her.**"

ETHEL: "**Against my will, I am sent to . . .**" Have you noticed what's going on in this assignment?

FRED: What do you mean?

ETHEL: We're all working with our first partners from back in the first acting class. At least I'm pretty sure that's true.

FRED: My god, I think you're right. Karen and John . . . and Tim and Ralph and . . . I think you're right.

ETHEL: I wonder why.

FRED: Probably supposed to give us some sense of perspective or something.
> [*He discovers a jacket someone has left in the room*]
>
> Hey, look!

ETHEL: What?

FRED: Who says there's no sweater here for you.
> [*Puts it around her shoulders*]

ETHEL: Do you even remember our first open scene?

FRED: Sure. The best thing I ever did.
> [*She looks at him witheringly*]
>
> Just kidding. But we did okay. How come we were never partners again? Until now?

ETHEL: You mean why didn't I ever ask you?

FRED: Yeah. I asked *you* the first time.

ETHEL: Well, as I recall you missed two rehearsals altogether, you were late more than a few times, and you didn't even get your lines until the day before it was due. How could I resist working with you again?

FRED: But I matured a lot after that term. You know that. I got much more disciplined. So how come we never worked together again?

ETHEL: I don't know. We're together now. Or . . . I guess it was our names.

FRED: Our names?

ETHEL: Fred and Ethel. I didn't like the idea of anyone thinking of us as the Mertzes.

FRED: The Mertzes?

ETHEL: Lucy and Ricky's neighbors.

FRED: Oh. Is that the real reason?

ETHEL: I don't know. Let's get back to it. From my entrance again?

FRED: Right. "I do spy some marks of love on her."

ETHEL: "Against my will I am sent to bid you come in to dinner." Did you know that Katharine Hepburn played Beatrice?

FRED: She did?

ETHEL: At the Stratford Festival. I just thought I'd impress you with some Hepburn trivia of my own.

FRED: **"You take pleasure in the message?"**

ETHEL: Now I can't stop thinking about all the rehearsals I've spent in this place. And it's just about over. From open scenes to Shakespeare.

FRED: And next comes graduation. Then we have to deal with "real life."

ETHEL: Alright. What the hell. It's almost over anyway. The real reason I avoided working with you is . . . God, I can't believe I'm going to say this. I always thought you were attractive. I mean I was attracted to you and I just didn't want to get distracted, so . . . Well, you know.

FRED: Seriously?

[She nods]

'Cause I've never been exactly indifferent to you either, but I never thought . . . No kidding?

ETHEL: **"Against my will I am sent to bid you to come to dinner."**

FRED: **"You take pleasure in the message?"** Don't you think we should talk about this?

ETHEL: No. I think we should rehearse. **"Yes, just so much as you may take upon a knife's point . . ."**

[She is getting emotional, skips lines]

"If it had been painful I would not have come. . ."

[She can't go on]

I'm sorry . . . I guess it's all this end of the year stuff and it's . . .

[She moves away from him to collect herself. Pause]

FRED: May I give you a hug? A very nonthreatening, nonsexual, supportive friend-type hug?

ETHEL: Please.

[They hug, at first tentatively, then relax into it]

Listen, this room has more memories than I'm up to today. Do you think we could go somewhere else?

FRED: Sure. Let's find someplace more Shakespearean. Then we can say we used sense memory in rehearsal.

ETHEL: And then, sometime soon, we'll talk.

FRED: Right, first we do a brilliant scene. Then we work out . . . then we talk about . . . us. Okay?

ETHEL: Good. Let's go.

[She returns as soon as they leave, having remembered the jacket she has on. She removes it, replaces it, and starts to leave]

Thanks, Katharine. Uh . . . Kate. Ummm . . . Ms. Hepburn. God, it's freezing in here.

[Exits]

APPENDIX I   Further Study

Almost any acting book is easier to appreciate with a group or at least a partner. However, each of the following can be studied independently. All are clear, approachable, and worth your time, whether you are in a class or working on your own.

Benedetti, Jean. *Stanislavski: An Introduction.* New York: Theatre Arts Books, 1982.
(Direct and interesting guide to Stanislavski's works, providing background and perspective on the System. A good book to review before reading Stanislavski's own works.)

Berry, Cecily. *Voice and the Actor.* New York: Macmillan, 1973.
(Compact, useful collection of voice exercises and insights. One of the few voice books which economically covers everything from simple relaxation through diction drills.)

Cohen, Robert. *Acting Power.* Palo Alto: Mayfield, 1978.
(Stimulating discussion of acting on a theoretical level, full of striking and original insights, connecting actor training with other areas of study, from computers to behavioral sciences.)

Gawain, Shakti. *Creative Visualization.* San Rafael: Whatever, 1978.
(Effective, accessible images for mental warm-ups and for achieving focus. Basic introduction to visualization and a help for actors in adding imaging to basic warm-up exercises.)

Hagen, Uta. *Respect for Acting.* New York: Macmillan, 1973.
(Highly entertaining and personal approach to performance, with memorable examples from the author's own distinguished acting and teaching careers.)

Hobbs, Robert. *Teach Yourself Transatlantic.* Palo Alto: Mayfield, 1978.
(Simple guide to eliminating distracting regional or nonstandard pronunciation for those wishing to perform classical or high style plays, requiring a more elevated level of speech than that of standard conversation.)

King, Nancy. *A Movement Approach to Acting.* Englewood Cliffs: Prentice-Hall, 1981.
(Straightforward program for developing physical awareness, movement skills, and the capacity for transformation.)

Markus, Tom. *The Professional Actor.* New York: Drama Books, 1979.
(Solid advice on achieving and maintaining high standards of

civilized behavior in each stage of rehearsal and performance.)

Moore, Sonia. *The Stanislavski System.* New York: Viking Press, 1965.
(A simple, straightforward discussion of basic ingredients of the system written by someone who was actually there, studying with the Moscow Art Theatre Studio in the early 1920s.)

Shurtleff, Michael. *Audition.* New York: Walker, 1978.
(Soundest available advice on the audition process, presented candidly and lucidly, dealing with specific mental preparation and instant text analysis as well as procedures.)

Silver, Fred. *Auditioning for Musical Theatre.* New York: Newmarket Press, 1985.
(Significant help in overcoming any actor's fears, not just of singing, but of facing a wide range of high pressure circumstances.)

Notes

Chapter 1

1. Bob Greene, "Jessica Lange Speaks for Herself," *Esquire,* 12/85, p. 332.
2. Bob Greene, "Streep," *Esquire,* 12/84, p. 442.
3. John Cottrell, *Laurence Olivier,* Prentice-Hall: 1975, p. 388.
4. William Shakespeare, *As You Like It,* II; vii; 139–166.
5. Richard Corliss, "Bette Steals Hollywod," *Time,* 3/2/87, p. 67.
6. Laurence Zuckerman, "Cosby, Inc.," *Time,* 9/28/87.
7. Dan Yakir, "The Future is Now," *Cabletime,* 4/87, p. 28.
8. Robert Edmund Jones, "The Theatre as It Was and as It Is," *The Dramatic Imagination,* Theatre Arts Books: 1941, pp. 45–49.
9. Corliss, p. 67.
10. Ron Rosenbaum, "Acting: The Creative Mind of Jack Nicholson," *The New York Times Magazine,* 7/13/86, p. 15.

Chapter 2

1. Jack Kroll, "William Hurt and the Curse of the Spider Man," *Esquire,* 10/86, p. 105.
2. Liz Smith, "The New Queen of the Screen," *People,* 11/3/86, p. 107.
3. Constantin Stanislavski, *An Actor Prepares,* Theatre Arts Books: 1948, p. 74.
4. Cottrell, p. 29.
5. Guy Martin, "Harrison Ford and the Jungle of Gloom," *Esquire,* 10/86, p. 116.
6. "Two Summer Shoot-outs," *Life,* 6/85, p. 139.

7. Maureen Dowd, "Testing Himself," *The New York Times Magazine*, 9/28/86, p. 16.
8. Hal Burton (Clive Goodwin, interviewer), *Acting in the Sixties*, BBC: 1970, p. 170.
9. Shirley MacLaine, "Shirley MacLaine Goes Out on a Limb," *TV Guide*, 1/17/87, p. 8.

Chapter 3
1. Gordon Hunt, *How to Audition*, Harper & Row: 1979, p. 304.
2. Cottrell, p. 389.
3. Douglas Brode, *The Films of Dustin Hoffman*, Citadel Press: 1983, p. 50.
4. Brad Gooch, "The Queen of Curves," *Vanity Fair*, 9/86, p. 76.
5. Richard Corliss, "Well, Hello Molly!" *Time*, 5/26/86, p. 71.
6. Hal Burton (David Jones, interviewer), *Great Acting*, Bonanza Books: 1967, p. 89.
7. "Bob Hoskins," *People*, 1/5/86, p. 53.
8. Dowd, p. 18.
9. J. Rovin, "Shirley!" *Ladies Home Journal*, 8/85, p. 154.
10. John Skow, "What Makes Meryl Magic," *Time*, 9/7/81, p. 47.

Chapter 4
1. Burton (Goodwin), p. 169.
2. Constantin Stanislavski, "The Evolution of My System," *Actors on Acting* (Cole and Chinoy, eds.), Crown Publishers: 1970, p. 491.
3. Jean Benedetti, *Stanislavski: An Introduction*, Theatre Arts Books: 1982, p. 2.
4. J. Benedetti, p. 3.
5. Constantin Stanislavski, "What Is My System," *An Actor's Handbook*, Theatre Arts Books: 1963, p. 159.
6. J. Benedetti, p. 73.
7. Constantin Stanislavski, *Building a Character*, Theatre Arts Books: 1949, p. 70.
8. Stanislavski, *Actors on Acting*, p. 494.
9. Stanislavski, *An Actor Prepares*, p. 192.
10. Hunt, p. 305.
11. Constantin Stanislavski, *Creating a Role*, Theatre Arts Books: 1961, p. 23.
12. *New York Theatre Review*, 3/79, p. 27.
13. Stanislavski, *An Actor Prepares*, p. 204.
14. Sonia Moore, *The Stanislavski System*, Viking Press: 1965, p. 27.
15. Stanislavksi, *An Actor's Handbook*, p. 114.
16. Stanislavski, *An Actor's Handbook*, p. 9.

17. Stanislavski, *An Actor Prepares,* p. 34.
18. Stanislavski, *An Actor Prepares,* p. 126.
19. Stanislavski, *Creating a Role,* p. 61.
20. Stanislavski, *Creating a Role,* p. 62.
21. Rosenbaum, p. 17.
22. Richard Corliss, "The Years of Living Splendidly," *Time,* 7/28/86, p. 60.
23. Stanislavski, *An Actor Prepares,* p. 166.
24. Stanislavski, *Building a Character,* pp. 69, 71, 82, 87, 126, 135, 146.
25. Stanislavski, *Building a Character,* p. 28.
26. Stanislavski, *Actors on Acting,* p. 493.
27. Stanislavski, *Building a Character,* p. 168.
28. Christine Edwards, *The Stanislavski Heritage,* New York University Press: 1965, p. 299.
29. Stanislavski, *An Actor Prepares,* p. 246.
30. Stanislavski, *Creating a Role,* p. 249.
31. Alvin H. Marill, *Katharine Hepburn,* Galahad Books: 1973, p. 138.
32. Stanislavski, *Building a Character,* p. 286.
33. Edward Albee, *The Zoo Story,* Dramatist's Play Service: 1960.
34. Uta Hagen, *Respect for Acting,* Macmillian: 1973.
35. Edwards, p. 311.
36. Sonia Moore (interviews Joshua Logan), *The Stanislavski System,* Viking Press: 1965, p. xv.

Chapter 5

1. Harry Hill, *A Voice for the Theatre,* Holt, Rinehart and Winston: 1985, p. 321.
2. Burton (Kenneth Tynan, interviewer), *Great Acting,* p. 31.
3. Chris Chase, "Lee Strasberg," *Viva,* 11/74, p. 37.
4. Burton (Jones), p. 92.
5. Kenneth Turan, "Harrison Ford Wants to Be Alone," *Gentlemen's Quarterly,* 10/86, p. 288.
6. Burton (Derek Hart, interviewer), *Great Acting,* p. 161.
7. Michael Shurtleff, *Audition,* Walker: 1978, p. 116.
8. Hill, p. 232.

Chapter 6

1. Brode, p. 20.
2. Helen Hayes, *A Gift of Joy,* Fawcett: 1966, p. 214.
3. Rovin, p. 152.
4. Stanislavski, *Building a Character,* p. 73.
5. Edwards, p. 304.
6. Kroll, p. 106.
7. Staats, p. 14.

Chapter 7

1. Christopher Connelly, "Ben Kingsley's Blessed Career," *Rolling Stone,* 3/17/83, p. 51.
2. Anne Edwards, *A Remarkable Woman,* William Morrow: 1985, p. 293.
3. Marrill, p. 138.
4. Bruce Buschel, "The Rise and Rise of Michael J. Fox," *Gentlemen's Quarterly,* 12/86, p. 229.
5. Brian Bates, *The Way of the Actor,* Shambhala: 1987, p. 7.
6. Dowd, p. 20.
7. Robert Benedetti, *The Actor at Work,* Prentice-Hall: 1986, p. xiv.
8. Elaine Dutka, "Talking with Meryl Streep," *Redbook,* 9/82, p. 12.
9. Tom Robbins, *Still Life with Woodpecker*, Bantam Books: 1980, p. 277.

Index